ANCIENT LAW

ANCIENT LAW

*Its Connection with the Early History
of Society and its Relation to
Modern Ideas*

SIR HENRY SUMNER MAINE

DORSET PRESS

First published in 1861.

This edition published by Dorset Press,
a division of
Marboro Books Corporation.

1986 Dorset Press.

ISBN 0-88029-092-7

Printed in the United States of America

M 9 8 7 6 5 4

CONTENTS

PREFACE

The chief object of the following pages is to indicate some of the earliest ideas of mankind, as they are reflected in Ancient Law, and to point out the relation of those ideas to modern thought. Much of the inquiry attempted could not have been prosecuted with the slightest hope of a useful result if there had not existed a body of law, like that of the Romans, bearing in its earliest portions the traces of the most remote antiquity and supplying from its later rules the staple of the civil institutions by which modern society is even now controlled. The necessity of taking the Roman law as a typical system, has compelled the author to draw from it what may appear a disproportionate number of his illustrations; but it has not been his intention to write a treatise on Roman jurisprudence, and he has as much as possible avoided all discussions which might give that appearance to his work. The space allotted in the Third and Fourth Chapters to certain philosophical theories of the Roman Jurisconsults, has been appropriated to them for two reasons. In the first place, those theories appear to the author to have had a much wider and more permanent influence on the thought and action of the world than is usually supposed. Secondly, they are believed to be the ultimate source of most of the views which have been prevalent, till quite recently, on the subjects treated of in this volume. It was impossible for the author to proceed far with his undertaking, without stating his opinion on the origin, meaning and value of those speculations.

H. S. M.

CHAPTER I

THE most celebrated system of jurisprudence known to the world begins, as it ends, with a Code. From the commencement to the close of its history, the expositors of Roman Law consistently employed language which implied that the body of their system rested on the Twelve Decemviral Tables, and therefore on a basis of written law. Except in one particular, no institutions anterior to the Twelve Tables were recognised at Rome. The theoretical descent of Roman jurisprudence from a code, the theoretical ascription of English law to immemorial unwritten tradition, were the chief reasons why the development of their system differed from the development of ours. Neither theory corresponded exactly with the facts, but each produced consequences of the utmost importance.

I need hardly say that the publication of the Twelve Tables is not the earliest point at which we can take up the history of law. The ancient Roman code belongs to a class of which almost every civilized nation in the world can show a sample, and which, so far as the Roman and Hellenic worlds were concerned, were largely diffused over them at epochs not widely distant from one another. They appeared under exceedingly similar circumstances, and were produced, to our knowledge, by very similar causes. Unquestionably, many jural phenomena lie behind these codes and preceded them in point of time. Not a few documentary records exist which profess to give us information concerning the early phenomena of law; but, until philology has effected a complete analysis of the Sanskrit literature, our best sources of knowledge are undoubtedly the Greek Homeric poems, considered of course not as a history of actual occurrences, but as a description, not wholly idealized, of a state of society known to the writer. However the fancy of the poet may have exaggerated certain features of the heroic age, the prowess of warriors and the potency of gods, there is no reason to believe that it has tampered with moral or metaphysical conceptions which were not yet the subjects of conscious observation; and in this respect the Homeric literature is far more trustworthy than those relatively later documents which pretend to give an account of times similarly early, but which were compiled under philosophical or theological influences. If by any means we can determine the early forms of jural conceptions, they will be invaluable to us. These rudimentary ideas are to the jurist what the primary crusts of the earth are to the geologist. They contain, potentially, all the forms in which law has subsequently exhibited itself. The haste or the prejudice which has generally refused them all but the most superficial examination, must bear the blame of the unsatisfactory condition in which we find the science of jurisprudence. The inquiries of the jurist are in truth prosecuted much as inquiry in physics and physiology was prosecuted before observation had taken the place of assumption. Theories, plausible and comprehensive, but absolutely unverified, such as the Law of Nature or the Social Compact, enjoy a universal preference over sober research into the primitive history of society and law; and they obscure the truth not only by diverting attention from the only quarter in which it can be found, but by that most real and most important influence which, when once entertained and believed in, they are enabled to exercise on the later stages of jurisprudence.

The earliest notions connected with the conception, now so fully developed, of a law or rule of life, are those contained in the Homeric words " Themis " and " Themistes." " Themis ", it is well known, appears in the later Greek pantheon as the Goddess of Justice, but this is a modern and much developed idea, and it is in a very different sense that Themis is described in the Iliad as the assessor of Zeus. It is now clearly seen by all trustworthy observers of the primitive condition of mankind that, in the infancy of the race, men could only account for sustained or periodically recurring action by supposing a personal agent. Thus, the wind blowing was a person and of course a divine person; the sun rising, culminating, and setting was a person and a divine person; the earth yielding her increase was a person and divine. As, then, in the physical world, so in the moral. When a king decided a dispute by a sentence, the judgment was assumed to be the result of direct inspiration. The divine agent, suggesting judicial awards to kings or to gods, the greatest of kings, was *Themis*. The peculiarity of the conception is brought out by the use of the plural.

Themistes, Themises, the plural of Themis, are
the awards themselves, divinely dictated to the
judge. Kings are spoken of as if they had a store
of " Themistes " ready to hand for use; but it
must be distinctly understood that they are not
laws, but judgments. " Zeus, or the human
king on earth," says Mr. Grote, in his History of
Greece, " is not a law-maker, but a judge." He
is provided with Themistes, but, consistently with
the belief in their emanation from above, they
cannot be supposed to be connected by any
thread of principle; they are separate, isolated
judgments.

Even in the Homeric poems, we can see that
these ideas are transient. Parities of circumstances were probably commoner in the simple
mechanism of ancient society than they are now,
and in the succession of similar cases awards are
likely to follow and resemble each other. Here
we have the germ or rudiment of a Custom, a
conception posterior to that of Themistes or judgments. However strongly we, with our modern
associations, may be inclined to lay down *a priori*
that the notion of a Custom must precede that of
a judicial sentence, and that a judgment must
affirm a Custom or punish its breach, it seems
quite certain that the historical order of the
ideas is that in which I have placed them.
The Homeric word for a custom in the embryo
is sometimes " Themis " in the singular—more
often " Dike," the meaning of which visibly
fluctuates between a " judgment " and a
" custom " or " usage." Νόμος, a Law, so great
and famous a term in the political vocabulary of
the later Greek society, does not occur in
Homer.

This notion of a divine agency, suggesting the
Themistes, and itself impersonated in Themis,
must be kept apart from other primitive beliefs
with which a superficial inquirer might confound
it.   The conception of the Deity dictating an
entire code or body of law, as in the case of the
Hindoo laws of Menu, seems to belong to a range
of ideas more recent and more advanced.
" Themis " and " Themistes " are much less
remotely linked with that persuasion which clung
so long and so tenaciously to the human mind,
of a divine influence underlying and supporting
every relation of life, every social institution. In
early law, and amid the rudiments of political
thought, symptoms of this belief meet us on all
sides.   A supernatural presidency is supposed to
consecrate and keep together all the cardinal institutions of those times, the State, the Race,
and the Family.   Men, grouped together in the
different relations which those institutions imply,
are bound to celebrate periodically common rites
and to offer common sacrifices; and every now
and then the same duty is even more significantly
recognized in the purifications and expiations
which they perform, and which appear intended
to deprecate punishment for involuntary or neg-
lectful disrespect.   Everybody acquainted with
ordinary classical literature will remember the
sacra gentilicia, which exercised so important an
influence on the early Roman law of adoption and
of wills.   And to this hour the Hindoo Customary Law, in which some of the most curious
features of primitive society are stereotyped,
makes almost all the rights of persons and all
the rules of succession hinge on the due solemn-
ization of fixed ceremonies at the dead man's

funeral, that is, at every point where a breach
occurs in the continuity of the family.

Before we quit this stage of jurisprudence, a
caution may be usefully given to the English
student. Bentham in his *Fragment on Government*, and Austin, in his *Province of Jurisprudence Determined*, resolve every law into a
command of the lawgiver, an *obligation* imposed
thereby on the citizen, and a *sanction* threatened
in the event of disobedience; and it is further pre-
dicated of the *command*, which is the first element
in a law, that it must prescribe, not a single act,
but a series or number of acts of the same class
or kind. The results of this separation of ingredients tally exactly with the facts of mature
jurisprudence; and, by a little straining of language, they may be made to correspond in form
with all law, of all kinds, at all epochs. It is
not, however, asserted that the notion of law
entertained by the generality is even now quite in
conformity with this dissection; and it is curious
that, the farther we penetrate into the primitive
history of thought, the farther we find ourselves
from a conception of law which at all resembles a
compound of the elements which Bentham determined. It is certain that, in the infancy of mankind, no sort of legislature, not even a distinct
author of law, is contemplated or conceived of.
Law has scarcely reached the footing of custom;
it is rather a habit. It is, to use a French phrase,
" in the air." The only authoritative statement
of right and wrong is a judicial sentence after the
facts, not one presupposing a law which has been
violated, but one which is breathed for the first
time by a higher power into the judge's mind at
the moment of adjudication. It is of course

extremely difficult for us to realize a view so far
removed from us in point both of time and of
association, but it will become more credible
when we dwell more at length on the constitution
of ancient society, in which every man, living
during the greater part of his life under the patriarchal despotism, was practically controlled in all
his actions by a regimen not of law but of caprice.
I may add that an Englishman should be better
able than a foreigner to appreciate the historical
fact that the " Themistes " preceded any conception of law, because, amid the many inconsistent
theories which prevail concerning the character of
English jurisprudence, the most popular, or at all
events the one which most affects practice, is
certainly a theory which assumes that adjudged
cases and precedents exist antecedently to rules,
principles, and distinctions. The " Themistes "
have too, it should be remarked, the characteristic which, in the view of Bentham and Austin,
distinguishes single or mere commands from laws.
A true law enjoins on all the citizens indifferently
a number of acts similar in class or kind; and
this is exactly the feature of a law which has
most deeply impressed itself on the popular mind,
causing the term " law " to be applied to mere
uniformities, successions, and similitudes. A
command prescribes only a single act, and it is to
commands, therefore, that " Themistes " are
more akin than to laws. They are simply adjudica-
tions on insulated states of fact, and do not necessarily follow each other in any orderly sequence.

The literature of the heroic age discloses to us
law in the germ under the " Themistes " and a
little more developed in the conception of
" Dike." The next stage which we reach in the

history of jurisprudence is strongly marked and
surrounded by the utmost interest. Mr. Grote,
in the second part and second chapter of his
History, has fully described the mode in which
society gradually clothed itself with a different
character from that delineated by Homer. Heroic
kingship depended partly on divinely given prerogative, and partly on the possession of supereminent strength, courage, and wisdom. Gradually, as the impression of the monarch's sacredness became weakened, and feeble members
occurred in the series of hereditary kings, the
royal power decayed, and at last gave way to the
dominion of aristocracies. If language so precise
can be used of the revolution, we might say that
the office of the king was usurped by that council
of chiefs which Homer repeatedly alludes to and
depicts. At all events from an epoch of kingly
rule we come everywhere in Europe to an era of
oligarchies; and even where the name of the
monarchical functions does not absolutely disappear, the authority of the king is reduced to a
mere shadow. He becomes a mere hereditary
general, as in Lacedæmon, a mere functionary, as
the King Archon at Athens, or a mere formal
hierophant, like the *Rex Sacrificulus* at Rome. In
Greece, Italy, and Asia Minor, the dominant
orders seem to have universally consisted of a
number of families united by an assumed relationship in blood, and, though they all appear at first
to have laid claim to a quasi-sacred character,
their strength does not seem to have resided in
their pretended sanctity. Unless they were pre-
maturely overthrown by the popular party, they
all ultimately approached very closely to what we
should now understand by a political aristocracy.

The changes which society underwent in the communities of the further Asia occurred of course at periods long anterior in point of time to these revolutions of the Italian and Hellenic worlds; but their relative place in civilization appears to have been the same, and they seem to have been exceedingly similar in general character. There is some evidence that the races which were subsequently united under the Persian monarchy, and those which peopled the peninsula of India, had all their heroic age and their era of aristocracies; but a military and a religious oligarchy appear to have grown up separately, nor was the authority of the king generally superseded. Contrary, too, to the course of events in the West, the religious element in the East tended to get the better of the military and political. Military and civil aristocracies disappear, annihilated or crushed into insignificance between the kings and the sacerdotal order; and the ultimate result at which we arrive is, a monarch enjoying great power, but circumscribed by the privileges of a caste of priests. With these differences, however, that in the East aristocracies became religious, in the West civil or political, the proposition that a historical era of aristocracies succeeded a historical era of heroic kings may be considered as true, if not of all mankind, at all events of all branches of the Indo-European family of nations.

The important point for the jurist is that these aristocracies were universally the depositaries and administrators of law. They seem to have succeeded to the prerogatives of the king, with the important difference, however, that they do not appear to have pretended to direct inspiration for each sentence. The connection of ideas which caused the judgments of the patriarchal chieftain to be attributed to superhuman dictation still shows itself here and there in the claim of a divine origin for the entire body of rules, or for certain parts of it, but the progress of thought no longer permits the solution of particular disputes to be explained by supposing an extra-human interposition. What the juristical oligarchy now claims is to monopolize the *knowledge* of the laws, to have the exclusive possession of the principles by which quarrels are decided. We have in fact arrived at the epoch of Customary Law. Customs or Observances now exist as a substantive aggregate, and are assumed to be precisely known to the aristocratic order or caste. Our authorities leave us no doubt that the trust lodged with the oligarchy was sometimes abused, but it certainly ought not to be regarded as a mere usurpation or engine of tyranny. Before the invention of writing, and during the infancy of the art, an aristocracy invested with judicial privileges formed the only expedient by which accurate preservation of the customs of the race or tribe could be at all approximated to. Their genuineness was, so far as possible, insured by confiding them to the recollection of a limited portion of the community.

The epoch of Customary Law, and of its custody by a privileged order, is a very remarkable one. The condition of the jurisprudence which it implies has left traces which may still be detected in legal and popular phraseology. The law, thus known exclusively to a privileged minority, whether a caste, an aristocracy, a priestly tribe, or a sacerdotal college, is true unwritten law.

Except this, there is no such thing as unwritten law in the world. English case-law is sometimes spoken of as unwritten, and there are some English theorists who assure us that if a code of English jurisprudence were prepared we should be turning unwritten law into written—a conversion, as they insist, if not of doubtful policy, at all events of the greatest seriousness. Now, it is quite true that there was once a period at which the English common law might reasonably have been termed unwritten. The elder English judges did really pretend to knowledge of rules, principles, and distinctions which were not entirely revealed to the bar and to the lay-public. Whether all the law which they claimed to monopolize was really unwritten, is exceedingly questionable; but at all events, on the assumption that there was once a large mass of civil and criminal rules known exclusively to the judges, it presently ceased to be unwritten law. As soon as the Courts at Westminster Hall began to base their judgments on cases recorded, whether in the year books or elsewhere, the law which they administered became written law. At the present moment a rule of English law has first to be disentangled from the recorded facts of adjudged printed precedents, then thrown into a form of words varying with the taste, precision, and knowledge of the particular judge, and then applied to the circumstances of the case for adjudication. But at no stage of this process has it any characteristic which distinguishes it from written law. It is written case-law, and only different from code-law because it is written in a different way.

From the period of Customary Law we come to another sharply defined epoch in the history of jurisprudence. We arrive at the era of Codes, those ancient codes of which the Twelve Tables of Rome were the most famous specimen. In Greece, in Italy, on the Hellenized sea-board of Western Asia, these codes all made their appearance at periods much the same everywhere, not, I mean, at periods identical in point of time, but similar in point of the relative progress of each community. Everywhere, in the countries I have named, laws engraven on tablets and published to the people take the place of usage deposited with the recollection of a privileged oligarchy. It must not for a moment be supposed that the refined considerations now urged in favour of what is called codification had any part or place in the change I have described. The ancient codes were doubtless originally suggested by the discovery and diffusion of the art of writing. It is true that the aristocracies seem to have abused their monopoly of legal knowledge; and at all events their exclusive possession of the law was a formidable impediment to the success of those popular movements which began to be universal in the western world. But, though democratic sentiment may have added to their popularity, the codes were certainly in the main a direct result of the invention of writing. Inscribed tablets were seen to be a better depositary of law, and a better security for its accurate preservation, than the memory of a number of persons however strengthened by habitual exercise.

The Roman code belongs to the class of codes I have been describing. Their value did not consist in any approach to symmetrical classifications, or to terseness and clearness of expression, but in their publicity, and in the knowledge which they furnished to everybody, as to what he was to do, and what not to do. It is, indeed, true that the Twelve Tables of Rome do exhibit some traces of systematic arrangement, but this is probably explained by the tradition that the framers of that body of law called in the assistance of Greeks who enjoyed the later Greek experience in the art of law-making. The fragments of the Attic Code of Solon show, however, that it had but little order, and probably the laws of Draco had even less. Quite enough too remains of these collections, both in the East and in the West, to show that they mingled up religious, civil, and merely moral ordinances, without any regard to differences in their essential character; and this is consistent with all we know of early thought from other sources, the severance of law from morality, and of religion from law, belonging very distinctly to the *later* stages of mental progress.

But, whatever to a modern eye are the singularities of these Codes, their importance to ancient societies was unspeakable. The question—and it was one which affected the whole future of each community—was not so much whether there there should be a code at all, for the majority of ancient societies seem to have obtained them sooner or later, and, but for the great interruption in the history of jurisprudence created by feudalism, it is likely that all modern law would be distinctly traceable to one or more of these fountainheads. But the point on which turned the history of the race was, at what period, at what stage of their social progress, they should have their laws put into writing. In the western world the plebeian or popular element in each State successfully assailed the oligarchical mono-

poly, and a code was nearly universally obtained
early in the history of the Commonwealth. But in
the East, as I have before mentioned, the ruling
aristocracies tended to become religious rather
than military or political, and gained, therefore,
rather than lost in power; while in some instances
the physical conformation of Asiatic countries had
the effect of making individual communities larger
and more numerous than in the West; and it is a
known social law that the larger the space over
which a particular set of institutions is diffused,
the greater is its tenacity and vitality. From
whatever cause, the codes obtained by Eastern
societies were obtained, relatively, much later
than by Western, and wore a very different
character. The religious oligarchies of Asia,
either for their own guidance, or for the relief of
their memory, or for the instruction of their
disciples, seem in all cases to have ultimately
embodied their legal learning in a code; but the
opportunity of increasing and consolidating their
influence was probably too tempting to be resisted.
Their complete monopoly of legal knowledge
appears to have enabled them to put off on the
world collections, not so much of the rules
actually observed as of the rules which the priestly
order considered proper to be observed. The
Hindoo code, called the Laws of Menu, which is
certainly a Brahmin compilation, undoubtedly enshrines many genuine observances of the Hindoo
race, but the opinion of the best contemporary
orientalists is, that it does not, as a whole, represent a set of rules ever actually administered in
Hindostan. It is, in great part, an ideal picture
of that which, in the view of the Brahmins, *ought*
to be the law. It is consistent with human nature

and with the special motives of their authors, that codes like that of Menu should pretend to the highest antiquity and claim to have emanated in their complete form from the Deity. Menu, according to Hindoo mythology, is an emanation from the supreme God; but the compilation which bears his name, though its exact date is not easily discovered, is, in point of the relative progress of Hindoo jurisprudence, a recent production.

Among the chief advantages which the Twelve Tables and similar codes conferred on the societies which obtained them, was the protection which they afforded against the frauds of the privileged oligarchy and also against the spontaneous depravation and debasement of the national institutions. The Roman Code was merely an enunciation in words of the existing customs of the Roman people. Relatively to the progress of the Romans in civilization, it was a remarkably early code, and it was published at a time when Roman society had barely emerged from that intellectual condition in which civil obligation and religious duty are inevitably confounded. Now a barbarous society practising a body of customs, is exposed to some especial dangers which may be absolutely fatal to its progress in civilization. The usages which a particular community is found to have adopted in its infancy and in its primitive seats are generally those which are on the whole best suited to promote its physical and moral well-being; and, if they are retained in their integrity until new social wants have taught new practices, the upward march of society is almost certain. But unhappily there is a law of development which ever threatens to operate upon unwritten usage. The customs are of course obeyed by multitudes who are incapable of understanding the true ground of their expediency, and who are therefore left inevitably to invent superstitious reasons for their permanence. A process then commences which may be shortly described by saying that usage which is reasonable generates usage which is unreasonable. Analogy, the most valuable of instruments in the maturity of jurisprudence, is the most dangerous of snares in its infancy. Prohibitions and ordinances, originally confined, for good reasons, to a single description of acts, are made to apply to all acts of the same class, because a man menaced with the anger of the gods for doing one thing, feels a natural terror in doing any other thing which is remotely like it. After one kind of food has been interdicted for sanitary reasons, the prohibition is extended to all food resembling it, though the resemblance occasionally depends on analogies the most fanciful. So, again, a wise provision for insuring general cleanliness dictates in time long routines of ceremonial ablution; and that division into classes which at a particular crisis of social history is necessary for the maintenance of the national existence degenerates into the most disastrous and blighting of all human institutions—Caste. The fate of the Hindoo law is, in fact, the measure of the value of the Roman code. Ethnology shows us that the Romans and the Hindoos sprang from the same original stock, and there is indeed a striking resemblance between what appear to have been their original customs. Even now, Hindoo jurisprudence has a substratum of forethought and sound judgment, but irrational imitation has engrafted in it an immense apparatus of cruel absurdities. From these corruptions the Romans were protected by their code. It was compiled while the usage was still wholesome, and a hundred years afterwards it might have been too late. The Hindoo law has been to a great extent embodied in writing, but, ancient as in one sense are the compendia which still exist in Sanskrit, they contain ample evidence that they were drawn up after the mischief had been done. We are not of course entitled to say that if the Twelve Tables had not been published the Romans would have been condemned to a civilization as feeble and perverted as that of the Hindoos, but thus much at least is certain, that *with* their code they were exempt from the very chance of so unhappy a destiny.

CHAPTER II

LEGAL FICTIONS

WHEN primitive law has once been embodied in a Code, there is an end to what may be called its spontaneous development. Henceforward the changes effected in it, if effected at all, are effected deliberately and from without. It is impossible to suppose that the customs of any race or tribe remained unaltered during the whole of the long —in some instances the immense—interval between their declaration by a patriarchal monarch and their publication in writing. It would be unsafe too to affirm that no part of the alteration was effected deliberately. But from the little we know of the progress of law during this period, we are justified in assuming that set

purpose had the very smallest share in producing
change. Such innovations on the earliest usages
as disclose themselves appear to have been dictated by feelings and modes of thought which,
under our present mental conditions, we are
unable to comprehend. A new era begins, however, with the Codes. Wherever, after this epoch,
we trace the course of legal modification we are
able to attribute it to the conscious desire of
improvement, or at all events of compassing
objects other than those which were aimed at in
the primitive times.

It may seem at first sight that no general propositions worth trusting can be elicited from the
history of legal systems subsequent to the codes.
The field is too vast. We cannot be sure that we
have included a sufficient number of phenomena
in our observations, or that we accurately understand those which we have observed. But the
undertaking will be seen to be more feasible, if
we consider that after the epoch of codes the
distinction between stationary and progressive
societies begins to make itself felt. It is only
with the progressive societies that we are concerned, and nothing is more remarkable than their
extreme fewness. In spite of overwhelming
evidence, it is most difficult for a citizen of
western Europe to bring thoroughly home to himself the truth that the civilization which surrounds
him is a rare exception in the history of the
world. The tone of thought common among
us, all our hopes, fears, and speculations,
would be materially affected, if we had vividly
before us the relation of the progressive races
to the totality of human life. It is indisputable
that much the greatest part of mankind has

never shown a particle of desire that its civil
institutions should be improved since the moment
when external completeness was first given to
them by their embodiment in some permanent
record. One set of usages has occasionally been
violently overthrown and superseded by another;
here and there a primitive code, pretending to a
supernatural origin, has been greatly extended,
and distorted into the most surprising forms, by
the perversity of sacerdotal commentators; but,
except in a small section of the world, there has
been nothing like the gradual amelioration of a
legal system. There has been material civilization, but, instead of the civilization expanding the
law, the law has limited the civilization. The
study of races in their primitive condition affords
us some clue to the point at which the development of certain societies has stopped. We can
see that Brahminical India has not passed beyond
a stage which occurs in the history of all the
families of mankind, the stage at which a rule of
law is not yet discriminated from a rule of
religion. The members of such a society consider that the transgression of a religious ordinance should be punished by civil penalties, and
that the violation of a civil duty exposes the delinquent to divine correction. In China this
point has been passed, but progress seems to
have been there arrested, because the civil laws
are coextensive with all the ideas of which the
race is capable. The difference between the
stationary and progressive societies is, however,
one of the great secrets which inquiry has yet to
penetrate. Among partial explanations of it I
venture to place the considerations urged at the
end of the last chapter. It may further be

remarked that no one is likely to succeed in the investigation who does not clearly realize that the stationary condition of the human race is the rule, the progressive the exception. And another indispensable condition of success is an accurate knowledge of Roman law in all its principal stages. The Roman jurisprudence has the longest known history of any set of human institutions. The character of all the changes which it underwent is tolerably well ascertained. From its commencement to its close, it was progressively modified for the better, or for what the authors of the modification conceived to be the better, and the course of improvement was continued through periods at which all the rest of human thought and action materially slackened its pace, and repeatedly threatened to settle down into stagnation.

I confine myself in what follows to the progressive societies. With respect to them it may be laid down that social necessities and social opinion are always more or less in advance of Law. We may come indefinitely near to the closing of the gap between them, but it has a perpetual tendency to reopen. Law is stable; the societies we are speaking of are progressive. The greater or less happiness of a people depends on the degree of promptitude with which the gulf is narrowed.

A general proposition of some value may be advanced with respect to the agencies by which Law is brought into harmony with society. These instrumentalities seem to me to be three in number, Legal Fictions, Equity, and Legislation. Their historical order is that in which I have placed them. Sometimes two of them will be seen operating together, and there are legal

systems which have escaped the influence of one
or other of them. But I know of no instance in
which the order of their appearance has been
changed or inverted. The early history of one of
them, Equity, is universally obscure, and hence it
may be thought by some that certain isolated
statutes, reformatory of the civil law, are older
than any equitable jurisdiction. My own belief is
that remedial Equity is everywhere older than
remedial Legislation; but, should this be not
strictly true, it would only be necessary to limit
the proposition respecting their order of sequence
to the periods at which they exercise a sustained
and substantial influence in transforming the
original law.

I employ the word " fiction " in a sense considerably wider than that in which English lawyers
are accustomed to use it, and with a meaning
much more extensive than that which belonged to
the Roman "fictiones." Fictio, in old Roman
law, is properly a term of pleading, and signifies
a false averment on the part of the plaintiff which
the defendant was not allowed to traverse; such,
for example, as an averment that the plaintiff was
a Roman citizen, when in truth he was a foreigner.
The object of these " fictiones " was, of course,
to give jurisdiction, and they therefore strongly
resembled the allegations in the writs of the English Queen's Bench and Exchequer, by which
those Courts contrived to usurp the jurisdiction
of the Common Pleas :—the allegation that the
defendant was in custody of the king's marshal,
or that the plaintiff was the king's debtor, and
could not pay his debt by reason of the defendant's default. But I now employ the expression
" Legal Fiction " to signify any assumption which

conceals, or affects to conceal, the fact that a rule
of law has undergone alteration, its letter remaining unchanged, its operation being modified. The
words, therefore, include the instances of fictions
which I have cited from the English and Roman
law, but they embrace much more, for I should
speak both of the English Case-law and of the
Roman Responsa Prudentum as resting on
fictions. Both these examples will be examined
presently. The *fact* is in both cases that the law
has been wholly changed; the *fiction* is that it
remains what it always was. It is not difficult
to understand why fictions in all their forms are
particularly congenial to the infancy of society.
They satisfy the desire for improvement, which is
not quite wanting, at the same time that they do
not offend the superstitious disrelish for change
which is always present. At a particular stage
of social progress they are invaluable expedients
for overcoming the rigidity of law, and, indeed,
without one of them, the Fiction of Adoption
which permits the family tie to be artificially
created, it is difficult to understand how society
would ever have escaped from its swaddling-
clothes, and taken its first steps towards civilization. We must, therefore, not suffer ourselves to
be affected by the ridicule which Bentham pours
on legal fictions wherever he meets them. To
revile them as merely fraudulent is to betray
ignorance of their peculiar office in the historical
development of law. But at the same time it
would be equally foolish to agree with those
theorists who, discerning that fictions have had
their uses, argue that they ought to be stereotyped in our system. They have had their day,
but it has long since gone by. It is unworthy of

us to effect an admittedly beneficial object by so rude a device as a legal fiction. I cannot admit any anomaly to be innocent, which makes the law either more difficult to understand or harder to arrange in harmonious order. Now legal fictions are the greatest of obstacles to symmetrical classification. The rule of law remains sticking in the system, but it is a mere shell. It has been long ago undermined, and a new rule hides itself under its cover. Hence there is at once a difficulty in knowing whether the rule which is actually operative should be classed in its true or in its apparent place, and minds of different casts will differ as to the branch of the alternative which ought to be selected. If the English law is ever to assume an orderly distribution, it will be necessary to prune away the legal fictions which, in spite of some recent legislative improvements, are still abundant in it.

The next instrumentality by which the adaptation of law to social wants is carried on I call Equity, meaning by that word any body of rules existing by the side of the original civil law, founded on distinct principles and claiming incidentally to supersede the civil law in virtue of a superior sanctity inherent in those principles. The Equity whether of the Roman Prætors or of the English Chancellors, differs from the Fictions which in each case preceded it, in that the interference with law is open and avowed. On the other hand, it differs from Legislation, the agent of legal improvement which comes after it, in that its claim to authority is grounded, not on the prerogative of any external person or body, not even on that of the magistrate who enunciates it, but on the special nature of its principles, to which

it is alleged that all law ought to conform. The
very conception of a set of principles, invested
with a higher sacredness than those of the original
law and demanding application independently of
the consent of any external body, belongs to a
much more advanced stage of thought than that
to which legal fictions originally suggested themselves.

Legislation, the enactments of a legislature
which, whether it take the form of an autocratic
prince or of a parliamentary assembly, is the assumed organ of the entire society, is the last of
the ameliorating instrumentalities.   It differs
from Legal Fictions just as Equity differs from
them, and it is also distinguished from Equity, as
deriving its authority from an external body or
person. Its obligatory force is independent of
its principles. The legislature, whatever be the
actual restraints imposed on it by public opinion,
is in theory empowered to impose what obligations
it pleases on the members of the community.
There is nothing to prevent its legislating in the
wantonness of caprice. Legislation may be dictated by equity, if that last word be used to indicate some standard of right and wrong to which
its enactments happen to be adjusted; but then
these enactments are indebted for their binding
force to the authority of the legislature and not to
that of the principles on which the legislature
acted; and thus they differ from rules of Equity,
in the technical sense of the word, which pretend
to a paramount sacredness entitling them at once
to the recognition of the courts even without the
concurrence of prince or parliamentary assembly.
It is the more necessary to note these differences,
because a student of Bentham would be apt to

confound Fictions, Equity, and Statute law under the single head of legislation. They all, he would say, involve *law-making*; they differ only in respect of the machinery by which the new law is produced. That is perfectly true, and we must never forget it; but it furnishes no reason why we should deprive ourselves of so convenient a term as Legislation in the special sense. Legislation and Equity are disjoined in the popular mind and in the minds of most lawyers; and it will never do to neglect the distinction between them, however conventional, when important practical consequences follow from it.

It would be easy to select from almost any regularly developed body of rules examples of *legal fictions*, which at once betray their true character to the modern observer. In the two instances which I proceed to consider, the nature of the expedient employed is not so readily detected. The first authors of these fictions did not perhaps intend to innovate, certainly did not wish to be suspected of innovating. There are, moreover, and always have been, persons who refuse to see any fiction in the process, and conventional language bears out their refusal. No examples, therefore, can be better calculated to illustrate the wide diffusion of legal fictions, and the efficiency with which they perform their two-fold office of transforming a system of laws and of concealing the transformation.

We in England are well accustomed to the extension, modification, and improvement of law by a machinery which, in theory, is incapable of altering one jot or one line of existing jurisprudence. The process by which this virtual legislation is effected is not so much insensible as unacknowledged. With respect to that great portion of our legal system which is enshrined in cases and recorded in law reports, we habitually employ a double language and entertain, as it would appear, a double and inconsistent set of ideas. When a group of facts come before an English Court for adjudication, the whole course of the discussion between the judge and the advocates assumes that no question is, or can be, raised which will call for the application of any principles but old ones, or of any distinctions but such as have long since been allowed. It is taken absolutely for granted that there is somewhere a rule of known law which will cover the facts of the dispute now litigated, and that, if such a rule be not discovered, it is only that the necessary patience, knowledge, or acumen is not forthcoming to detect it. Yet the moment the judgment has been rendered and reported, we slide unconsciously or unavowedly into a new language and a new train of thought. We now admit that the new decision *has* modified the law. The rules applicable have, to use the very inaccurate expression sometimes employed, become more elastic. In fact they have been changed. A clear addition has been made to the precedents, and the canon of law elicited by comparing the precedents is not the same with that which would have been obtained if the series of cases had been curtailed by a single example. The fact that the old rule has been repealed, and that a new one has replaced it, eludes us, because we are not in the habit of throwing into precise language the legal formulas which we derive from the precedents, so that a change in their tenor is not easily detected unless it is violent and glaring. I shall not now pause

to consider at length the causes which have led
English lawyers to acquiesce in these curious
anomalies. Probably it will be found that originally it was the received doctrine that somewhere,
in nubibus or *in gremio magistratuum*, there
existed a complete, coherent, symmetrical body
of English law, of an amplitude sufficient to furnish principles which would apply to any conceiv-
able combination of circumstances. The theory
was at first much more thoroughly believed in
than it is now, and indeed it may have had a
better foundation. The judges of the thirteenth
century may have really had at their command a
mine of law unrevealed to the bar and to the lay-
public, for there is some reason for suspecting
that in secret they borrowed freely, though not
always wisely, from current compendia of the
Roman and Canon laws. But that storehouse
was closed so soon as the points decided at Westminster Hall became numerous enough to supply
a basis for a substantive system of jurisprudence;
and now for centuries English practitioners have
so expressed themselves as to convey the paradoxical proposition that, except by Equity and
Statute law, nothing has been added to the basis
since it was first constituted. We do not admit
that our tribunals legislate; we imply that they
have never legislated; and yet we maintain that
the rules of the English common law, with some
assistance from the Court of Chancery and from
Parliament, are coextensive with the complicated
interests of modern society.

A body of law bearing a very close and very instructive resemblance to our case-law in those
particulars which I have noticed, was known to
the Romans under the name of the Responsa Pru-

dentum, the " answers of the learned in the law."
The form of these Responses varied a good deal
at different periods of the Roman jurisprudence,
but throughout its whole course they consisted of
explanatory glosses on authoritative written documents, and at first they were exclusively collections of opinions interpretative of the Twelve
Tables. As with us, all legal language adjusted
itself to the assumption that the text of the old
Code remained unchanged. There was the express rule. It overrode all glosses and comments,
and no one openly admitted that any interpretation of it, however eminent the interpreter, was
safe from revision on appeal to the venerable
texts. Yet in point of fact, Books of Responses
bearing the names of leading jurisconsults
obtained an authority at least equal to that of our
reported cases, and constantly modified, extended,
limited or practically overruled the provisions of
the Decemviral law. The authors of the new
jurisprudence during the whole progress of its
formation professed the most sedulous respect for
the letter of the Code. They were merely explaining it, deciphering it, bringing out its full meaning; but then, in the result, by piecing texts
together, by adjusting the law to states of fact
which actually presented themselves and by
speculating on its possible application to others
which might occur, by introducing principles of
interpretation derived from the exegesis of other
written documents which fell under their observation, they educed a vast variety of canons which
had never been dreamed of by the compilers of
the Twelve Tables and which were in truth rarely
or never to be found there. All these treatises of
the jurisconsults claimed respect on the ground of

their assumed conformity with the Code, but their comparative authority depended on the reputation of the particular jurisconsults who gave them to the world. Any name of universally acknowledged greatness clothed a Book of Responses with a binding force hardly less than that which belonged to enactments of the legislature; and such a book in its turn constituted a new foundation on which a further body of jurisprudence might rest. The Responses of the early lawyers were not however published, in the modern sense, by their author. They were recorded and edited by his pupils, and were not therefore in all probability arranged according to any scheme of classification. The part of the students in these publications must be carefully noted, because the service they rendered to their teacher seems to have been generally repaid by his sedulous attention to the pupils' education. The educational treatises called Institutes or Commentaries, which are a later fruit of the duty then recognised, are among the most remarkable features of the Roman system. It was apparently in these Institutional works, and not in the books intended for trained lawyers, that the jurisconsults gave to the public their classifications and their proposals for modifying and improving the technical phraseology.

In comparing the Roman Responsa Prudentum with their nearest English counterpart, it must be carefully borne in mind that the authority by which this part of the Roman jurisprudence was expounded was not the *bench*, but the *bar*. The decision of a Roman tribunal, though conclusive in the particular case, had no ulterior authority except such as was given by the professional repute of the magistrate who happened to be in

office for the time. Properly speaking, there was
no institution at Rome during the republic analogous to the English Bench, the Chambers of
Imperial Germany, or the Parliaments of Monarchical France. There were magistrates indeed,
invested with momentous judicial functions in
their several departments, but the tenure of the
magistracies was but for a single year, so that
they are much less aptly compared to a permanent
judicature than to a cycle of offices briskly cir-
culating among the leaders of the bar. Much
might be said on the origin of a condition of things
which looks to us like a startling anomaly, but
which was in fact much more congenial than our
own system to the spirit of ancient societies,
tending, as they always did, to split into distinct
orders which, however exclusive themselves,
tolerated no professional hierarchy above them.

It is remarkable that this system did not produce certain effects which might on the whole
have been expected from it. It did not, for
example, *popularize* the Roman law,—it did not,
as in some of the Greek republics, lessen the
effort of intellect required for the mastery of the
science, although its diffusion and authoritative
exposition were opposed by no artificial barriers.
On the contrary, if it had not been for the operation of a separate set of causes, there were strong
probabilities that the Roman jurisprudence would
have become as minute, technical, and difficult as
any system which has since prevailed. Again, a
consequence which might still more naturally
have been looked for, does not appear at any time
to have exhibited itself. The jurisconsults, until
the liberties of Rome were overthrown, formed a
class which was quite undefined and must have

fluctuated greatly in numbers; nevertheless, there does not seem to have existed a doubt as to the particular individuals whose opinion, in their generation, was conclusive on the cases submitted to them. The vivid pictures of a leading jurisconsult's daily practice which abound in Latin literature—the clients from the country flocking to his antechamber in the early morning, and the students standing round with their note-books to record the great lawyer's replies —are seldom or never identified at any given period with more than one or two conspicuous names. Owing too to the direct contact of the client and the advocate, the Roman people itself seems to have been always alive to the rise and fall of professional reputation, and there is abundance of proof, more particularly in the well-known oration of Cicero, *Pro Muræna*, that the reverence of the commons for forensic success was apt to be excessive rather than deficient.

We cannot doubt that the peculiarities which have been noted in the instrumentality by which the development of the Roman law was first effected, were the source of its characteristic excellence, its early wealth in principles. The growth and exuberance of principle was fostered, in part, by the competition among the expositors of the law, an influence wholly unknown where there exists a Bench, the depositaries intrusted by king or commonwealth with the prerogative of justice. But the chief agency, no doubt, was the uncontrolled multiplication of cases for legal decision. The state of facts which caused genuine perplexity to a country client was not a whit more entitled to form the basis of the jurisconsult's Response, or legal decision, than a set of hypothe-

tical circumstances propounded by an ingenious
pupil. All combinations of fact were on precisely
the same footing, whether they were real or
imaginary. It was nothing to the jurisconsult
that his opinion was overruled for the moment by
the magistrate who adjudicated on his client's
case, unless that magistrate happened to rank
above him in legal knowledge or the esteem of
his profession. I do not, indeed, mean it to be
inferred that he would wholly omit to consider
his client's advantage, for the client was in
earlier times the great lawyer's constituent and
at a later period his paymaster, but the main
road to the rewards of ambition lay through the
good opinion of his order, and it is obvious that
under such a system as I have been describing
this was much more likely to be secured by viewing each case as an illustration of a great principle, or an exemplification of a broad rule, than
by merely shaping it for an insulated forensic
triumph. A still more powerful influence must
have been exercised by the want of any distinct
check on the suggestion or invention of possible
questions. Where the data can be multiplied at
pleasure, the facilities for evolving a general rule
are immensely increased. As the law is administered among ourselves, the judge cannot
travel out of the sets of facts exhibited before
him or before his predecessors. Accordingly
each group of circumstances which is adjudicated
upon receives, to employ a Gallicism, a sort of
consecration. It acquires certain qualities which
distinguish it from every other case genuine or
hypothetical. But at Rome, as I have attempted
to explain, there was nothing resembling a Bench
or Chamber of judges; and therefore no combina-

tion of facts possessed any particular value more than another. When a difficulty came for opinion before the jurisconsult, there was nothing to prevent a person endowed with a nice perception of analogy from at once proceeding to adduce and consider an entire class of supposed questions with which a particular feature connected it. Whatever were the practical advice given to the client, the *responsum* treasured up in the note-books of listening pupils would doubtless contemplate the circumstances as governed by a great principle, or included in a sweeping rule. Nothing like this has ever been possible among ourselves, and it should be acknowledged that in many criticisms passed on the English law the manner in which it has been enunciated seems to have been lost sight of. The hesitation of our courts in declaring principles may be much more reasonably attributed to the comparative scantiness of our precedents, voluminous as they appear to him who is acquainted with no other system, than to the temper of our judges. It is true that in the wealth of legal principle we are considerably poorer than several modern European nations. But they, it must be remembered, took the Roman jurisprudence for the foundation of their civil institutions. They built the *débris* of the Roman law into their walls; but in the materials and workmanship of the residue there is not much which distinguishes it favourably from the structure erected by the English judicature.

The period of Roman freedom was the period during which the stamp of a distinctive character was impressed on the Roman jurisprudence; and through all the earlier part of it, it was by the Responses of the jurisconsults that the development of the law was mainly carried on. But as we approach the fall of the republic there are signs that the Responses are assuming a form which must have been fatal to their farther expansion. They are becoming systematized and reduced into compendia. Q. Mucius Scævola, the Pontifex, is said to have published a manual of the entire Civil Law, and there are traces in the writings of Cicero of growing disrelish for the old methods, as compared with the more active instruments of legal innovation. Other agencies had in fact by this time been brought to bear on the law. The Edict, or annual proclamation of the Prætor, had risen into credit as the principal engine of law reform, and L. Cornelius Sylla, by causing to be enacted the great group of statutes called the *Leges Corneliæ*, had shown what rapid and speedy improvements can be effected by direct legislation. The final blow to the Responses was dealt by Augustus, who limited to a few leading jurisconsults the right of giving binding opinions on cases submitted to them, a change which, though it brings us nearer the ideas of the modern world, must obviously have altered fundamentally the characteristics of the legal profession and the nature of its influence on Roman law. At a later period another school of jurisconsults arose, the great lights of jurisprudence for all time. But Ulpian and Paulus, Gaius and Papinian, were not authors of Responses. Their works were regular treatises on particular departments of the law, more especially on the Prætor's Edict.

The *Equity* of the Romans and the Prætorian

Edict by which it was worked into their system, will be considered in the next chapter. Of the Statute Law it is only necessary to say that it was scanty during the republic, but became very voluminous under the empire. In the youth and infancy of a nation it is a rare thing for the legislature to be called into action for the general reform of private law. The cry of the people is not for change in the laws, which are usually valued above their real worth, but solely for their pure, complete, and easy administration; and recourse to the legislative body is generally directed to the removal of some great abuse, or the decision of some incurable quarrel between classes and dynasties. There seems in the minds of the Romans to have been some association between the enactment of a large body of statutes and the settlement of society after a great civil commotion. Sylla signalized his reconstitution of the republic by the Leges Corneliæ; Julius Cæsar contemplated vast additions to the Statute Law; Augustus caused to be passed the all-important group of Leges Juliæ; and among later emperors the most active promulgators of constitutions are princes who, like Constantine, have the concerns of the world to readjust. The true period of Roman Statute Law does not begin till the establishment of the empire. The enactments of the emperors, clothed at first in the pretence of popular sanction, but afterwards emanating undisguisedly from the imperial prerogative, extend in increasing massiveness from the consolidation of Augustus's power to the publication of the Code of Justinian. It will be seen that even in the reign of the second emperor a considerable approximation is made to that

condition of the law and that mode of administering it with which we are all familiar. A
statute law and a limited board of expositors have
risen into being; a permanent court of appeal
and a collection of approved commentaries will
very shortly be added; and thus we are brought
close on the ideas of our own day.

CHAPTER III

LAW OF NATURE AND EQUITY

THE theory of a set of legal principles, entitled
by their intrinsic superiority to supersede the
older law, very early obtained currency both in
the Roman state and in England. Such a body
of principles, existing in any system, has in the
foregoing chapters been denominated Equity, a
term which, as will presently be seen, was one
(though only one) of the designations by which
this agent of legal change was known to the
Roman jurisconsults. The jurisprudence of the
Court of Chancery, which bears the name of
Equity in England, could only be adequately
discussed in a separate treatise. It is extremely
complex in its texture and derives its materials
from several heterogeneous sources. The early
ecclesiastical chancellors contributed to it, from
the Canon Law, many of the principles which lie
deepest in its structure. The Roman law, more
fertile than the Canon Law in rules applicable to
secular disputes, was not seldom resorted to by
a later generation of Chancery judges, amid
whose recorded dicta we often find entire texts
from the *Corpus Juris Civilis* imbedded, with

their terms unaltered, though their origin is never acknowledged. Still more recently, and particularly at the middle and during the latter half of the 18th century, the mixed systems of jurisprudence and morals constructed by the publicists of the Low Countries appear to have been much studied by English lawyers, and from the chancellorship of Lord Talbot to the commencement of Lord Eldon's chancellorship these works had considerable effect on the rulings of the Court of Chancery. The system, which obtained its ingredients from these various quarters, was greatly controlled in its growth by the necessity imposed on it of conforming itself to the analogies of the common law, but it has always answered the description of a body of comparatively novel legal principles claiming to override the older jurisprudence of the country on the strength of an intrinsic ethical superiority.

The Equity of Rome was a much simpler structure, and its development from its first appearance can be much more easily traced. Both its character and its history deserve attentive examination. It is the root of several conceptions which have exercised profound influence on human thought, and through human thought have seriously affected the destinies of mankind.

The Romans described their legal system as consisting of two ingredients. "All nations," says the Institutional Treatise published under the authority of the Emperor Justinian, "who are ruled by laws and customs, are governed partly by their own particular laws, and partly by those laws which are common to all mankind. The law which a people enacts is called the Civil Law of that people, but that which natural

reason appoints for all mankind is called the
Law of Nations, because all nations use it."
The part of the law " which natural reason appoints for all mankind " was the element which
the Edict of the Prætor was supposed to have
worked into Roman jurisprudence. Elsewhere it
is styled more simply Jus Naturale, or the Law
of Nature; and its ordinances are said to be
dictated by Natural Equity (*naturalis æquitas*)
as well as by natural reason. I shall attempt to
discover the origin of these famous phrases, Law
of Nations, Law of Nature, Equity, and to determine how the conceptions which they indicate
are related to one another.

The most superficial student of Roman history
must be struck by the extraordinary degree in
which the fortunes of the republic were affected
by the presence of foreigners, under different
names, on her soil. The causes of this immigra-
tion are discernible enough at a later period, for
we can readily understand why men of all races
should flock to the mistress of the world; but
the same phenomenon of a large population of
foreigners and denizens meets us in the very
earliest records of the Roman State. No doubt,
the instability of society in ancient Italy, composed as it was in great measure of robber tribes,
gave men considerable inducement to locate
themselves in the territory of any community
strong enough to protect itself and them from
external attack, even though protection should
be purchased at the cost of heavy taxation, political disfranchisement, and much social humilia-
tion. It is probable, however, that this explanation is imperfect, and that it could only be completed by taking into account those active

commercial relations which, though they are little reflected in the military traditions of the republic, Rome appears certainly to have had with Carthage and with the interior of Italy in pre-historic times. Whatever were the circumstances to which it was attributable, the foreign element in the commonwealth determined the whole course of its history, which, at all its stages, is little more than a narrative of conflicts between a stubborn nationality and an alien population. Nothing like this has been seen in modern times; on the one hand, because modern European communities have seldom or never received any accession of foreign immigrants which was large enough to make itself felt by the bulk of the native citizens, and on the other, because modern states, being held together by allegiance to a king or political superior, absorb considerable bodies of immigrant settlers with a quickness unknown to the ancient world, where the original citizens of a commonwealth always believed themselves to be united by kinship in blood, and resented a claim to equality of privilege as a usurpation of their birthright. In the early Roman republic the principle of the absolute exclusion of foreigners pervaded the Civil Law no less than the Constitution. The alien or denizen could have no share in any institution supposed to be coeval with the State. He could not have the benefit of Quiritarian law. He could not be a party to the *nexum* which was at once the conveyance and the contract of the primitive Romans. He could not sue by the Sacramental Action, a mode of litigation of which the origin mounts up to the very infancy of civilization. Still, neither the interest nor the security of

Rome permitted him to be quite outlawed. All
ancient communities ran the risk of being overthrown by a very slight disturbance of equili-
brium, and the mere instinct of self-preservation
would force the Romans to devise some method
of adjusting the rights and duties of foreigners,
who might otherwise—and this was a danger of
real importance in the ancient world—have
decided their controversies by armed strife.
Moreover, at no period of Roman history was
foreign trade entirely neglected. It was therefore probably half as a measure of police and half
in furtherance of commerce that jurisdiction was
first assumed in disputes to which the parties
were either foreigners or a native and a foreigner.
The assumption of such a jurisdiction brought
with it the immediate necessity of discovering
some principles on which the questions to be
adjudicated upon could be settled, and the principles applied to this object by the Roman
lawyers were eminently characteristic of the
time. They refused, as I have said before, to
decide the new cases by pure Roman Civil Law.
They refused, no doubt because it seemed to involve some kind of degradation, to apply the law
of the particular State from which the foreign
litigant came. The expedient to which they resorted was that of selecting the rules of law common to Rome and to the different Italian communities in which the immigrants were born.
In other words, they set themselves to form a
system answering to the primitive and literal
meaning of Jus Gentium, that is, Law common
to all Nations. Jus Gentium was, in fact, the
sum of the common ingredients in the customs
of the old Italian tribes, for they were *all the*

nations whom the Romans had the means of observing, and who sent successive swarms of immigrants to Roman soil. Whenever a particular usage was seen to be practised by a large number of separate races in common it was set down as part of the Law common to all Nations, or Jus Gentium. Thus, although the conveyance of property was certainly accompanied by very different forms in the different commonwealths surrounding Rome, the actual transfer, tradition, or delivery of the article intended to be conveyed was a part of the ceremonial in all of them. It was, for instance, a part, though a subordinate part, in the Mancipation or conveyance peculiar to Rome. Tradition, therefore, being in all probability the only common ingredient in the modes of conveyance which the jurisconsults had the means of observing, was set down as an institution Juris Gentium, or rule of the Law common to all Nations. A vast number of other observances were scrutinized with the same result. Some common characteristic was discovered in all of them, which had a common object, and this characteristic was classed in the Jus Gentium. The Jus Gentium was accordingly a collection of rules and principles, determined by observation to be common to the institutions which prevailed among the various Italian tribes.

The circumstances of the origin of the Jus Gentium are probably a sufficient safeguard against the mistake of supposing that the Roman lawyers had any special respect for it. It was the fruit in part of their disdain for all foreign law, and in part of their disinclination to give the foreigner the advantage of their own indigenous

Jus Civile. It is true that we, at the present day,
should probably take a very different view of the
Jus Gentium, if we were performing the operation which was effected by the Roman jurisconsults. We should attach some vague superiority
or precedence to the element which we had thus
discerned underlying and pervading so great a
variety of usage. We should have a sort of
respect for rules and principles so universal.
Perhaps we should speak of the common ingredient as being of the essence of the transaction
into which it entered, and should stigmatize the
remaining apparatus of ceremony, which varied in
different communities, as adventitious and accidental. Or it may be, we should infer that the
races which we were comparing had once obeyed
a great system of common institutions of which
the Jus Gentium was the reproduction, and that
the complicated usages of separate commonwealths were only corruptions and depravations
of the simpler ordinances which had once
regulated their primitive state. But the results
to which modern ideas conduct the observer are,
as nearly as possible, the reverse of those which
were instinctively brought home to the primitive
Roman. What we respect or admire, he disliked
or regarded with jealous dread. The parts of
jurisprudence which he looked upon with affection were exactly those which a modern theorist
leaves out of consideration as accidental and
transitory; the solemn gestures of the mancipation; the nicely adjusted questions and answers
of the verbal contract; the endless formalities of
pleading and procedure. The Jus Gentium was
merely a system forced on his attention by a
political necessity. He loved it as little as he

loved the foreigners from whose institutions it was
derived and for whose benefit it was intended.
A complete revolution in his ideas was required
before it could challenge his respect, but so complete was it when it did occur, that the true reason
why our modern estimate of the Jus Gentium
differs from that which has just been described,
is that both modern jurisprudence and modern
philosophy have inherited the matured views of
the later jurisconsults on this subject. There did
come a time when, from an ignoble appendage of
the Jus Civile, the Jus Gentium came to be considered a great though as yet imperfectly
developed model to which all law ought as far as
possible to conform. This crisis arrived when the
Greek theory of a Law of Nature was applied to
the practical Roman administration of the Law
common to all Nations.

The Jus Naturale, or Law of Nature, is simply
the Jus Gentium or Law of Nations seen in the
light of a peculiar theory. An unfortunate attempt to discriminate them was made by the jurisconsult Ulpian, with the propensity to distinguish
characteristic of a lawyer, but the language of
Gaius, a much higher authority, and the passage
quoted before from the Institutes leave no room
for doubt, that the expressions were practically
convertible. The difference between them was
entirely historical, and no distinction in essence
could ever be established between them. It is
almost unnecessary to add that the confusion
between Jus Gentium, or Law common to all
Nations, and *international law* is entirely modern.
The classical expression for international law is
Jus Feciale or the law of negotiation and diplo-
macy. It is, however, unquestionable that indis-

tinct impressions as to the meaning of Jus Gentium had considerable share in producing the
modern theory that the relations of independent
states are governed by the Law of Nature.

It becomes necessary to investigate the Greek
conceptions of nature and her law. The word
φύσις, which was rendered in the Latin *natura*
and our *nature*, denoted beyond all doubt originally the material universe, but it was the material
universe contemplated under an aspect which—
such is our intellectual distance from those times
—it is not very easy to delineate in modern language. Nature signified the physical world regarded as the result of some primordial element or
law. The oldest Greek philosophers had been accustomed to explain the fabric of creation as the
manifestation of some single principle which they
variously asserted to be movement, force, fire,
moisture, or generation. In its simplest and most
ancient sense, Nature is precisely the physical universe looked upon in this way as the manifestation
of a principle. Afterwards, the later Greek sects,
returning to a path from which the greatest intel-
lects of Greece had meanwhile strayed, added the
moral to the *physical* world in the conception of
Nature. They extended the term till it embraced
not merely the visible creation, but the thoughts,
observances, and aspirations of mankind.   Still, as
before, it was not solely the moral phenomena of
human society which they understood by *Nature*,
but these phenomena considered as resolvable into
some general and simple laws.

Now, just as the oldest Greek theorists supposed
that the sports of chance had changed the material
universe from its simple primitive form into its
present heterogeneous condition, so their intel-

lectual descendants imagined that but for un-
toward accident the human race would have conformed itself to simpler rules of conduct and a
less tempestuous life. To live according to *nature*
came to be considered as the end for which man
was created, and which the best men were bound
to compass. To live according to *nature* was to
rise above the disorderly habits and gross indulgences of the vulgar to higher laws of action which
nothing but self-denial and self-command would
enable the aspirant to observe. It is notorious
that this proposition—live according to nature—
was the sum of the tenets of the famous Stoic
philosophy. Now on the subjugation of Greece
that philosophy made instantaneous progress in
Roman society. It possessed natural fascinations
for the powerful class who, in theory at least,
adhered to the simple habits of the ancient
Italian race, and disdained to surrender themselves to the innovations of foreign fashion. Such
persons began immediately to affect the Stoic
precepts of life according to nature—an affecta-
tion all the more grateful, and, I may add, all
the more noble, from its contrast with the unbounded profligacy which was being diffused
through the imperial city by the pillage of the
world and by the example of its most luxurious
races. In the front of the disciples of the new
Greek school, we might be sure, even if we did
not know it historically, that the Roman lawyers
figured. We have abundant proof that, there
being substantially but two professions in the
Roman republic, the military men were generally
identified with the party of movement, but the
lawyers were universally at the head of the party
of resistance.

The alliance of the lawyers with the Stoic philosophers lasted through many centuries. Some of the earliest names in the series of renowned jurisconsults are associated with Stoicism, and ultimately we have the golden age of Roman jurisprudence fixed by general consent at the era of the Antonine Cæsars, the most famous disciples to whom that philosophy has given a rule of life. The long diffusion of these doctrines among the members of a particular profession was sure to affect the art which they practised and influenced. Several positions which we find in the remains of the Roman jurisconsults are scarcely intelligible, unless we use the Stoic tenets as our key; but at the same time it is a serious, though a very common, error to measure the influence of Stoicism on Roman law by counting up the number of legal rules which can be confidently affiliated on Stoical dogmas. It has often been observed that the strength of Stoicism resided not in its canons of conduct, which were often repulsive or ridiculous, but in the great though vague principle which it inculcated of resistance to passion. Just in the same way the influence on jurisprudence of the Greek theories, which had their most distinct expression in Stoicism, consisted not in the number of specific positions which they contributed to Roman law, but in the single fundamental assumption which they lent to it. After Nature had become a household word in the mouths of the Romans, the belief gradually prevailed among the Roman lawyers that the old Jus Gentium was in fact the lost code of Nature, and that the Prætor in framing an Edictal jurisprudence on the principles of the Jus Gentium

was gradually restoring a type from which law
had only departed to deteriorate. The inference
from this belief was immediate, that it was the
Prætor's duty to supersede the Civil Law as much
as possible by the Edict, to revive as far as might
be the institutions by which Nature had governed
man in the primitive state. Of course, there were
many impediments to the amelioration of law by
this agency. There may have been prejudices to
overcome even in the legal profession itself, and
Roman habits were far too tenacious to give way
at once to mere philosophical theory. The indirect methods by which the Edict combated certain technical anomalies, show the caution which
its authors were compelled to observe, and down
to the very days of Justinian there was some part
of the old law which had obstinately resisted its
influence. But, on the whole, the progress of the
Romans in legal improvement was astonishingly
rapid as soon as stimulus was applied to it by the
theory of Natural Law. The ideas of simplifica-
tion and generalization had always been associated with the conception of Nature; simplicity,
symmetry, and intelligibility came therefore to
be regarded as the characteristics of a good legal
system, and the taste for involved language, multiplied ceremonials, and useless difficulties disappeared altogether. The strong will and unusual opportunities of Justinian were needed to
bring the Roman law to its existing shape, but
the ground plan of the system had been sketched
long before the imperial reforms were effected.

What was the exact point of contact between
the old Jus Gentium and the Law of Nature? I
think that they touch and blend through Æquitas,
or Equity in its original sense; and here we seem

to come to the first appearance in jurisprudence
of this famous term, Equity. In examining an
expression which has so remote an origin and so
long a history as this, it is always safest to penetrate, if possible, to the simple metaphor or figure
which at first shadowed forth the conception. It
has generally been supposed that Æquitas is the
equivalent of the Greek ἰσότης, i.e., the principle
of equal or proportionate distribution. The equal
division of numbers or physical magnitudes is
doubtless closely entwined with our perceptions of
justice; there are few associations which keep
their ground in the mind so stubbornly or are
dismissed from it with such difficulty by the
deepest thinkers. Yet in tracing the history of
this association, it certainly does not seem to have
suggested itself to very early thought, but is
rather the offspring of a comparatively late philosophy. It is remarkable too that the " equality "
of laws on which the Greek democracies prided
themselves—that equality which, in the beautiful
drinking song of Callistratus, Harmodius and
Aristogiton are said to have given to Athens—
had little in common with the " equity " of the
Romans. The first was an equal administration
of civil laws among the citizens, however limited
the class of citizens might be; the last implied the
applicability of a law, which was not civil law, to
a class which did not necessarily consist of citizens. The first excluded a despot; the last included foreigners, and for some purposes slaves.
On the whole, I should be disposed to look in
another direction for the germ of the Roman
" Equity." The Latin word " æquus " carries
with it more distinctly than the Greek " ἴσος "
the sense of *levelling*. Now its levelling tendency

was exactly the characteristic of the Jus Gentium, which would be most striking to a primitive Roman. The pure Quiritarian law recognized a multitude of arbitrary distinctions between classes of men and kinds of property; the Jus Gentium, generalized from a comparison of various customs, neglected the Quiritarian divisions. The old Roman law established, for example, a fundamental difference between " Agnatic " and " Cognatic " relationship, that is, between the Family considered as based upon common subjection to patriarchal authority and the Family considered (in conformity with modern ideas) as united through the mere fact of a common descent. This distinction disappears in the " law common to all nations," as also does the difference between the archaic forms of property, Things " Mancipi " and Things " nec Mancipi." The neglect of demarcations and boundaries seems to me, therefore, the feature of the Jus Gentium which was depicted in Æquitas. I imagine that the word was at first a mere description of that constant *levelling* or removal of irregularities which went on wherever the prætorian system was applied to the cases of foreign litigants. Probably no colour of ethical meaning belonged at first to the expression; nor is there any reason to believe that the process which it indicated was otherwise than extremely distasteful to the primitive Roman mind.

On the other hand, the feature of the Jus Gentium which was presented to the apprehension of a Roman by the word Equity, was exactly the first and most vividly realised characteristic of the hypothetical state of nature. Nature implied symmetrical order, first in the physical world, and next in the moral, and the earliest notion of order

doubtless involved straight lines, even surfaces,
and measured distances. The same sort of picture or figure would be unconsciously before the
mind's eye, whether it strove to form the outlines
of the supposed natural state, or whether it took
in at a glance the actual administration of the
" law common to all nations "; and all we know
of primitive thought would lead us to conclude
that this ideal similarity would do much to
encourage the belief in an identity of the two
conceptions. But then, while the Jus Gentium
had little or no antecedent credit at Rome, the
theory of a Law of Nature came in surrounded
with all the prestige of philosophical authority,
and invested with the charms of association with
an elder and more blissful condition of the race.
It is easy to understand how the difference in the
point of view would affect the dignity of the term
which at once described the operation of the old
principles and the results of the new theory. Even
to modern ears it is not at all the same thing to
describe a process as one of " levelling " and to
call it the " correction of anomalies ", though the
metaphor is precisely the same. Nor do I doubt
that, when once Æquitas was understood to convey an allusion to the Greek theory, associations
which grew out of the Greek notion of ἰσότης began
to cluster round it. The language of Cicero
renders it more than likely that this was so, and
it was the first stage of a transmutation of the
conception of Equity, which almost every ethical
system which has appeared since those days has
more or less helped to carry on.

Something must be said of the formal instrumentality by which the principles and distinctions
associated, first with the Law common to all

Nations, and afterwards with the Law of Nature, were gradually incorporated with the Roman law. At the crisis of primitive Roman history which is marked by the expulsion of the Tarquins, a change occurred which has its parallel in the early annals of many ancient states, but which had little in common with those passages of political affairs which we now term revolutions. It may best be described by saying that the monarchy was put into commission. The powers heretofore accumulated in the hands of a single person were parcelled out among a number of elective functionaries, the very name of the kingly office being retained and imposed on a personage known subsequently as the Rex Sacrorum or Rex Sacrificulus. As part of the change, the settled duties of the supreme judicial office devolved on the Prætor, at the time the first functionary in the commonwealth, and together with these duties was transferred the undefined supremacy over law and legislation which always attached to ancient sovereigns and which is not obscurely related to the patriarchal and heroic authority they had once enjoyed. The circumstances of Rome gave great importance to the more indefinite portion of the functions thus transferred, as with the establishment of the republic began that series of recurrent trials which overtook the state, in the difficulty of dealing with a multitude of persons who, not coming within the technical description of indigenous Romans, were nevertheless permanently located within Roman jurisdiction. Controversies between such persons, or between such persons and native-born citizens, would have remained without the pale of the remedies provided by Roman law, if the Prætor had not undertaken to decide them, and he must

soon have addressed himself to the more critical
disputes which in the extension of commerce arose
between Roman subjects and avowed foreigners.
The great increase of such cases in the Roman
Courts about the period of the first Punic War
is marked by the appointment of a special Prætor,
known subsequently as the Prætor Peregrinus,
who gave them his undivided attention. Meantime, one precaution of the Roman people against
the revival of oppression, had consisted in obliging
every magistrate whose duties had any tendency
to expand their sphere, to publish, on commencing his year of office, an Edict or proclamation,
in which he declared the manner in which he intended to administer his department. The
Prætor fell under the rule with other magistrates;
but as it was necessarily impossible to construct
each year a separate system of principles, he
seems to have regularly republished his predeces-
sor's Edict with such additions and changes as the
exigency of the moment or his own views of the
law compelled him to introduce. The Prætor's
proclamation, thus lengthened by a new portion
every year, obtained the name of the Edictum
Perpetuum, that is, the *continuous* or *unbroken*
edict. The immense length to which it extended,
together perhaps with some distaste for its necessarily disorderly texture, caused the practice of increasing it to be stopped in the year of Salvius
Julianus, who occupied the magistracy in the
reign of the Emperor Hadrian. The edict of that
Prætor embraced therefore the whole body of
equity jurisprudence, which it probably disposed
in new and symmetrical order, and the perpetual
edict is therefore often cited in Roman law merely
as the Edict of Julianus.

Perhaps the first inquiry which occurs to an Englishman who considers the peculiar mechanism of the Edict is, what were the limitations by which these extensive powers of the Prætor were restrained? How was authority so little definite reconciled with a settled condition of society and of law? The answer can only be supplied by careful observation of the conditions under which our own English law is administered. The Prætor, it should be recollected, was a jurisconsult himself, or a person entirely in the hands of advisers who were jurisconsults, and it is probable that every Roman lawyer waited impatiently for the time when he should fill or control the great judicial magistracy. In the interval, his tastes, feelings, prejudices, and degree of enlightenment were inevitably those of his own order, and the qualifications which he ultimately brought to office were those which he had acquired in the practice and study of his profession. An English Chancellor goes through precisely the same training, and carries to the woolsack the same qualifications. It is certain when he assumes office that he will have, to some extent, modified the law before he leaves it; but until he has quitted his seat, and the series of his decisions in the Law Reports has been completed, we cannot discover how far he has elucidated or added to the principles which his predecessors bequeathed to him. The influence of the Prætor on Roman jurisprudence differed only in respect of the period at which its amount was ascertained. As was before stated, he was in office but for a year, and his decisions rendered during his year, though of course irreversible as regarded the litigants, were of no ulterior value. The most natural moment for declaring the changes he proposed to effect occurred therefore at his entrance on the prætorship, and hence, when commencing his duties, he did openly and avowedly that which in the end his English representative does insensibly and sometimes unconsciously. The checks on his apparent liberty are precisely those imposed on an English judge. Theoretically there seems to be hardly any limit to the powers of either of them, but practically the Roman Prætor, no less than the English Chancellor, was kept within the narrowest bounds by the prepossessions imbibed from early training and by the strong restraints of professional opinion, restraints of which the stringency can only be appreciated by those who have personally experienced them. It may be added that the lines within which movement is permitted, and beyond which there is to be no travelling, were chalked with as much distinctness in the one case as in the other. In England the judge follows the analogies of reported decisions on insulated groups of facts. At Rome, as the intervention of the Prætor was at first dictated by simple concern for the safety of the state, it is likely that in the earliest times it was proportioned to the difficulty which it attempted to get rid of. Afterwards, when the taste for principle had been diffused by the Responses, he no doubt used the Edict as the means of giving a wider application to those fundamental principles which he and the other practising jurisconsults, his contemporaries, believed themselves to have detected underlying the law. Latterly he acted wholly under the influence of Greek phiiosophical theories, which at once tempted him to advance and confined him to a particular course of progress.

The nature of the measures attributed to Salvius Julianus has been much disputed. Whatever they were, their effects on the Edict are sufficiently plain. It ceased to be extended by annual additions, and henceforward the equity jurisprudence of Rome was developed by the labours of a succession of great jurisconsults who fill with their writings the interval between the reign of Hadrian and the reign of Alexander Severus. A fragment of the wonderful system which they built up survives in the Pandects of Justinian, and supplies evidence that their works took the form of treatises on all parts of Roman law, but chiefly that of commentaries on the Edict. Indeed, whatever be the immediate subject of a jurisconsult of this epoch, he may always be called an expositor of Equity. The principles of the Edict had, before the epoch of its cessation, made their way into every part of Roman jurisprudence. The Equity of Rome, it should be understood, even when most distinct from the Civil Law, was always administered by the same tribunals. The Prætor was the chief equity judge as well as the great common law magistrate, and as soon as the Edict had evolved an equitable rule the Prætor's court began to apply it in place of or by the side of the old rule of the Civil Law, which was thus directly or indirectly repealed without any express enactment of the legislature. The result, of course, fell considerably short of a complete fusion of law and equity, which was not carried out till the reforms of Justinian. The technical severance of the two elements of jurisprudence entailed some confusion and some inconvenience, and there were certain of the stubborner doctrines of the Civil Law with which neither the

authors nor the expositors of the Edict had ventured to interfere. But at the same time there was
no corner of the field of jurisprudence which was
not more or less swept over by the influence of
Equity.   It supplied the jurist with all his
materials for generalization, with all his method;
of interpretation, with his elucidations of first
principles, and with that great mass of limiting
rules which are rarely interfered with by the legislator, but which seriously control the application
of every legislative act.

The period of jurists ends with Alexander
Severus. From Hadrian to that emperor the improvement of law was carried on, as it is at the
present moment in most continental countries,
partly by approved commentaries and partly by
direct legislation. But in the reign of Alexander
Severus the power of growth in Roman Equity
seems to be exhausted, and the succession of
jurisconsults comes to a close. The remaining
history of the Roman law is the history of the
imperial constitutions, and, at the last, of attempts to codify what had now become the un-
wieldy body of Roman jurisprudence. We have
the latest and most celebrated experiment of this
kind in the *Corpus Juris* of Justinian.

It would be wearisome to enter on a detailed
comparison or contrast of English and Roman
Equity, but it may be worth while to mention
two features which they have in common. The
first may be stated as follows. Each of them
tended, and all such systems tend, to exactly the
same state in which the old common law was
when Equity first interfered with it. A time
always comes at which the moral principles
originally adopted have been carried out to all

their legitimate consequences, and then the system founded on them becomes as rigid, as unexpansive, and as liable to fall behind moral progress as the sternest code of rules avowedly legal. Such an epoch was reached at Rome in the reign of Alexander Severus; after which, though the whole Roman world was undergoing a moral revolution, the Equity of Rome ceased to expand. The same point of legal history was attained in England under the chancellorship of Lord Eldon, the first of our equity judges who, instead of enlarging the jurisprudence of his court by indirect legislation, devoted himself through life to explaining and harmonizing it. If the philosophy of legal history were better understood in England, Lord Eldon's services would be less exaggerated on the one hand and better appreciated on the other than they appear to be among contemporary lawyers. Other misapprehensions too, which bear some practical fruit, would perhaps be avoided. It is easily seen by English lawyers that English Equity is a system founded on moral rules; but it is forgotten that these rules are the morality of past centuries—not of the present—that they have received nearly as much application as they are capable of, and that, though of course they do not differ largely from the ethical creed of our own day, they are not necessarily on a level with it. The imperfect theories of the subject which are commonly adopted have generated errors of opposite sorts. Many writers of treatises on Equity, struck with the completeness of the system in its present state, commit themselves expressly or implicitly to the paradoxical assertion that the founders of the chancery jurisprudence contemplated its present fixity of form when they were settling its first bases. Others, again, complain—and this is a grievance frequently observed upon in forensic arguments—that the moral rules enforced by the Court of Chancery fall short of the ethical standard of the present day. They would have each Lord Chancellor perform precisely the same office for the jurisprudence which he finds ready to his hand, which was performed for the old common law by the fathers of English Equity. But this is to invert the order of the agencies by which the improvement of the law is carried on. Equity has its place and its time; but I have pointed out that another instrumentality is ready to succeed it when its energies are spent.

Another remarkable characteristic of both English and Roman Equity is the falsehood of the assumptions upon which the claim of the equitable to superiority over the legal rule is originally defended. Nothing is more distasteful to men, either as individuals or as masses, than the admission of their moral progress as a substantive reality. This unwillingness shows itself, as regards individuals, in the exaggerated respect which is ordinarily paid to the doubtful virtue of consistency. The movement of the collective opinion of a whole society is too palpable to be ignored, and is generally too visibly for the better to be decried; but there is the greatest disinclination to accept it as a primary phenomenon, and it is commonly explained as the recovery of a lost perfection—the gradual return to a state from which the race has lapsed. This tendency to look backward instead of forward for the goal of moral progress produced anciently, as we have seen, on Roman jurisprudence effects the most serious and permanent. The Roman jurisconsults, in order to account for the improvement of their jurisprudence by the Prætor, borrowed from Greece the doctrine of a Natural state of man—a Natural society—anterior to the organization of commonwealths governed by positive laws. In England, on the other hand, a range of ideas especially congenial to Englishmen of that day, explained the claim òf Equity to override the common law by supposing a general right to superintend the administration of justice which was assumed to be vested in the king as a natural result of his paternal authority. The same view appears in a different and a quainter form in the old doctrine that Equity flowed from the king's conscience— the improvement which had in fact taken place in the moral standard of the community being thus referred to an inherent elevation in the moral sense of the sovereign. The growth of the English constitution rendered such a theory unpalatable after a time; but, as the jurisdiction of the Chancery was then firmly established, it was not worth while to devise any formal substitute for it. The theories found in modern manuals of Equity are very various, but all are alike in their untenability. Most of them are modifications of the Roman doctrine of a natural law, which is indeed adopted in tenour by those writers who begin a discussion of the jurisdiction of the Court of Chancery by laying down a distinction between natural justice and civil.

CHAPTER IV.

THE MODERN HISTORY OF THE LAW OF NATURE.

It will be inferred from what has been said that the theory which transformed the Roman jurisprudence had no claim to philosophical precision. It involved, in fact, one of those " mixed modes of thought " which are now acknowledged to have characterized all but the highest minds during the infancy of speculation, and which are far from undiscoverable even in the mental efforts of our own day. The Law of Nature confused the Past and the Present. Logically, it implied a state of Nature which had once been regulated by natural law; yet the jurisconsults do not speak clearly or confidently of the existence of such a state, which indeed is little noticed by the ancients except where it finds a poetical expression in the fancy of a golden age. Natural law, for all practical purposes, was something belonging to the present, something entwined with existing institutions, something which could be distinguished from them by a competent observer. The test which separated the ordinances of Nature from the gross ingredients with which they were mingled was a sense of simplicity and harmony; yet it was not on account of their simplicity and harmony that these finer elements were primarily respected, but on the score of their descent from the aboriginal reign of Nature. This confusion has not been successfully explained away by the modern disciples of the jurisconsults, and in truth modern speculations on the Law of Nature betray much more indistinctness of perception and are vitiated by much more hopeless ambiguity of language than the Roman lawyers can be justly charged with. There are some writers on the subject who attempt to evade the fundamental difficulty by contending that the code of Nature exists in the future and is the goal to which all civil laws are moving, but this is to reverse the assumptions on which the old theory rested, or rather perhaps to mix together two inconsistent theories. The tendency to look not to the past but to the future for types of perfection was brought into the world by Christianity. Ancient literature gives few or no hints of a belief that the progress of society is necessarily from worse to better.

But the importance of this theory to mankind has been very much greater than its philosophical deficiencies would lead us to expect. Indeed, it is not easy to say what turn the history of thought, and therefore, of the human race, would have taken, if the belief in a law natural had not become universal in the ancient world.

There are two special dangers to which law, and society which is held together by law, appear to be liable in their infancy. One of them is that law may be too rapidly developed. This occurred with the codes of the more progressive Greek communities, which disembarrassed themselves with astonishing facility from cumbrous forms of procedure and needless terms of art, and soon ceased to attach any superstitious value to rigid rules and prescriptions. It was not for the ultimate advantage of mankind that they did so, though the immediate benefit conferred on their citizens may have been considerable. One of the rarest quali-

ties of national character is the capacity for applying and working out the law, as such, at the cost
of constant miscarriages of abstract justice, without at the same time losing the hope or the wish
that law may be conformed to a higher ideal. The
Greek intellect, with all its nobility and elasticity,
was quite unable to confine itself within the strait
waistcoat of a legal formula; and, if we may judge
them by the popular courts of Athens of whose
working we possess accurate knowledge, the Greek
tribunals exhibited the strongest tendency to confound law and fact. The remains of the Orators
and the forensic commonplaces preserved by Aristotle in his Treatise on Rhetoric, show that questions of pure law were constantly argued on every
consideration which could possibly influence the
mind of the judges. No durable system of jurisprudence could be produced in this way. A community which never hesitated to relax rules of
written law whenever they stood in the way of
an ideally perfect decision on the facts of
particular cases, would only, if it bequeathed any
body of judicial principles to posterity, bequeath
one consisting of the ideas of right and wrong
which happened to be prevalent at the time.
Such a jurisprudence would contain no frame-
work to which the more advanced conceptions of
subsequent ages could be fitted. It would amount
at best to a philosophy, marked with the imper-
fections of the civilization under which it grew
up.

Few national societies have had their jurisprudence menaced by this peculiar danger of pre-
cocious maturity and untimely disintegration. It
is certainly doubtful whether the Romans were
ever seriously threatened by it, but at any rate

they had adequate protection in their theory of Natural Law. For the Natural Law of the jurisconsults was distinctly conceived by them as a system which ought gradually to absorb civil laws, without superseding them so long as they remained unrepealed. There was no such impression of its sanctity abroad, that an appeal to it would be likely to overpower the mind of a judge who was charged with the superintendence of a particular litigation. The value and serviceableness of the conception arose from its keeping before the mental vision a type of perfect law, and from its inspiring the hope of an indefinite approximation to it, at the same time that it never tempted the practitioner or the citizen to deny the obligation of existing laws which had not yet been adjusted to the theory. It is important too to observe that this model system, unlike many of those which have mocked men's hopes in later days, was not entirely the product of imagination. It was never thought of as founded on quite untested principles. The notion was that it underlay existing law and must be looked for through it. Its functions were in short remedial, not revolutionary or anarchical. And this, unfortunately, is the exact point at which the modern view of a Law of Nature has often ceased to resemble the ancient.

The other liability to which the infancy of society is exposed has prevented or arrested the progress of far the greater part of mankind. The rigidity of primitive law, arising chiefly from its early association and identification with religion, has chained down the mass of the human race to those views of life and conduct which they entertained at the time when their usages were first con-

solidated into a systematic form. There were one
or two races exempted by a marvellous fate from
this calamity, and grafts from these stocks have
fertilized a few modern societies, but it is still
true that, over the larger part of the world, the
perfection of law has always been considered as
consisting in adherence to the ground plan supposed to have been marked out by the original
legislator. If intellect has in such cases been
exercised on jurisprudence, it has uniformly prided
itself on the subtle perversity of the conclusions
it could build on ancient texts, without discoverable departure from their literal tenour. I know
no reason why the law of the Romans should be
superior to the laws of the Hindoos, unless the
theory of Natural Law had given it a type of
excellence different from the usual one. In this
one exceptional instance, simplicity and symmetry were kept before the eyes of a society
whose influence on mankind was destined to be
prodigious from other causes, as the characteristics of an ideal and absolutely perfect law. It is
impossible to overrate the importance to a nation
or profession of having a distinct object to aim
at in the pursuit of improvement. The secret
of Bentham's immense influence in England
during the past thirty years is his success in
placing such an object before the country. He
gave us a clear rule of reform. English lawyers
of the last century were probably too acute to be
blinded by the paradoxical commonplace that
English law was the perfection of human reason,
but they acted as if they believed it for want of
any other principle to proceed upon. Bentham
made the good of the community take precedence
of every other object, and thus gave escape to a

current which had long been trying to find its
way outwards.

It is not an altogether fanciful comparison if
we call the assumptions we have been describing
the ancient counterpart of Benthamism. The
Roman theory guided men's efforts in the same
direction as the theory put into shape by the
Englishman; its practical results were not widely
different from those which would have been
attained by a sect of law-reformers who maintained a steady pursuit of the general good of the
community. It would be a mistake, however, to
suppose it a conscious anticipation of Bentham's
principles. The happiness of mankind is, no
doubt, sometimes assigned, both in the popular
and in the legal literature of the Romans, as the
proper object of remedial legislation, but it is very
remarkable how few and faint are the testimonies
to this principle compared with the tributes which
are constantly offered to the overshadowing claims
of the Law of Nature. It was not to anything
resembling philanthropy, but to their sense of
simplicity and harmony—of what they significantly termed " elegance "—that the Roman
jurisconsults freely surrendered themselves. The
coincidence of their labours with those which a
more precise philosophy would have counselled
has been part of the good fortune of mankind.

Turning to the modern history of the law of
nature, we find it easier to convince ourselves of
the vastness of its influence than to pronounce
confidently whether that influence has been
exerted for good or for evil. The doctrines and
institutions which may be attributed to it are the
material of some of the most violent controversies
debated in our time, as will be seen when it is

stated that the theory of Natural Law is the source of almost all the special ideas as to law, politics, and society which France during the last hundred years has been the instrument of diffusing over the western world. The part played by jurists in French history, and the sphere of jural conceptions in French thought, have always been remarkably large. It was not indeed in France, but in Italy, that the juridical science of modern Europe took its rise, but of the schools founded by emissaries of the Italian universities in all parts of the continent, and attempted (though vainly) to be set up in our island, that established in France produced the greatest effect on the fortunes of the country. The lawyers of France immediately formed a strict alliance with the kings of the house of Capet, and it was as much through their assertions of royal prerogative, and through their interpretations of the rules of feudal succession, as by the power of the sword, that the French monarchy at last grew together out of the agglomeration of provinces and dependencies. The enormous advantage which their understanding with the lawyers conferred on the French kings in the prosecution of their struggle with the great feudatories, the aristocracy, and the church, can only be appreciated if we take into account the ideas which prevailed in Europe far down into the middle ages. There was, in the first place, a great enthusiasm for generalization and a curious admiration for all general propositions, and consequently, in the field of law, an involuntary reverence for every general formula which seemed to embrace and sum up a number of the insulated rules which were practised as usages in various localities. Such general formulas it was, of course, not difficult for practitioners familiar with the Corpus Juris or the Glosses to supply in almost any quantity. There was, however, another cause which added yet more considerably to the lawyers' power. At the period of which we are speaking, there was universal vagueness of ideas as to the degree and nature of the authority residing in written texts of law. For the most part, the peremptory preface, *Ita scriptum est,* seems to have been sufficient to silence all objections. Where a mind of our own day would jealously scrutinize the formula which had been quoted, would inquire its source, and would (if necessary) deny that the body of law to which it belonged had any authority to supersede local customs, the elder jurist would not probably have ventured to do more than question the applicability of the rule, or at best cite some counter-proposition from the Pandects or the Canon Law. It is extremely necessary to bear in mind the uncertainty of men's notions on this most important side of juridical controversies, not only because it helps to explain the weight which the lawyers threw into the monarchical scale, but on account of the light which it sheds on several curious historical problems. The motives of the author of the Forged Decretals and his extraordinary success are rendered more intelligible by it. And, to take a phenomenon of smaller interest, it assists us, though only partially, to understand the plagiarisms of Bracton. That an English writer of the time of Henry III. should have been able to put off on his countrymen as a compendium of pure English law a treatise of which the entire form and a third of the contents were directly borrowed from the Corpus Juris, and that he should have ventured on this experiment in a country where the systematic study of the Roman law was formally proscribed, will always be among the most hopeless enigmas in the history of jurisprudence; but still it is something to lessen our surprise when we comprehend the state of opinion at the period as to the obligatory force of written texts, apart from all consideration of the source whence they were derived.

When the kings of France had brought their long struggle for supremacy to a successful close, an epoch which may be placed roughly at the accession of the branch of Valois-Angoulême to the throne, the situation of the French jurists was peculiar and continued to be so down to the outbreak of the revolution. On the one hand, they formed the best instructed and nearly the most powerful class in the nation. They had made good their footing as a privileged order by the side of the feudal aristocracy, and they had assured their influence by an organization which distributed their profession over France in great chartered corporations possessing large defined powers and still larger indefinite claims. In all the qualities of the advocate, the judge, and the legislator, they far excelled their compeers throughout Europe. Their juridical tact, their ease of expression, their fine sense of analogy and harmony, and (if they may be judged by the highest names among them) their passionate devotion to their conceptions of justice, were as remarkable as the singular variety of talent which they included, a variety covering the whole ground between the opposite poles of Cujas and Montesquieu, of D'Aguesseau and Dumoulin. But, on the other hand, the system of laws which

they had to admininster stood in striking contrast
with the habits of mind which they had cultivated.
The France which had been in great part constituted by their efforts was smitten with the
curse of an anomalous and dissonant jurisprudence beyond every other country in Europe.
One great division ran through the country and
separated it into *Pays du Droit Ecrit* and *Pays du
Droit Coutumier*, the first acknowledging the
written Roman law as the basis of their jurisprudence, the last admitting it only so far as it
supplied general forms of expression, and courses
of juridical reasoning which were reconcilable
with the local usages. The sections thus formed
were again variously sub-divided. In the *Pays du
Droit Coutumier* province differed from province,
county from county, municipality from municipality, in the nature of its customs. In the *Pays
du Droit Ecrit* the stratum of feudal rules which
overlay the Roman law was of the most miscellaneous composition. No such confusion as this
ever existed in England. In Germany it did exist,
but was too much in harmony with the deep
political and religious divisions of the country to
be lamented or even felt. It was the special
peculiarity of France that an extraordinary diver-
sity of laws continued without sensible alteration
while the central authority of the monarchy was
constantly strengthening itself, while rapid
approaches were being made to complete adminis-
trative unity, and while a fervid national spirit
had been developed among the people. The contrast was one which fructified in many serious
results, and among them we must rank the effect
which it produced on the minds of the French
lawyers. Their speculative opinions and their

intellectual bias were in the strongest opposition
to their interests and professional habits. With tne
keenest sense and the fullest recognition of those
perfections of jurisprudence which consist in simplicity and uniformity, they believed, or seemed
to believe, that the vices which actually infested
French law were ineradicable; and in practice
they often resisted the reformation of abuses with
an obstinacy which was not shown by many among
their less enlightened countrymen. But there
was a way to reconcile these contradictions. They
became passionate enthusiasts for Natural Law.
The Law of Nature overleapt all provincial and
municipal boundaries; it disregarded all distinctions between noble and burgess, between burgess
and peasant; it gave the most exalted place to
lucidity, simplicity and system; but it committed
its devotees to no specific improvement, and did
not directly threaten any venerable or lucrative
technicality. Natural law may be said to have
become the common law of France, or, at all
events, the admission of its dignity and claims
was the one tenet which all French practitioners
alike subscribed to. The language of the præ-
revolutionary jurists in its eulogy is singularly unqualified, and it is remarkable that the writers
on the Customs, who often made it their duty to
speak disparagingly of the pure Roman law, speak
even more fervidly of Nature and her rules than
the civilians who professed an exclusive respect
for the Digest and the Code. Dumoulin, the
highest of all authorities on old French Customary
Law, has some extravagant passages on the Law
of Nature; and his panegyrics have a peculiar
rhetorical turn which indicates a considerable
departure from the caution of the Roman juris-

consults. The hypothesis of a Natural Law had become not so much a theory guiding practice as an article of speculative faith, and accordingly we shall find that, in the transformation which it more recently underwent, its weakest parts rose to the level of its strongest in the esteem of its supporters.

The eighteenth century was half over when the most critical period in the history of Natural Law was reached. Had the discussion of the theory and of its consequences continued to be exclusively the employment of the legal profession, there would possibly have been an abatement of the respect which it commanded; for by this time the *Esprit des Lois* had appeared. Bearing in some exaggerations the marks of the excessive violence with which its author's mind had recoiled from assumptions usually suffered to pass without scrutiny, yet showing in some ambiguities the traces of a desire to compromise with existing prejudice, the book of Montesquieu, with all its defects, still proceeded on that Historical Method before which the Law of Nature has never maintained its footing for an instant. Its influence on thought ought to have been as great as its general popularity; but, in fact, it was never allowed time to put it forth, for the counter-hypothesis which it seemed destined to destroy passed suddenly from the forum to the street, and became the key-note of controversies far more exciting than are ever agitated in the courts or the schools. The person who launched it on its new career was that remarkable man who, without learning, with few virtues, and with no strength of character, has nevertheless stamped himself ineffaceably on history by the force of a vivid imagination, and by the help of a genuine and burning love for his fellow-men, for which much will always have to be forgiven him. We have never seen in our own generation—indeed the world has not seen more than once or twice in all the course of history—a literature which has exercised such prodigious influence over the minds of men, over every cast and shade of intellect, as that which emanated from Rousseau between 1749 and 1762. It was the first attempt to re-erect the edifice of human belief after the purely iconoclastic efforts commenced by Bayle, and in part by our own Locke, and consummated by Voltaire; and besides the superiority which every constructive effort will always enjoy over one that is merely destructive, it possessed the immense advantage of appearing amid an all but universal scepticism as to the soundness of all foregone knowledge in matters speculative. Now, in all the speculations of Rousseau, the central figure, whether arrayed in an English dress as the signatory of a social compact, or simply stripped naked of all historical qualities, is uniformly Man, in a supposed state of nature. Every law or institution which would misbeseem this imaginary being under these ideal circumstances is to be condemned as having lapsed from an original perfection; every transformation of society which would give it a closer resemblance to the world over which the creature of Nature reigned, is admirable and worthy to be effected at any apparent cost. The theory is still that of the Roman lawyers, for in the phantasmagoria with which the Natural Condition is peopled, every feature and characteristic eludes the mind except the simplicity and harmony which possessed such charms for the jurisconsult; but the theory is, as it were, turned upside down. It is not the Law of Nature, but the State of Nature, which is now the primary subject of contemplation. The Roman had conceived that by careful observation of existing institutions parts of them could be singled out which either exhibited already, or could by judicious purification be made to exhibit, the vestiges of that reign of nature whose reality he faintly affirmed. Rousseau's belief was that a perfect social order could be evolved from the unassisted consideration of the natural state, a social order wholly irrespective of the actual condition of the world and wholly unlike it. The great difference between the views is that one bitterly and broadly condemns the present for its unlikeness to the ideal past; while the other, assuming the present to be as necessary as the past, does not affect to disregard or censure it. It is not worth our while to analyse with any particularity that philosophy of politics, art, education, ethics, and social relation which was constructed on the basis of a state of nature. It still possesses singular fascination for the looser thinkers of every country, and is no doubt the parent, more or less remote, of almost all the prepossessions which impede the employment of the Historical Method of inquiry, but its discredit with the higher minds of our day is deep enough to astonish those who are familiar with the extraordinary vitality of speculative error. Perhaps the question most frequently asked nowadays is not what is the value of these opinions, but what were the causes which gave them such overshadowing prominence a hundred years ago. The answer is, I conceive, a simple one. The study which in the last century would best have

corrected the misapprehensions into which an
exclusive attention to legal antiquities is apt to
betray was the study of religion. But Greek
religion, as then understood, was dissipated in
imaginative myths. The Oriental religions, if
noticed at all, appeared to be lost in vain cosmo-
gonies. There was but one body of primitive
records which was worth studying—the early history of the Jews. But resort to this was prevented
by the prejudices of the time. One of the few
characteristics which the school of Rousseau had
in common with the school of Voltaire was an
utter disdain of all religious antiquities; and, more
than all, of those of the Hebrew race. It is well
known that it was a point of honour with the
reasoners of that day to assume not merely that
the institutions called after Moses were not
divinely dictated, nor even that they were codified
at a later date than that attributed to them, but
that they and the entire Pentateuch were a
gratuitous forgery, executed after the return from
the Captivity. Debarred, therefore, from one
chief security against speculative delusion, the
philosophers of France, in their eagerness to
escape from what they deemed a superstition of
the priests, flung themselves headlong into a
superstition of the lawyers.

But though the philosophy founded on the hypothesis of a state of nature has fallen low in general
esteem, in so far as it is looked upon under its
coarser and more palpable aspect, it does not
follow that in its subtler disguises it has lost
plausibility, popularity, or power. I believe, as I
have said, that it is still the great antagonist of
the Historical Method; and whenever (religious
objections apart) any mind is seen to resist or

contemn that mode of investigation, it will
generally be found under the influence of a prejudice or vicious bias traceable to a conscious or
unconscious reliance on a non-historic, natural,
condition of society or the individual. It is chiefly,
however, by allying themselves with political and
social tendencies that the doctrines of Nature and
her law have preserved their energy. Some of
these tendencies they have stimulated, others
they have actually created, to a great number
they have given expression and form. They
visibly enter largely into the ideas which constantly radiate from France over the civilized
world, and thus become part of the general body
of thought by which its civilisation is modified.
The value of the influence which they thus exercise over the fortunes of the race is of course one
of the points which our age debates most warmly,
and it is beside the purpose of this treatise to
discuss it. Looking back, however, to the period at
which the theory of the state of nature acquired the
maximum of political importance, there are few
who will deny that it helped most powerfully to
bring about the grosser disappointments of which
the first French Revolution was fertile. It gave
birth, or intense stimulus, to the vices of mental
habit all but universal at the time, disdain of
positive law, impatience of experience, and the
preference of *à priori* to all other reasoning. In
proportion too as this philosophy fixes its grasp
on minds which have thought less than others and
fortified themselves with smaller observation, its
tendency is to become distinctly anarchical. It is
surprising to note how many of the *Sophismes
Anarchiques* which Dumont published for
Bentham, and which embody Bentham's exposure

of errors distinctively French, are derived from the
Roman hypothesis in its French transformation,
and are unintelligible unless referred to it. On
this point too it is a curious exercise to consult
the *Moniteur* during the principal eras of the
Revolution. The appeals to the Law and State of
Nature become thicker as the times grow darker.
They are comparatively rare in the Constituent
Assembly; they are much more frequent in the
Legislative; in the Convention, amid the din of
debate on conspiracy and war, they are perpetual.

There is a single example which very strikingly
illustrates the effects of the theory of natural law
on modern society, and indicates how very far are
those effects from being exhausted. There cannot, I conceive, be any question that to the
assumption of a Law Natural we owe the doctrine
of the fundamental equality of human beings.
That " all men are equal " is one of a large number of legal propositions which, in progress of
time, have become political. The Roman jurisconsults of the Antonine era lay down that
" omnes homines naturâ æquales sunt ", but in
their eyes this is a strictly juridical axiom. They
intend to affirm that, under the hypothetical Law
of Nature, and in so far as positive law approxi-
mates to it, the arbitrary distinctions which the
Roman Civil Law maintained between classes of
persons cease to have a legal existence. The rule
was one of considerable importance to the Roman
practitioner, who required to be reminded that,
wherever Roman jurisprudence was assumed to
conform itself exactly to the code of Nature, there
was no difference in the contemplation of the
Roman tribunals between citizen and foreigner,
between freeman and slave, between Agnate and

Cognate. The jurisconsults who thus expressed themselves most certainly never intended to censure the social arrangements under which civil law fell somewhat short of its speculative type; nor did they apparently believe that the world would ever see human society completely assimilated to the economy of nature. But when the doctrine of human equality makes its appearance in a modern dress it has evidently clothed itself with a new shade of meaning. Where the Roman jurisconsult had written " æquales sunt," meaning exactly what he said, the modern civilian wrote " all men are equal " in the sense of " all men ought to be equal." The peculiar Roman idea that natural law coexisted with civil law and gradually absorbed it, had evidently been lost sight of, or had become unintelligible, and the words which had at most conveyed a theory concerning the origin, composition, and development of human institutions, were beginning to express the sense of a great standing wrong suffered by mankind. As early as the beginning of the fourteenth century, the current language concerning the birth-state of men, though visibly intended to be identical with that of Ulpian and his contemporaries, has assumed an altogether different form and meaning. The preamble to the celebrated ordinance of King Louis Hutin enfranchising the serfs of the royal domains would have sounded strangely to Roman ears. ' Whereas, according to natural law, everybody ought to be born free; and by some usages and customs which, from long antiquity, have been introduced and kept until now in our realm, and peradventure by reason of the misdeeds of their predecessors, many persons of our common people have fallen into servitude,

therefore, We, &c.' This is the enunciation not
of a legal rule but of a political dogma; and from
this time the equality of men is spoken of by the
French lawyers just as if it were a political truth
which happened to have been preserved among
the archives of their science. Like all other
deductions from the hypothesis of a Law Natural,
and like the belief itself in a Law of Nature, it
was languidly assented to and suffered to have
little influence on opinion and practice until it
passed out of the possession of the lawyers into
that of the literary men of the eighteenth century
and of the public which sat at their feet. With
them it became the most distinct tenet of their
creed, and was even regarded as a summary of all
the others. It is probable, however, that the
power which it ultimately acquired over the
events of 1789 was not entirely owing to its popularity in France, for in the middle of the century
it passed over to America. The American lawyers
of the time, and particularly those of Virginia,
appear to have possessed a stock of knowledge
which differed chiefly from that of their English
contemporaries in including much which could
only have been derived from the legal literature
of continental Europe. A very few glances at the
writings of Jefferson will show how strongly his
mind was affected by the semi-juridical, semi-
popular opinions which were fashionable in
France, and we cannot doubt that it was sympathy with the peculiar ideas of the French jurists
which led him and the other colonial lawyers who
guided the course of events in America to join
the specially French assumption that ' all men
are born equal ' with the assumption, more
familiar to Englishmen, that ' all men are born

free,' in the very first lines of their Declaration of Independence. The passage was one of great importance to the history of the doctrine before us. The American lawyers, in thus prominently and emphatically affirming the fundamental equality of human beings, gave an impulse to political movements in their own country, and in a less degree in Great Britain, which is far from having yet spent itself; but besides this they returned the dogma they had adopted to its home in France, endowed with vastly greater energy and enjoying much greater claims on general reception and respect. Even the more cautious politicians of the first Constituent Assembly repeated Ulpian's proposition as if it at once commended itself to the instincts and intuitions of mankind; and of all the ' principles of 1789 ' it is the one which has been least strenuously assailed, which has most thoroughly leavened modern opinion, and which promises to modify most deeply the constitution of societies and the politics of states.

The grandest function of the Law of Nature was discharged in giving birth to modern International Law and to the modern Law of War, but this part of its effects must here be dismissed with consideration very unequal to its importance.

Among the postulates which form the foundation of International Law, or of so much of it as retains the figure which it received from its original architects, there are two or three of pre-eminent importance. The first of all is expressed in the position that there is a determinable Law of Nature. Grotius and his successors took the assumption directly from the Romans, but they differed widely from the Roman jurisconsults and from

each other in their ideas as to the mode of deter-
mination. The ambition of almost every Publicist
who has flourished since the revival of letters has
been to provide new and more manageable definitions of Nature and of her law, and it is indisputable that the conception in passing through the
long series of writers on Public Law has gathered
round it a large accretion, consisting of fragments
of ideas derived from nearly every theory of
ethics which has in its turn taken possession of
the schools. Yet it is a remarkable proof of the
essentially historical character of the conception
that, after all the efforts which have been made
to evolve the code of nature from the necessary
characteristics of the natural state, so much of
the result is just what it would have been if men
had been satisfied to adopt the dicta of the Roman
lawyers without questioning or reviewing them.
Setting aside the Conventional or Treaty Law of
Nations, it is surprising how large a part of the
system is made up of pure Roman law. Wherever
there is a doctrine of the jurisconsults affirmed
by them to be in harmony with the Jus Gentium,
the publicists have found a reason for borrowing
it, however plainly it may bear the marks of a
distinctively Roman origin. We may observe too
that the derivative theories are afflicted with the
weakness of the primary notion. In the majority
of the Publicists, the mode of thought is still
' mixed.' In studying these writers, the great
difficulty is always to discover whether they are
discussing law or morality—whether the state of
international relations they describe is actual or
ideal—whether they lay down that which is, or
that which, in their opinion, ought to be.

The assumption that Natural Law is binding on

states *inter se* is the next in rank of those which underlie International Law. A series of assertions or admissions of this principle may be traced up to the very infancy of modern juridical science, and at first sight it seems a direct inference from the teaching of the Romans. The civil condition of society being distinguished from the natural by the fact that in the first there is a distinct author of law, while in the last there is none, it appears as if the moment a number of *units* were acknowledged to obey no common sovereign or political superior they were thrown back on the ulterior behests of the Law Natural. States are such units; the hypothesis of their independence excludes the notion of a common lawgiver, and draws with it, therefore, according to a certain range of ideas, the notion of subjection to the primeval order of nature. The alternative is to consider independent communities as not related to each other by any law, but this condition of lawlessness is exactly the vacuum which the Nature of the jurisconsults abhorred. There is certainly apparent reason for thinking that if the mind of a Roman lawyer rested on any sphere from which civil law was banished, it would instantly fill the void with the ordinances of Nature. It is never safe, however, to assume that conclusions, however certain and immediate in our own eyes, were actually drawn at any period of history. No passage has ever been adduced from the remains of Roman law which, in my judgment, proves the jurisconsults to have believed natural law to have obligatory force between independent commonwealths; and we cannot but see that to citizens of the Roman empire, who regarded their sovereign's dominions

as conterminous with civilisation, the equal subjection of states to the Law of Nature, if contemplated at all, must have seemed at most an
extreme result of curious speculation. The truth
appears to be that modern International Law,
undoubted as is its descent from Roman law, is
only connected with it by an irregular filiation.
The early modern interpreters of the jurisprudence
of Rome, misconceiving the meaning of Jus
Gentium, assumed without hesitation that the
Romans had bequeathed to them a system of rules
for the adjustment of international transactions.
This ' Law of Nations ' was at first an authority
which had formidable competitors to strive with,
and the condition of Europe was long such as to
preclude its universal reception. Gradually, however, the western world arranged itself in a form
more favourable to the theory of the civilians;
circumstances destroyed the credit of rival doctrines; and at last, at a peculiarly felicitous con-
juncture, Ayala and Grotius were able to obtain
for it the enthusiastic assent of Europe, an assent
which has been over and over again renewed in
every variety of solemn engagement. The great
men to whom its triumph is chiefly owing attempted, it need scarcely be said, to place it on an
entirely new basis, and it is unquestionable that
in the course of this displacement they altered
much of its structure, though far less of it than is
commonly supposed. Having adopted from the
Antonine jurisconsults the position that the Jus
Gentium and the Jus Naturæ were identical,
Grotius, with his immediate predecessors and his
immediate successors, attributed to the Law of
Nature an authority which would never perhaps
have been claimed for it, if ' Law of Nations '

had not in that age been an ambiguous expression.
They laid down unreservedly that Natural Law
is the code of states, and thus put in operation a
process which has continued almost down to our
own day, the process of engrafting on the international system rules which are supposed to have
been evolved from the unassisted contemplation
of the conception of Nature. There is too one
consequence of immense practical importance to
mankind which, though not unknown during the
early modern history of Europe, was never clearly
or universally acknowledged till the doctrines of
the Grotian school had prevailed. If the society
of nations is governed by Natural Law, the atoms
which compose it must be absolutely equal. Men
under the sceptre of Nature are all equal, and
accordingly commonwealths are equal if the international state be one of nature. The proposition
that independent communities, however different
in size and power, are all equal in the view of the
law of nations, has largely contributed to the
happiness of mankind, though it is constantly
threatened by the political tendencies of each successive age. It is a doctrine which probably would
never have obtained a secure footing at all if
International Law had not been entirely derived
from the majestic claims of Nature by the Publicists who wrote after the revival of letters.

On the whole, however, it is astonishing, as I
have observed before, how small a proportion the
additions made to International Law since Grotius's day bear to the ingredients which have been
simply taken from the most ancient stratum of
the Roman Jus Gentium. Acquisition of territory
has always been the great spur of national ambition, and the rules which govern this acquisition,

together with the rules which moderate the wars
in which it too frequently results, are merely
transcribed from the part of the Roman law which
treats of the modes of acquiring property *jure
gentium*. These modes of acquisition were
obtained by the elder jurisconsults, as I have
attempted to explain, by abstracting a common
ingredient from the usages observed to prevail
among the various tribes surrounding Rome; and,
having been classed on account of their origin in
the 'law common to all nations,' they were
thought by the later lawyers to fit in, on the score
of their simplicity, with the more recent conception of a Law Natural. They thus made their
way into the modern Law of Nations, and the
result is that those parts of the international
system which refer to *dominion*, its nature, its
limitations, the modes of acquiring and securing
it, are pure Roman Property Law—so much, that
is to say, of the Roman Law of Property as the
Antonine jurisconsults imagined to exhibit a certain congruity with the natural state. In order
that these chapters of International Law may be
capable of application, it is necessary that sovereigns should be related to each other like the
members of a group of Roman proprietors. This is
another of the postulates which lie at the threshold
of the International Code, and it is also one which
could not possibly have been subscribed to during
the first centuries of modern European history.
It is resolvable into the double proposition that
' sovereignty is territorial ', *i.e.*, that it is always
associated with the proprietorship of a limited
portion of the earth's surface, and that ' sovereigns *inter se* are to be deemed not *paramount*,
but *absolute*, owners of the state's territory '.

Many contemporary writers on International Law tacitly assume that the doctrines of their system, founded on principles of equity and common sense, were capable of being readily reasoned out in every stage of modern civilisation. But this assumption, while it conceals some real defects of the international theory, is altogether untenable so far as regards a large part of modern history. It is not true that the authority of the Jus Gentium in the concerns of nations was always uncontradicted; on the contrary, it had to struggle long against the claims of several competing systems. It is again not true that the territorial character of sovereignty was always recognised, for long after the dissolution of the Roman dominion the minds of men were under the empire of ideas irreconcileable with such a conception. An old order of things, and of views founded on it, had to decay—a new Europe, and an apparatus of new notions congenial to it, had to spring up—before two of the chiefest postulates of International Law could be universally conceded.

It is a consideration well worthy to be kept in view, that during a large part of what we usually term modern history no such conception was entertained as that of ' *territorial sovereignty* '. Sovereignty was not associated with dominion over a portion or subdivision of the earth. The world had lain for so many centuries under the shadow of Imperial Rome as to have forgotten that distribution of the vast spaces comprised in the empire which had once parcelled them out into a number of independent commonwealths, claiming immunity from extrinsic interference, and pretending to equality of national rights.

After the subsidence of the barbarian irruptions, the notion of sovereignty that prevailed seems to have been twofold. On the one hand it assumed the form of what may be called ' *tribe*-sovereignty '. The Franks, the Burgundians, the Vandals, the Lombards, and Visigoths were masters, of course, of the territories which they occupied, and to which some of them have given a geographical appellation; but they based no claim of right upon the fact of territorial possession, and indeed attached no importance to it whatever. They appear to have retained the traditions which they brought with them from the forest and the steppe, and to have still been in their own view a patriarchal society, a nomad horde, merely encamped for the time upon the soil which afforded them sustenance. Part of Transalpine Gaul, with part of Germany, had now become the country *de facto* occupied by the Franks—it was France; but the Merovingian line of chieftains, the descendants of Clovis, were not Kings of France, they were Kings of the Franks. The alternative to this peculiar notion of sovereignty appears to have been—and this is the important point—the idea of universal dominion. The moment a monarch departed from the special relation of chief to clansmen, and became solicitous, for purposes of his own, to invest himself with a novel form of sovereignty, the only precedent which suggested itself for his adoption was the domination of the Emperors of Rome. To parody a common quotation, he became ' *aut Cæsar aut nullus* '. Either he pretended to the full prerogative of the Byzantine Emperor, or he had no political status whatever. In our own age, when a new dynasty is desirous of obliterating the prescriptive title of a deposed line of sovereigns, it takes its designation from the *people*, instead of the *territory*. Thus we have Emperors and Kings of the French, and a King of the Belgians. At the period of which we have been speaking, under similar circumstances a different alternative presented itself. The Chieftain who would no longer call himself King of the tribe must claim to be Emperor of the world. Thus, when the hereditary Mayors of the Palace had ceased to compromise with the monarchs they had long since virtually dethroned, they soon became unwilling to call themselves Kings of the Franks, a title which belonged to the displaced Merovings; but they could not style themselves Kings of France, for such a designation, though apparently not unknown, was not a title of dignity. Accordingly they came forward as aspirants to universal empire. Their motive has been greatly misapprehended. It has been taken for granted by recent French writers that Charlemagne was far before his age, quite as much in the character of his designs as in the energy with which he prosecuted them. Whether it be true or not that anybody is at any time before his age, it is certainly true that Charlemagne, in aiming at an unlimited dominion, was emphatically taking the only course which the characteristic ideas of his age permitted him to follow. Of his intellectual eminence there cannot be a question, but it is proved by his acts and not by his theory.

These singularities of view were not altered on the partition of the inheritance of Charlemagne among his three grandsons. Charles the Bald, Lewis, and Lothair were still theoretically—if it be proper to use the word—Emperors of Rome.

Just as the Cæsars of the Eastern and Western Empires had each been *de jure* emperor of the whole world, with *de facto* control over half of it, so the three Carlovingians appear to have considered their power as limited, but their title as unqualified. The same speculative universality of sovereignty continued to be associated with the Imperial throne after the second division on the death of Charles the Fat, and, indeed, was never thoroughly dissociated from it so long as the empire of Germany lasted. Territorial sovereignty—the view which connects sovereignty with the possession of a limited portion of the earth's surface—was distinctly an offshoot, though a tardy one, of *feudalism*. This might have been expected *à priori*, for it was feudalism which for the first time linked personal duties, and by consequence personal rights, to the ownership of land. Whatever be the proper view of its origin and legal nature, the best mode of vividly picturing to ourselves the feudal organisation is to begin with the basis, to consider the relation of the tenant to the patch of soil which created and limited his services—and then to mount up, through narrowing circles of super-feudation, till we approximate to the apex of the system. Where that summit exactly was during the later portion of the dark ages it is not easy to decide. Probably, wherever the conception of tribe sovereignty had really decayed, the topmost point was always assigned to the supposed successor of the Cæsars of the West. But before long, when the actual sphere of Imperial authority had immensely contracted, and when the emperors had concentrated the scanty remains of their power upon Germany and North Italy, the highest

feudal superiors in all the outlying portions
of the former Carlovingian empire found themselves practically without a supreme head.
Gradually they habituated themselves to the
new situation, and the fact of immunity put
at last out of sight the theory of dependence; but there are many symptoms that
this change was not quite easily accomplished;
and, indeed, to the impression that in the nature
of things there must necessarily be a culminating
domination somewhere, we may, no doubt, refer
the increasing tendency to attribute secular
superiority to the See of Rome. The completion
of the first stage in the revolution of opinion is
marked, of course, by the accession of the Cape-
tian dynasty in France. When the feudal prince
of a limited territory surrounding Paris began,
from the accident of his uniting an unusual number of suzerainties in his own person, to call himself *King of France*, he became king in quite a
new sense, a sovereign standing in the same
relation to the soil of France as the baron to his
estate, the tenant to his freehold. The precedent,
however, was as influential as it was novel, and
the form of the monarchy in France had visible
effects in hastening changes which were elsewhere
proceeding in the same direction. The kingship
of our Anglo-Saxon regal houses was midway
between the chieftainship of a tribe and a territorial supremacy; but the superiority of the
Norman monarchs, imitated from that of the
King of France, was distinctly a territorial sovereignty. Every subsequent dominion which was
established or consolidated was formed on the
later model. Spain, Naples, and the principalities
founded on the ruins of municipal freedom in

Italy, were all under rulers whose sovereignty was
territorial. Few things, I may add, are more
curious than the gradual lapse of the *Venetians*
from one view to the other. At the commencement of its foreign conquests, the republic regarded itself as an antitype of the Roman commonwealth, governing a number of subject provinces. Move a century onwards, and you find
that it wishes to be looked upon as a corporate
sovereign, claiming the rights of a feudal suzerain
over its possessions in Italy and the Ægean.

During the period through which the popular
ideas on the subject of sovereignty were undergoing this remarkable change, the system which
stood in the place of what we now call International Law, was heterogeneous in form and
inconsistent in the principles to which it appealed.
Over so much of Europe as was comprised in the
Romano-German empire, the connection of the
confederate states was regulated by the complex
and as yet incomplete mechanism of the Imperial
constitution; and, surprising as it may seem to us,
it was a favourite notion of German lawyers that
the relations of commonwealths, whether inside
or outside the empire, ought to be regulated not
by the *Jus Gentium*, but by the pure Roman
jurisprudence, of which Cæsar was still the centre.
This doctrine was less confidently repudiated in
the outlying countries than we might have supposed antecedently; but, substantially, through
the rest of Europe feudal subordinations furnished
a substitute for a public law; and when those
were undetermined or ambiguous, there lay behind, in theory at least, a supreme regulating
force in the authority of the head of the Church.
It is certain, however, that both feudal and

ecclesiastical influences were rapidly decaying during the fifteenth, and even the fourteenth century; and if we closely examine the current pretexts of wars, and the avowed motives of alliances, it will be seen that, step by step with the displacement of the old principles, the views afterwards harmonised and consolidated by Ayala and Grotius were making considerable progress, though it was silent and but slow. Whether the fusion of all the sources of authority would ultimately have evolved a system of international relations, and whether that system would have exhibited material differences from the fabric of Grotius, is not now possible to decide, for as a matter of fact the Reformation annihilated all its potential elements except one. Beginning in Germany, it divided the princes of the empire by a gulf too broad to be bridged over by the Imperial supremacy, even if the Imperial superior had stood neutral. He, however, was forced to take colour with the church against the reformers; the Pope was, as a matter of course, in the same predicament; and thus the two authorities to whom belonged the office of mediation between combatants became themselves the chiefs of one great faction in the schism of the nations. Feudalism, already enfeebled and discredited as a principle of public relations, furnished no bond whatever which was stable enough to countervail the alliances of religion. In a condition, therefore, of public law which was little less than chaotic, those views of a state system to which the Roman jurisconsults were supposed to have given their sanction alone remained standing. The shape, the symmetry, and the prominence which they assumed in the hands of Grotius are

known to every educated man; but the great
marvel of the Treatise ' De Jure Belli et Pacis ',
was its rapid, complete, and universal success.
The horrors of the Thirty Years' War, the boundless terror and pity which the unbridled license of
the soldiery was exciting, must, no doubt, be
taken to explain that success in some measure,
but they do not wholly account for it. Very little
penetration into the ideas of that age is required
to convince one that, if the ground plan of the
international edifice which was sketched in the
great book of Grotius had not appeared to be
theoretically perfect, it would have been discarded
by jurists and neglected by statesmen and
soldiers.

It is obvious that the speculative perfection of
the Grotian system is intimately connected with
that conception of territorial sovereignty which we
have been discussing. The theory of International
Law assumes that commonwealths are, relatively to each other, in a state of nature; but
the component atoms of a natural society must,
by the fundamental assumption, be insulated and
independent of each other. If there be a higher
power connecting them, however slightly and
occasionally, by the claim of common supremacy,
the very conception of a common superior introduces the notion of positive law, and excludes
the idea of a law natural. It follows, therefore,
that if the universal suzerainty of an Imperial
head had been admitted even in bare theory, the
labours of Grotius would have been idle. Nor is
this the only point of junction between modern
public law and those views of sovereignty of
which I have endeavoured to describe the development. I have said that there are entire depart-

ments of international jurisprudence which consist of the Roman Law of Property. What then is the inference? It is, that if there had been no such change as I have described in the estimate of sovereignty—if sovereignty had not been associated with the proprietorship of a limited portion of the earth, had not, in other words, become territorial—three parts of the Grotian theory would have been incapable of application.

CHAPTER V.

PRIMITIVE SOCIETY AND ANCIENT LAW.

THE necessity of submitting the subject of jurisprudence to scientific treatment has never been entirely lost sight of in modern times, and the essays which the consciousness of this necessity has produced have proceeded from minds of very various calibre, but there is not much presumption, I think, in asserting that what has hitherto stood in the place of a science has for the most part been a set of guesses, those very guesses of the Roman lawyers which were examined in the two preceding chapters. A series of explicit statements, recognising and adopting these conjectural theories of a natural state, and of a system of principles congenial to it, has been continued with but brief interruption from the days of their inventors to our own. They appear in the annotations of the Glossators who founded modern jurisprudence, and in the writings of the scholastic jurists who succeeded them. They are visible in the dogmas of the canonists. They are thrust into prominence by those civilians of marvellous erudition, who flourished at the revival of ancient letters. Grotius and his successors invested them not less with brilliancy and plausibility than with practical importance. They may be read in the introductory chapters of our own Blackstone, who has transcribed them textually from Burlamaqui, and wherever the manuals published in the present day for the guidance of the student or the practitioner begin with any discussion of the first principles of law, it always resolves itself into a restatement of the Roman hypothesis. It is however from the disguises with which these conjectures sometimes clothe themselves, quite as much as from their native form, that we gain an adequate idea of the subtlety with which they mix themselves in human thought. The Lockeian theory of the origin of Law in a Social Compact scarcely conceals its Roman derivation, and indeed is only the dress by which the ancient views were rendered more attractive to a particular generation of the moderns; but on the other hand the theory of Hobbes on the same subject was purposely devised to repudiate the reality of a law of nature as conceived by the Romans and their disciples. Yet these two theories, which long divided the reflecting politicians of England into hostile camps, resemble each other strictly in their fundamental assumption of a non-historic, unverifiable, condition of the race. Their authors differed as to the characteristics of the præ-social state, and as to the nature of the abnormal action by which men lifted themselves out of it into that social organisation with which alone we are acquainted, but they agreed in thinking that a great chasm separated man in his primitive condition from man in society, and this notion we

cannot doubt that they borrowed, consciously or
unconsciously, from the Romans. If indeed the
phenomena of law be regarded in the way in
which these theorists regarded them—that is, as
one vast complex whole—it is not surprising that
the mind should often evade the task it has set
to itself by falling back on some ingenious conjecture which (plausibly interpreted) will seem to
reconcile everything, or else that it should sometimes abjure in despair the labour of systematiza-
tion.

From the theories of jurisprudence which have
the same speculative basis as the Roman doctrine
two of much celebrity must be excepted. The
first of them is that associated with the great
name of Montesquieu. Though there are some
ambiguous expressions in the early part of the
Esprit des Lois, which seem to show its writer's
unwillingness to break quite openly with the
views hitherto popular, the general drift of the
book is certainly to indicate a very different conception of its subject from any which had been
entertained before. It has often been noticed
that, amidst the vast variety of examples which,
in its immense width of survey, it sweeps together
from supposed systems of jurisprudence, there is
an evident anxiety to thrust into especial prominence those manners and institutions which
astonish the civilised reader by their uncouthness,
strangeness, or indecency. The inference constantly suggested is, that laws are the creatures
of climate, local situation, accident, or impos-
ture—the fruit of any causes except those which
appear to operate with tolerable constancy. Montesquieu seems, in fact, to have looked on the
nature of man as entirely plastic, as passively

reproducing the impressions, and submitting implicitly to the impulses, which it receives from without. And here no doubt lies the error which vitiates his system as a system. He greatly underrates the stability of human nature. He pays little or no regard to the inherited qualities of the race, those qualities which each generation receives from its predecessors, and transmits but slightly altered to the generation which follows it. It is quite true, indeed, that no complete account can be given of social phenomena, and consequently of laws, till due allowance has been made for those modifying causes which are noticed in the *Esprit des Lois;* but their number and their force appear to have been overestimated by Montesquieu. Many of the anomalies which he parades have since been shown to rest on false report or erroneous construction, and of those which remain not a few prove the permanence rather than the variableness of man's nature, since they are relics of older stages of the race which have obstinately defied the influences that have elsewhere had effect. The truth is that the stable part of our mental, moral, and physical constitution is the largest part of it, and the resistance it opposes to change is such that, though the variations of human society in a portion of the world are plain enough, they are neither so rapid nor so extensive that their amount, character, and general direction cannot be ascertained. An approximation to truth may be all that is attainable with our present knowledge, but there is no reason for thinking that is so remote, or (what is the same thing) that it requires so much future correction, as to be entirely useless and uninstructive.

The other theory which has been adverted to is the historical theory of Bentham. This theory which is obscurely (and, it might even be said, timidly) propounded in several parts of Bentham's works is quite distinct from that analysis of the conception of law which he commenced in the "Fragment on Government," and which was more recently completed by Mr. John Austin. The resolution of a law into a command of a particular nature, imposed under special conditions, does not affect to do more than protect us against a difficulty—a most formidable one certainly—of language. The whole question remains open as to the motives of societies in imposing these commands on themselves, as to the connexion of these commands with each other, and the nature of their dependence on those which preceded them, and which they have superseded. Bentham suggests the answer that societies modify, and have always modified, their laws according to modifications of their views of general expediency. It is difficult to say that this proposition is false, but it certainly appears to be unfruitful. For that which seems expedient to a society, or rather to the governing part of it, when it alters a rule of law is surely the same thing as the object, whatever it may be, which it has in view when it makes the change. Expediency and the greatest good are nothing more than different names for the impulse which prompts the modification; and when we lay down expediency as the rule of change in law or opinion, all we get by the proposition is the substitution of an express term for a term which is necessarily implied when we say that a change takes place.

There is such wide-spread dissatisfaction with existing theories of jurisprudence, and so general a conviction that they do not really solve the questions they pretend to dispose of, as to justify the suspicion that some line of inquiry necessary to a perfect result has been incompletely followed or altogether omitted by their authors. And indeed there is one remarkable omission with which all these speculations are chargeable, except perhaps those of Montesquieu. They take no account of what law has actually been at epochs remote from the particular period at which they made their appearance. Their originators carefully observed the institutions of their own age and civilisation, and those of other ages and civilisations with which they had some degree of intellectual sympathy, but, when they turned their attention to archaic states of society which exhibited much superficial difference from their own, they uniformly ceased to observe and began guessing. The mistake which they committed is therefore analogous to the error of one who, in investigating the laws of the material universe, should commence by contemplating the existing physical world as a world, instead of beginning with the particles which are its simplest ingredients. One does not certainly see why such a scientific solecism should be more defensible in jurisprudence than in any other region of thought. It would seem antecedently that we ought to commence with the simplest social forms in a state as near as possible to their rudimentary condition. In other words, if we followed the course usual in such inquiries, we should penetrate as far up as we could in the history of primitive societies. The phenomena which early societies present us with are not easy at first to understand, but the difficulty of grappling with them bears no proportion to the perplexities which beset us in considering the baffling entanglement of modern social organisation. It is a difficulty arising from their strangeness and uncouthness, not from their number and complexity. One does not readily get over the surprise which they occasion when looked at from a modern point of view; but when that is surmounted they are few enough and simple enough. But, even if they gave more trouble than they do, no pains would be wasted in ascertaining the germs out of which has assuredly been unfolded every form of moral restraint which controls our actions and shapes our conduct at the present moment.

The rudiments of the social state, so far as they are known to us at all, are known through testimony of three sorts—accounts by contemporary observers of civilisations less advanced than their own, the records which particular races have preserved concerning their primitive history, and ancient law. The first kind of evidence is the best we could have expected. As societies do not advance concurrently, but at different rates of progress, there have been epochs at which men trained to habits of methodical observation have really been in a position to watch and describe the infancy of mankind. Tacitus made the most of such an opportunity; but the *Germany*, unlike most celebrated classical books, has not induced others to follow the excellent example set by its author, and the amount of this sort of testimony which we possess is exceedingly small. The lofty contempt which a civilised people entertains for barbarous neighbours has caused a remarkable

negligence in observing them, and this careless-
ness has been aggravated at times by fear, by
religious prejudice, and even by the use of these
very terms—civilisation and barbarism—which
convey to most persons the impression of a difference not merely in degree but in kind. Even the
Germany has been suspected by some critics of
sacrificing fidelity to poignancy of contrast and
picturesqueness of narrative. Other histories too,
which have been handed down to us among the
archives of the people to whose infancy they
relate, have been thought distorted by the pride of
race or by the religious sentiment of a newer age.
It is important then to observe that these sus-
picions, whether groundless or rational, do not
attach to a great deal of archaic law. Much of the
old law which has descended to us was preserved
merely because it was old. Those who practised
and obeyed it did not pretend to understand it;
and in some cases they even ridiculed and despised it. They offered no account of it except
that it had come down to them from their ancestors. If we confine our attention, then, to those
fragments of ancient institutions which cannot
reasonably be supposed to have been tampered
with, we are able to gain a clear conception of
certain great characteristics of the society to
which they originally belonged. Advancing a step
further, we can apply our knowledge to systems
of law which, like the Code of Menu, are as a
whole of suspicious authenticity; and, using the
key we have obtained, we are in a position to discriminate those portions of them which are truly
archaic from those which have been affected by
the prejudices, interests, or ignorance of the com-
piler. It will at least be acknowledged that, if

the materials for this process are sufficient, and if the comparisons be accurately executed, the methods followed are as little objectionable as those which have led to such surprising results in comparative philology.

The effect of the evidence derived from comparative jurisprudence is to establish that view of the primeval condition of the human race which is known as the Patriarchal Theory. There is no doubt, of course, that this theory was originally based on the Scriptural history of the Hebrew patriarchs in Lower Asia; but, as has been explained already, its connexion with Scripture rather militated than otherwise against its reception as a complete theory, since the majority of the inquirers who till recently addressed themselves with most earnestness to the colligation of social phenomena, were either influenced by the strongest prejudice against Hebrew antiquities or by the strongest desire to construct their system without the assistance of religious records. Even now there is perhaps a disposition to undervalue these accounts, or rather to decline generalising from them, as forming part of the traditions of a Semitic people. It is to be noted, however, that the legal testimony comes nearly exclusively from the institutions of societies belonging to the Indo-European stock, the Romans, Hindoos, and Sclavonians supplying the greater part of it; and indeed the difficulty, at the present stage of the inquiry, is to know where to stop, to say of what races of men it is *not* allowable to lay down that the society in which they are united was originally organised on the patriarchal model. The chief lineaments of such a society, as collected from the early chapters in Genesis, I need

not attempt to depict with any minuteness, both
because they are familiar to most of us from our
earliest childhood, and because, from the interest
once attaching to the controversy which takes its
name from the debate between Locke and Filmer,
they fill a whole chapter, thought not a very pro-
fitable one, in English literature. The points
which lie on the surface of the history are these :—
The eldest male parent—the eldest ascendant—is
absolutely supreme in his household. His dominion extends to life and death, and is as unqualified over his children and their houses as
over his slaves; indeed the relations of sonship
and serfdom appear to differ in little beyond the
higher capacity which the child in blood possesses
of becoming one day the head of a family himself.
The flocks and herds of the children are the flocks
and herds of the father, and the possessions of the
parent, which he holds in a representative rather
than in a proprietary character, are equally divided
at his death among his descendants in the first
degree, the eldest son sometimes receiving a
double share under the name of birthright, but
more generally endowed with no hereditary advantage beyond an honorary precedence. A less
obvious inference from the Scriptural accounts is
that they seem to plant us on the traces of the
breach which is first effected in the empire of the
parent. The families of Jacob and Esau separate
and form two nations; but the families of Jacob's
children hold together and become a people. This
looks like the immature germ of a state or commonwealth, and of an order of rights superior to
the claims of family relation.

If I were attempting for the more special purposes of the jurist to express compendiously the

characteristics of the situation in which mankind
disclose themselves at the dawn of their history,
I should be satisfied to quote a few verses from
the *Odyssey* of Homer :

τοῖσιν δ᾽ οὔτ᾽ ἀγοραὶ βουληφόροι οὔτε θέμιστες.
        .   .   θεμιστεύει δὲ ἕκαστος
παίδων ἠδ᾽ ἀλόχων, οὐδ᾽ ἀλλήλων ἀλέγουσιν.

' They have neither assemblies for consultation
nor *themistes*, but every one exercises jurisdiction
over his wives and his children, and they pay no
regard to one another '. These lines are applied
to the Cyclops, and it may not perhaps be an
altogether fanciful idea when I suggest that the
Cyclops is Homer's type of an alien and less
advanced civilisation; for the almost physical
loathing which a primitive community feels for
men of widely different manners from its own
usually expresses itself by describing them as
monsters, such as giants, or even (which is almost
always the case in Oriental mythology) as demons.
However that may be, the verses condense in
themselves the sum of the hints which are given
us by legal antiquities. Men are first seen distributed in perfectly insulated groups, held together
by obedience to the parent. Law is the parent's
word, but it is not yet in the condition of those
themistes which were analysed in the first chapter
of this work. When we go forward to the state
of society in which these early legal conceptions
show themselves as formed, we find that they still
partake of the mystery and spontaneity which
must have seemed to characterise a despotic
father's commands, but that at the same time,
inasmuch as they proceed from a sovereign, they

presuppose a union of family groups in some wider organisation. The next question is, what is the nature of this union and the degree of intimacy which it involves. It is just here that archaic law renders us one of the greatest of its services and fills up a gap which otherwise could only have been bridged by conjecture. It is full, in all its provinces, of the clearest indications that society in primitive times was not what it is assumed to be at present, a collection of *individuals*. In fact, and in the view of the men who composed it, it was *an aggregation of families*. The contrast may be most forcibly expressed by saying that the *unit* of an ancient society was the Family, of a modern society the Individual. We must be prepared to find in ancient law all the consequences of this difference. It is so framed as to be adjusted to a system of small independent corporations. It is therefore scanty, because it is supplemented by the despotic commands of the heads of households. It is ceremonious, because the transactions to which it pays regard resemble international concerns much more than the quick play of intercourse between individuals. Above all it has a peculiarity of which the full importance cannot be shown at present. It takes a view of *life* wholly unlike any which appears in developed jurisprudence. Corporations *never die*, and accordingly primitive law considers the entities with which it deals, i.e., the patriarchal or family groups, as perpetual and inextinguishable. This view is closely allied to the peculiar aspect under which, in very ancient times, moral attributes present themselves. The moral elevation and moral debasement of the individual appear to be confounded with, or postponed to, the merits and offences of the group to which the individual belongs. If the community sins, its guilt is much more than the sum of the offences committed by its members; the crime is a corporate act, and extends in its consequences to many more persons than have shared in its actual perpetration. If, on the other hand, the individual is conspicuously guilty, it is his children, his kinsfolk, his tribesmen, or his fellow-citizens, who suffer with him, and sometimes for him. It thus happens that the ideas of moral responsibility and retribution often seem to be more clearly realised at very ancient than at more advanced periods, for, as the family group is immortal, and its liability to punishment indefinite, the primitive mind is not perplexed by the questions which become troublesome as soon as the individual is conceived as altogether separate from the group. One step in the transition from the ancient and simple view of the matter to the theological or metaphysical explanations of later days is marked by the early Greek notion of an inherited curse. The bequest received by his posterity from the original criminal was not a liability to punishment, but a liability to the commission of fresh offences which drew with them a condign retribution; and thus the responsibility of the family was reconciled with the newer phase of thought which limited the consequences of crime to the person of the actual delinquent.

It would be a very simple explanation of the origin of society if we could base a general conclusion on the hint furnished us by the Scriptural example already adverted to, and could suppose that communities began to exist wherever a family held together instead of separating at the death of its patriarchal chieftain. In most of the Greek states and in Rome there long remained the vestiges of an ascending series of groups out of which the State was at first constituted. The Family, House, and Tribe of the Romans may be taken as the type of them, and they are so described to us that we can scarcely help conceiving them as a system of concentric circles which have gradually expanded from the same point. The elementary group is the Family, connected by common subjection to the highest male ascendant. The aggregation of Families forms the Gens or House. The aggregation of Houses makes the Tribe. The aggregation of Tribes constitutes the Commonwealth. Are we at liberty to follow these indications, and to lay down that the commonwealth is a collection of persons united by common descent from the progenitor of an original family? Of this we may at least be certain, that all ancient societies regarded themselves as having proceeded from one original stock, and even laboured under an incapacity for comprehending any reason except this for their holding together in political union. The history of political ideas begins, in fact, with the assumption that kinship in blood is the sole possible ground of community in political functions; nor is there any of those subversions of feeling, which we term emphatically revolutions, so startling and so complete as the change which is accomplished when some other principle—such as that, for instance, of *local contiguity*—establishes itself for the first time as the basis of common political action. It may be affirmed then of early commonwealths that their citizens considered all the groups in which they claimed membership to be founded on common lineage. What was obviously true of the Family was believed to be true first of the House, next of the Tribe, lastly of the State. And yet we find that along with this belief, or, if we may use the word, this theory, each community preserved records or traditions which distinctly showed that the fundamental assumption was false. Whether we look to the Greek states, or to Rome, or to the Teutonic aristocracies in Ditmarsh which furnished Niebuhr with so many valuable illustrations, or to the Celtic clan associations, or to that strange social organisation of the Sclavonic Russians and Poles which has only lately attracted notice, everywhere we discover traces of passages in their history when men of alien descent were admitted to, and amalgamated with, the original brotherhood. Adverting to Rome singly, we perceive that the primary group, the Family, was being constantly adulterated by the practice of adoption, while stories seem to have been always current respecting the exotic extraction of one of the original Tribes and concerning a large addition to the Houses made by one of the early kings. The composition of the state, uniformly assumed to be natural, was nevertheless known to be in great measure artificial. This conflict between belief or theory and notorious fact is at first sight extremely perplexing; but what it really illustrates is the efficiency with which Legal Fictions do their work in the infancy of society. The earliest and most extensively employed of legal fictions was that which permitted family relations to be created artificially, and there is none to which I conceive mankind to be more deeply indebted. If it had never existed, I do not see how any one of the primitive groups, whatever were their nature, could have absorbed another, or on what terms any two of them could have combined, except those of absolute superiority on one side and absolute subjection on the other. No doubt, when with our modern ideas we contemplate the union of independent communities, we can suggest a hundred modes of carrying it out, the simplest of all being that the individuals comprised in the coalescing groups shall vote or act together according to local propinquity; but the idea that a number of persons should exercise political rights in common simply because they happened to live within the same topographical limits was utterly strange and monstrous to primitive antiquity. The expedient which in those times commanded favour was that the incoming population should *feign themselves* to be descended from the same stock as the people on whom they were engrafted; and it is precisely the good faith of this fiction, and the closeness with which it seemed to imitate reality, that we cannot now hope to understand. One circumstance, however, which it is important to recollect, is that the men who formed the various political groups were certainly in the habit of meeting together periodically, for the purpose of acknowledging and consecrating their association by common sacrifices. Strangers amalgamated with the brotherhood were doubtless admitted to these sacrifices; and when that was once done, we can believe that it seemed equally easy, or not more difficult, to conceive them as sharing in the common lineage. The conclusion then which is suggested by the evidence is, not that all early societies were formed by descent from the same ancestor, but that all of them which had any permanence and solidity either were so descended or assumed that they were. An indefinite number of causes may have shattered the primitive groups, but wherever their ingredients recombined, it was on the model or principle of an association of kindred. Whatever were the fact all thought, language, and law adjusted themselves to the assumption. But though all this seems to me to be established with reference to the communities with whose records we are acquainted, the remainder of their history sustains the position before laid down as to the essentially transient and terminable influence of the most powerful Legal Fictions. At some point of time—probably as soon as they felt themselves strong enough to resist extrinsic pressure—all these states ceased to recruit themselves by factitious extensions of consanguinity. They necessarily, therefore, became Aristocracies, in all cases where a fresh population from any cause collected around them which could put in no claim to community of origin. Their sternness in maintaining the central principle of a system under which political rights were attainable on no terms whatever except connexion in blood, real or artificial, taught their inferiors another principle, which proved to be endowed with a far higher measure of vitality. This was the principle of *local contiguity*, now recognised everywhere as the condition of community in political functions. A new set of political ideas came at once into existence, which, being those of ourselves, our contemporaries, and in great measure of our ancestors, rather obscure our perception of the older theory which they vanquished and dethroned.

The Family then is the type of an archaic society in all the modifications which it was capable of assuming; but the family here spoken of is not exactly the family as understood by a modern. In order to reach the ancient conception we must give to our modern ideas an important extension and an important limitation. We must look on the family as constantly enlarged by the absorption of strangers within its circle, and we must try to regard the fiction of adoption as so closely simulating the reality of kinship that neither law nor opinion makes the slightest difference between a real and an adoptive connexion. On the other hand, the persons theoretically amalgamated into a family by their common descent are practically held together by common obedience to their highest living ascendant, the father, grandfather, or great-grandfather. The patriarchal authority of a chieftain is as necessary an ingredient in the notion of the family group as the fact (or assumed fact) of its having sprung from his loins; and hence we must understand that if there be any persons who, however truly included in the brotherhood by virtue of their blood-relationship, have nevertheless *de facto* withdrawn themselves from the empire of its ruler, they are always, in the beginnings of law, considered as lost to the family. It is this patriarchal aggregate—the modern family thus cut down on one side and extended on the other— which meets us on the threshold of primitive jurisprudence. Older probably than the State, the Tribe, and the House, it left traces of itself on private law long after the House and the Tribe had been forgotten, and long after consanguinity had ceased to be associated with the composition of States. It will be found to have stamped itself on all the great departments of jurisprudence,

and may be detected, I think, as the true source
of many of their most important and most durable
characteristics. At the outset, the peculiarities
of law in its most ancient state lead us irresistibly
to the conclusion that it took precisely the same
view of the family group which is taken of individual men by the systems of rights and duties
now prevalent throughout Europe. There are
societies open to our observation at this very
moment whose laws and usages can scarcely be
explained unless they are supposed never to have
emerged from this primitive condition; but in
communities more fortunately circumstanced the
fabric of jurisprudence fell gradually to pieces,
and if we carefully observe the disintegration we
shall perceive that it took place principally in
those portions of each system which were most
deeply affected by the primitive conception of the
family. In one all-important instance, that of
the Roman law, the change was effected so slowly,
that from epoch to epoch we can observe the line
and direction which it followed, and can even
give some idea of the ultimate result to which it
was tending. And, in pursuing this last inquiry,
we need not suffer ourselves to be stopped by the
imaginary barrier which separates the modern
from the ancient world. For one effect of that
mixture of refined Roman law with primitive bar-
baric usage, which is known to us by the deceptive name of feudalism, was to revive many
features of archaic jurisprudence which had died
out of the Roman world, so that the decom-
position which had seemed to be over commenced
again, and to some extent is still proceeding.

On a few systems of law the family organisation
of the earliest society has left a plain and broad

mark in the life-long authority of the Father or
other ancestor over the person and property of
his descendants, an authority which we may con-
veniently call by its later Roman name of Patria
Potestas. No feature of the rudimentary associations of mankind is deposed to by a greater
amount of evidence than this, and yet none seems
to have disappeared so generally and so rapidly
from the usages of advancing communities.
Gaius, writing under the Antonines, describes the
institution as distinctively Roman. It is true
that, had he glanced across the Rhine or the
Danube to those tribes of barbarians which were
exciting the curiosity of some among his contemporaries, he would have seen examples of
patriarchal power in its crudest form; and in the
far East a branch of the same ethnical stock from
which the Romans sprang was repeating their
Patria Potestas in some of its most technical
incidents. But among the races understood to be
comprised within the Roman empire, Gaius could
find none which exhibited an institution resembling the Roman " Power of the Father," except
only the Asiatic Galatæ. There are reasons, indeed, as it seems to me, why the direct authority
of the ancestor should, in the greater number of
progressive societies, very shortly assume humbler proportions than belonged to it in their
earliest state. The implicit obedience of rude
men to their parent is doubtless a primary fact,
which it would be absurd to explain away altogether by attributing to them any calculation of
its advantages; but, at the same time, if it is
natural in the sons to obey the father, it is equally
natural that they should look to him for superior
strength or superior wisdom. Hence, when

societies are placed under circumstances which cause an especial value to be attached to bodily and mental vigour, there is an influence at work which tends to confine the Patria Potestas to the cases where its possessor is actually skilful and strong. When we obtain our first glimpse of organised Hellenic society, it seems as if supereminent wisdom would keep alive the father's power in persons whose bodily strength had decayed; but the relations of Ulysses and Laertes in the *Odyssey* appear to show that, where extraordinary valour and sagacity were united in the son, the father in the decrepitude of age was deposed from the headship of the family. In the mature Greek jurisprudence, the rule advances a few steps on the practice hinted at in the Homeric literature; and though very many traces of stringent family obligation remain, the direct authority of the parent is limited, as in European codes, to the nonage or minority of the children, or, in other words, to the period during which their mental and physical inferiority may always be presumed. The Roman law, however, with its remarkable tendency to innovate on ancient usage only just so far as the exigency of the commonwealth may require, preserves both the primeval institution and the natural limitation to which I conceive it to have been subject. In every relation of life in which the collective community might have occasion to avail itself of his wisdom and strength, for all purposes of counsel or of war, the filius familias, or Son under Power, was as free as his father. It was a maxim of Roman jurisprudence that the Patria Potestas did not extend to the Jus Publicum. Father and son voted together in the city, and fought side by side in the field; indeed, the son, as general, might happen to command the father, or, as magistrate, decide on his contracts and punish his delinquencies. But in all the relations created by Private Law, the son lived under a domestic despotism which, considering the severity it retained to the last, and the number of centuries through which it endured, constitutes one of the strangest problems in legal history.

The Patria Potestas of the Romans, which is necessarily our type of the primeval paternal authority, is equally difficult to understand as an institution of civilised life, whether we consider its incidence on the person or its effects on property. It is to be regretted that a chasm which exists in its history cannot be more completely filled. So far as regards the person, the parent, when our information commences, has over his children the *jus vitæ necisque*, the power of life and death, and *à fortiori* of uncontrolled corporal chastisement; he can modify their personal condition at pleasure; he can give a wife to his son; he can give his daughter in marriage; he can divorce his children of either sex; he can transfer them to another family by adoption; and he can sell them. Late in the Imperial period we find vestiges of all these powers, but they are reduced within very narrow limits. The unqualified right of domestic chastisement has become a right of bringing domestic offences under the cognisance of the civil magistrate; the privilege of dictating marriage has declined into a conditional veto; the liberty of selling has been virtually abolished, and adoption itself, destined to lose almost all its ancient importance in the reformed system of Justinian, can no longer be effected without the assent of the child transferred to the adoptive parentage. In short, we are brought very close to the verge of the ideas which have at length prevailed in the modern world. But between these widely distant epochs there is an interval of obscurity, and we can only guess at the causes which permitted the Patria Potestas to last as long as it did by rendering it more tolerable than it appears. The active discharge of the most important among the duties which the son owed to the state must have tempered the authority of his parent if they did not annul it. We can readily persuade ourselves that the paternal despotism could not be brought into play without great scandal against a man of full age occupying a high civil office. During the earlier history, however, such cases of practical emancipation would be rare compared with those which must have been created by the constant wars of the Roman republic. The military tribune and the private soldier who were in the field three quarters of a year during the earlier contests, at a later period the proconsul in charge of a province, and the legionaries who ocupied it, cannot have had practical reason to regard themselves as the slaves of a despotic master; and all these avenues of escape tended constantly to multiply themselves. Victories led to conquests, conquests to occupations; the mode of occupation by colonies was exchanged for the system of occupying provinces by standing armies. Each step in advance was a call for the expatriation of more Roman citizens and a fresh draft on the blood of the failing Latin race. We may infer, I think, that a strong sentiment in favour of the relaxation of the Patria Potestas had become fixed by the time that the pacifica-

tion of the world commenced on the establishment of the Empire. The first serious blows at
the ancient institution are attributed to the earlier
Cæsars, and some isolated interferences of Trajan
and Hadrian seem to have prepared the ground
for a series of express enactments which, though
we cannot always determine their dates, we know
to have limited the father's powers on the one
hand, and on the other to have multiplied facilities for their voluntary surrender. The older mode
of getting rid of the Potestas, by effecting a triple
sale of the son's person, is evidence, I may
remark, of a very early feeling against the unnecessary prolongation of the powers. The rule
which declared that the son should be free after
having been three times sold by his father seems
to have been originally meant to entail penal consequences on a practice which revolted even the
imperfect morality of the primitive Roman. But
even before the publication of the Twelve Tables
it had been turned, by the ingenuity of the jurisconsults, into an expedient for destroying the
parental authority wherever the father desired
that it should cease.

Many of the causes which helped to mitigate
the stringency of the father's power over the
persons of his children are doubtless among those
which do not lie upon the face of history. We
cannot tell how far public opinion may have
paralysed an authority which the law conferred,
or how far natural affection may have rendered it
endurable. But though the powers over the
person may have been latterly nominal, the whole
tenour of the extant Roman jurisprudence suggests that the father's rights over the son's *property* were always exercised without scruple to

the full extent to which they were sanctioned by law. There is nothing to astonish us in the latitude of these rights when they first show themselves. The ancient law of Rome forbade the Children under Power to hold property apart from their parent, or (we should rather say) never contemplated the possibility of their claiming a separate ownership. The father was entitled to take the whole of the son's acquisitions, and to enjoy the benefit of his contracts without being entangled in any compensating liability. So much as this we should expect from the constitution of the earliest Roman society, for we can hardly form a notion of the primitive family group unless we suppose that its members brought their earnings of all kinds into the common stock while they were unable to bind it by improvident individual engagements. The true enigma of the Patria Potestas does not reside here, but in the slowness with which these proprietary privileges of the parent were curtailed, and in the circumstance that, before they were seriously diminished, the whole civilised world was brought within their sphere. No innovation of any kind was attempted till the first years of the Empire, when the acquisitions of soldiers on service were withdrawn from the operation of the Patria Potestas, doubtless as part of the reward of the armies which had overthrown the free commonwealth. Three centuries afterwards the same immunity was extended to the earnings of persons who were in the civil employment of the state. Both changes were obviously limited in their application, and they were so contrived in technical form as to interfere as little as possible with the principle of Patria Potestas. A certain qualified and dependent ownership had always been recognised by the Roman law in the perquisites and savings which slaves and sons under power were not compelled to include in the household accounts, and the special name of this permissive property, Peculium, was applied to the acquisitions newly relieved from Patria Potestas, which were called in the case of soldiers Castrense Peculium, and Quasi-castrense Peculium in the case of civil servants. Other modifications of the parental privileges followed, which showed a less studious outward respect for the ancient principle. Shortly after the introduction of the Quasi-castrense Peculium, Contantine the Great took away the father's absolute control over property which his children had inherited from their mother, and reduced it to a *usufruct*, or life-interest. A few more changes of slight importance followed in the Western Empire, but the furthest point reached was in the East, under Justinian, who enacted that unless the acquisitions of the child were derived from the parent's own property, the parent's rights over them should not extend beyond enjoying their produce for the period of his life. Even this, the utmost relaxation of the Roman Patria Potestas, left it far ampler and severer than any analogous institution of the modern world. The earliest modern writers on jurisprudence remark that it was only the fiercer and ruder of the conquerors of the empire, and notably the nations of Sclavonic origin, which exhibited a Patria Potestas at all resembling that which was described in the Pandects and the Code. All the Germanic immigrants seem to have recognised a corporate union of the family under the *mund*, or authority of a patriarchal chief; but his powers are obviously only the relics of a decayed Patria Potestas, and fell far short of those enjoyed by the Roman father. The Franks are particularly mentioned as not having the Roman Institution, and accordingly the old French lawyers, even when most busily engaged in filling the interstices of barbarous custom with rules of Roman law, were obliged to protect themselves against the intrusion of the Potestas by the express maxim, *Puyssance de père en France n'a lieu.* The tenacity of the Romans in maintaining this relic of their most ancient condition is in itself remarkable, but it is less remarkable than the diffusion of the Potestas over the whole of a civilisation from which it had once disappeared. While the Castrense Peculium constituted as yet the sole exception to the father's power over property, and while his power over his children's persons was still extensive, the Roman citizenship, and with it the Patria Potestas, were spreading into every corner of the empire. Every African or Spaniard, every Gaul, Briton, or Jew, who received this honour by gift, purchase, or inheritance, placed himself under the Roman Law of Persons, and, though our authorities intimate that children born before the acquisition of citizenship could not be brought under Power against their will, children born after it and all ulterior descendants were on the ordinary footing of a Roman *filius familias.* It does not fall within the province of this treatise to examine the mechanism of the later Roman society, but I may be permitted to remark that there is little foundation for the opinion which represents the constitution of Antoninus Caracalla conferring Roman citizenship on the whole of his subjects as a

measure of small importance. However we may
interpret it, it must have enormously enlarged
the sphere of the Patria Potestas, and it seems to
me that the tightening of family relations which
it effected is an agency which ought to be kept
in view more than it has been, in accounting for
the great moral revolution which was transforming the world.

Before this branch of our subject is dismissed,
it should be observed that the Paterfamilias was
answerable for the delicts (or *torts*) of his Sons
under Power. He was similarly liable for the
torts of his slaves; but in both cases he originally
possessed the singular privilege of tendering the
delinquent's person in full satisfaction of the
damage. The responsibility thus incurred on behalf
of sons, coupled with the mutual incapacity of
Parent and Child under Power to sue one another,
has seemed to some jurists to be best explained
by the assumption of a ' unity of person '
between the Pater-familias and the Filius-
familias. In the Chapter on Successions I shall
attempt to show in what sense, and to what
extent, this ' unity ' can be accepted as a reality.
I can only say at present that these responsi-
bilities of the Paterfamilias, and other legal phenomena which will be discussed hereafter, appear
to me to point at certain *duties* of the primitive
Patriarchal chieftain which balanced his *rights*. I
conceive that, if he disposed absolutely of the
persons and fortune of his clansmen, this representative ownership was coextensive with a
liability to provide for all members of the brotherhood out of the common fund. The difficulty is
to throw ourselves out of our habitual associations sufficiently for conceiving the nature of his

obligation. It was not a legal duty, for law had not yet penetrated into the precinct of the Family. To call it *moral* is perhaps to anticipate the ideas belonging to a later stage of mental development; but the expression " moral obligation " is significant enough for our purpose, if we understand by it a duty semi-consciously followed and enforced rather by instinct and habit than by definite sanctions.

The Patria Potestas, in its normal shape, has not been, and, as it seems to me, could not have been, a generally durable institution. The proof of its former universality is therefore incomplete so long as we consider it by itself; but the demonstration may be carried much further by examining other departments of ancient law which depend on it ultimately, but not by a thread of connexion visible in all its parts or to all eyes. Let us turn for example to Kinship, or in other words, to the scale on which the proximity of relatives to each other is calculated in archaic jurisprudence. Here again it will be convenient to employ the Roman terms, Agnatic and Cognatic relationship. *Cognatic* relationship is simply the conception of kinship familiar to modern ideas; it is the relationship arising through common descent from the same pair of married persons, whether the descent be traced through males or females. *Agnatic* relationship is something very different : it excludes a number of persons whom we in our day should certainly consider of kin to ourselves, and it includes many more whom we should never reckon among our kindred. It is in truth the connexion existing between the members of the Family, conceived as it was in the most ancient times. The limits

of this connexion are far from conterminous with
those of modern relationship.

Cognates then are all those persons who can
trace their blood to a single ancestor and ances-
tress; or, if we take the strict technical meaning
of the word in Roman law, they are all who trace
their blood to the legitimate marriage of a common pair. " Cognation " is therefore a relative
term, and the degree of connexion in blood which
it indicates depends on the particular marriage
which is selected as the commencement of the
calculation. If we begin with marriage of father
and mother, Cognation will only express the relationship of brothers and sisters; if we take that
of the grandfather and grandmother, then uncles,
aunts, and their descendants will also be included
in the notion of Cognation, and following the
same process a larger number of Cognates may be
continually obtained by choosing the starting point
higher and higher up in the line of ascent. All
this is easily understood by a modern; but who
are the Agnates? In the first place, they are all
the Cognates who trace their connexion exclusively through males. A table of Cognates is,
of course, formed by taking each lineal ancestor
in turn and including all his descendants of both
sexes in the tabular view; if then, in tracing the
various branches of such a genealogical table or
tree, we stop whenever we come to the name of
a female and pursue that particular branch or
ramification no further, all who remain after the
descendants of women have been excluded are
Agnates, and their connexion together is Agnatic
Relationship. I dwell a little on the process which
is practically followed in separating them from
the Cognates, because it explains a memorable

legal maxim, 'Mulier est finis familiæ'—a woman is the terminus of the family. A female name closes the branch or twig of the genealogy in which it occurs. None of the descendants of a female are included in the primitive notion of family relationship.

If the system of archaic law at which we are looking be one which admits Adoption, we must add to the Agnates thus obtained all persons, male or female, who have been brought into the Family by the artificial extension of its boundaries. But the descendants of such persons will only be Agnates, if they satisfy the conditions which have just been described.

What then is the reason of this arbitrary inclusion and exclusion? Why should a conception of Kinship, so elastic as to include strangers brought into the family by adoption, be nevertheless so narrow as to shut out the descendants of a female member? To solve these questions, we must recur to the Patria Potestas. The foundation of Agnation is not the marriage of Father and Mother, but the authority of the Father. All persons are Agnatically connected together who are under the same Paternal Power, or who have been under it, or who might have been under it if their lineal ancestor had lived long enough to exercise his empire. In truth, in the primitive view, Relationship is exactly limited by Patria Potestas. Where the Potestas begins, Kinship begins; and therefore adoptive relatives are among the kindred. Where the Potestas ends, Kinship ends; so that a son emancipated by his father loses all rights of Agnation. And here we have the reason why the descendants of females are outside the limits of archaic kinship. If a

woman died unmarried, she could have no legitimate descendants. If she married, her children
fell under the Patria Potestas, not of her Father,
but of her Husband, and thus were lost to her
own family. It is obvious that the organisation
of primitive societies would have been confounded, if men had called themselves relatives
of their mother's relatives. The inference would
have been that a person might be subject
to two distinct Patriæ Potestates; but distinct
Patriæ Potestates implied distinct jurisdictions, so
that anybody amenable to two of them at the
same time would have lived under two different
dispensations. As long as the Family was an
imperium in imperio, a community within the
commonwealth, governed by its own institutions
of which the parent was the source, the limitation
of relationship to the Agnates was a necessary
security against a conflict of laws in the domestic
forum.

The Parental Powers proper are extinguished by
the death of the Parent, but Agnation is as it
were a mould which retains their imprint after
they have ceased to exist. Hence comes the
interest of Agnation for the inquirer into the history of jurisprudence. The Powers themselves
are discernible in comparatively few monuments
of ancient law, but Agnatic Relationship, which
implies their former existence, is discoverable
almost everywhere. There are few indigenous
bodies of law belonging to communities of the
Indo-European stock, which do not exhibit
peculiarities in the most ancient part of their
structure which are clearly referable to Agnation.
In Hindoo law, for example, which is saturated
with the primitive notions of family dependency,

kinship is entirely Agnatic, and I am informed
that in Hindoo genealogies the names of women
are generally omitted altogether. The same view
of relationship pervades so much of the laws of
the races who overran the Roman Empire as
appears to have really formed part of their primitive usage, and we may suspect that it would
have perpetuated itself even more than it has in
modern European jurisprudence, if it had not
been for the vast influence of the later Roman
law on modern thought. The Prætors early laid
hold on Cognation as the *natural* form of kinship,
and spared no pains in purifying their system
from the older conception. Their ideas have
descended to us, but still traces of Agnation are
to be seen in many of the modern rules of succession after death. The exclusion of females
and their children from governmental functions,
commonly attributed to the usage of the Salian
Franks, has certainly an agnatic origin, being
descended from the ancient German rule of succession to allodial property. In Agnation too is
to be sought the explanation of that extraordinary
rule of English Law, only recently repealed,
which prohibited brothers of the half-blood from
succeeding to one another's lands. In the Customs of Normandy, the rule applies to *uterine*
brothers only, that is, to brothers by the same
mother but not by the same father; and, limited
in this way, it is a strict deduction from the
system of Agnation, under which uterine brothers
are no relations at all to one another. When it
was transplanted to England, the English judges,
who had no clue to its principle, interpreted it
as a general prohibition against the succession of
the half-blood, and extended it to *consanguineous*

brothers, that is to sons of the same father by different wives. In all the literature which enshrines the pretended philosophy of law, there is nothing more curious than the pages of elaborate sophistry in which Blackstone attempts to explain and justify the exclusion of the half-blood.

It may be shown, I think, that the Family, as held together by the Patria Potestas, is the nidus out of which the entire Law of Persons has germinated. Of all the chapters of that Law the most important is that which is concerned with the status of Females. It has just been stated that Primitive Jurisprudence, though it does not allow a Woman to communicate any rights of Agnation to her descendants, includes herself nevertheless in the Agnatic bond. Indeed, the relation of a female to the family in which she was born is much stricter, closer, and more durable than that which unites her male kinsmen. We have several times laid down that early law takes notice of Families only; this is the same thing as saying that it only takes notice of persons exercising Patria Potestas, and accordingly the only principle on which it enfranchises a son or grandson at the death of his Parent, is a consideration of the capacity inherent in such son or grandson to become himself the head of a new family and the root of a new set of Parental Powers. But a woman, of course, has no capacity of the kind, and no title accordingly to the liberation which it confers. There is therefore a peculiar contrivance of archaic jurisprudence for retaining her in the bondage of the Family for life. This is the institution known to the oldest Roman law as the Perpetual Tutelage of Women, under which a Female, though relieved from her

Parent's authority by his decease, continues subject through life to her nearest male relations as her Guardians. Perpetual Guardianship is obviously neither more nor less than an artificial prolongation of the Patria Potestas, when for other purposes it has been dissolved. In India, the system survives in absolute completeness, and its operation is so strict that a Hindoo Mother frequently becomes the ward of her own sons. Even in Europe, the laws of the Scandinavian nations respecting women preserved it until quite recently. The invaders of the Western Empire had it universally among their indigenous usages, and indeed their ideas on the subject of Guardianship, in all its forms, were among the most retrogressive of those which they introduced into the Western world. But from the mature Roman jurisprudence it had entirely disappeared. We should know almost nothing about it, if we had only the compilations of Justinian to consult; but the discovery of the manuscript of Gaius discloses it to us at a most interesting epoch, just when it had fallen into complete discredit and was verging on extinction. The great jurisconsult himself scouts the popular apology offered for it in the mental inferiority of the female sex, and a considerable part of his volume is taken up with descriptions of the numerous expedients, some of them displaying extraordinary ingenuity, which the Roman lawyers had devised for enabling Women to defeat the ancient rules. Led by their theory of Natural Law, the jurisconsults had evidently at this time assumed the equality of the sexes as a principle of their code of equity. The restrictions which they attacked were, it is to be observed, restrictions on the disposition of property, for which the assent of the woman's guardians was still formally required. Control of her person was apparently quite obsolete.

Ancient law subordinates the woman to her blood-relations, while a prime phenomenon of modern jurisprudence has been her subordination to her husband. The history of the change is remarkable. It begins far back in the annals of Rome. Anciently, there were three modes in which marriage might be contracted according to Roman usage, one involving a religious solemnity, the other two the observance of certain secular formalities. By the religious marriage or *Confarreation;* by the higher form of civil marriage, which was called *Coemption;* and by the lower form, which was termed *Usus*, the Husband acquired a number of rights over the person and property of his wife, which were on the whole in excess of such as are conferred on him in any system of modern jurisprudence. But in what capacity did he acquire them? Not as *Husband*, but as *Father*. By the Confarreation, Coemption, and Usus, the woman passed *in manum viri*, that is, in law she became the *Daughter* of her husband. She was included in his Patria Potestas. She incurred all the liabilities springing out of it while it subsisted, and surviving it when it had expired. All her property became absolutely his, and she was retained in tutelage after his death to the guardian whom he had appointed by will. These three ancient forms of marriage fell, however, gradually into disuse, so that, at the most splendid period of Roman greatness, they had almost entirely given place to a fashion of wedlock—old apparently, but not hitherto considered reputable—which was founded on a modification

of the lower form of civil marriage. Without
explaining the technical mechanism of the institution now generally popular, I may describe it
as amounting in law to little more than a temporary deposit of the woman by her family. The
rights of the family remained unimpaired, and the
lady continued in the tutelage of guardians whom
her parents had appointed and whose privileges
of control overrode, in many material respects,
the inferior authority of her husband. The consequence was that the situation of the Roman
female, whether married or unmarried, became
one of great personal and proprietary independence, for the tendency of the later law, as I have
already hinted, was to reduce the power of the
guardian to a nullity, while the form of marriage
in fashion conferred on the husband no compensating superiority. But Christianity tended somewhat from the very first to narrow this remarkable liberty. Led at first by justifiable disrelish
for the loose practices of the decaying heathen
world, but afterwards hurried on by a passion of
asceticism, the professors of the new faith looked
with disfavour on a marital tie which was in fact
the laxest the Western world has seen. The
latest Roman law, so far as it is touched by the
Constitutions of the Christian Emperors, bears
some marks of a reaction against the liberal doctrines of the great Antonine jurisconsults. And
the prevalent state of religious sentiment may
explain why it is that modern jurisprudence,
forged in the furnace of barbarian conquest, and
formed by the fusion of Roman jurisprudence with
patriarchal usage, has absorbed, among its rudiments, much more than usual of those rules concerning the position of women which belong

peculiarly to an imperfect civilisation. During the troubled era which begins modern history, and while the laws of the Germanic and Sclavonic immigrants remained superposed like a separate layer above the Roman jurisprudence of their provincial subjects, the women of the dominant races are seen everywhere under various forms of archaic guardianship, and the husband who takes a wife from any family except his own pays a money-price to her relations for the tutelage which they surrender to him. When we move onwards, and the code of the middle ages has been formed by the amalgamation of the two systems, the law relating to women carries the stamp of its double origin. The principle of the Roman jurisprudence is so far triumphant that unmarried females are generally (though there are local exceptions to the rule) relieved from the bondage of the family; but the archaic principle of the barbarians has fixed the position of married women, and the husband has drawn to himself in his marital character the powers which had once belonged to his wife's male kindred, the only difference being that he no longer purchases his privileges. At this point therefore the modern law of Western and Southern Europe begins to be distinguished by one of its chief characteristics, the comparative freedom it allows to unmarried women and widows, the heavy disabilities it imposes on wives. It was very long before the subordination entailed on the other sex by marriage was sensibly diminished. The principal and most powerful solvent of the revived barbarism of Europe was always the codified jurisprudence of Justinian, wherever it was studied with that passionate enthusiasm which it seldom failed to

awaken. It covertly but most efficaciously undermined the customs which it pretended merely to
interpret. But the Chapter of law relating to
married women was for the most part read by the
light, not of Roman, but of Canon Law, which in
no one particular departs so widely from the
spirit of the secular jurisprudence as in the view
it takes of the relations created by marriage.
This was in part inevitable, since no society which
preserves any tincture of Christian institution is
likely to restore to married women the personal
liberty conferred on them by the middle Roman
law, but the proprietary disabilities of married
females stand on quite a different basis from their
personal incapacities, and it is by keeping alive
and consolidating the former that the expositors
of the Canon Law have deeply injured civilisation.
There are many vestiges of a struggle between the
secular and ecclesiastical principles, but the
Canon Law nearly everywhere prevailed. In
some of the French provinces married women,
of a rank below nobility, obtained all the powers
of dealing with property which Roman jurisprudence had allowed, and this local law has been
largely followed by the Code Napoleon; but the
state of the Scottish law shows that scrupulous
deference to the doctrines of the Roman jurisconsults did not always extend to mitigating the
disabilities of wives. The systems however which
are least indulgent to married women are invariably those which have followed the Canon
Law exclusively, or those which, from the late-
ness of their contact with European civilisation,
have never had their archaisms weeded out. The
Scandinavian laws, harsh till lately to all females,
are still remarkable for their severity to wives.

And scarcely less stringent in the proprietary
incapacities it imposes is the English Common
Law, which borrows far the greatest number of
its fundamental principles from the jurisprudence
of the Canonists. Indeed, the part of the Common Law which prescribes the legal situation of
married women may serve to give an Englishman
clear notions of the great institution which has
been the principal subject of this chapter. I do
not know how the operation and nature of the
ancient Patria Potestas can be brought so vividly
before the mind as by reflecting on the prerogatives attached to the husband by the pure English
Common Law, and by recalling the rigorous consistency with which the view of a complete legal
subjection on the part of the wife is carried by
it, where it is untouched by equity or statutes,
through every department of rights, duties, and
remedies. The distance between the eldest and
latest Roman law on the subject of Children under
Power may be considered as equivalent to the
difference between the Common Law and the
jurisprudence of the Court of Chancery in the
rules which they respectively apply to wives.

If we were to lose sight of the true origin of
Guardianship in both its forms and were to employ the common language on these topics, we
should find ourselves remarking that, while the
Tutelage of Women is an instance in which
systems of archaic law push to an extravagant
length the fiction of suspended rights, the rules
which they lay down for the Guardianship of
Male Orphans are an example of a fault in precisely the opposite direction. All such systems
terminate the Tutelage of males at an extraordinarily early period. Under the ancient Roman

law, which may be taken as their type, the son
who was delivered from Patria Potestas by the
death of his Father or Grandfather remained
under guardianship till an epoch which for
general purposes may be described as arriving
with his fifteenth year; but the arrival of that
epoch placed him at once in the full enjoyment
of personal and proprietary independence. The
period of minority appears therefore to have been
as unreasonably short as the duration of the disabilities of women was preposterously long. But,
in point of fact, there was no element either of
excess or of shortcoming in the circumstances
which gave their original form to the two kinds
of guardianship. Neither the one nor the other
of them was based on the slightest consideration
of public or private convenience. The guardianship of male orphans was no more designed
originally to shield them till the arrival of years
of discretion than the tutelage of women was intended to protect the other sex against its own
feebleness. The reason why the death of the
father delivered the son from the bondage of the
family was the son's capacity for becoming himself the head of a new family and the founder of
a new Patria Potestas; no such capacity was
possessed by the woman and therefore she was
never enfranchised. Accordingly the Guardianship of Male Orphans was a contrivance for keeping alive the semblance of subordination to the
family of the Parent, up to the time when the
child was supposed capable of becoming a parent
himself. It was a prolongation of the Patria
Potestas up to the period of bare physical man-
hood. It ended with puberty, for the rigour of
the theory demanded that it should do so. Inas-

much, however, as it did not profess to conduct the orphan ward to the age of intellectual maturity or fitness for affairs, it was quite unequal to the purposes of general convenience; and this the Romans seem to have discovered at a very early stage of their social progress. One of the very oldest monuments of Roman legislation is the *Lex Lætoria* or *Plætoria* which placed all free males who were of full years and rights under the temporary control of a new class of guardians, called *Curatores*, whose sanction was required to validate their acts or contracts. The twenty-sixth year of the young man's age was the limit of this statutory supervision; and it is exclusively with reference to the age of twenty-five that the terms " majority " and " minority " are employed in Roman law. *Pupilage* or *wardship* in modern jurisprudence had adjusted itself with tolerable regularity to the simple principle of protection to the immaturity of youth both bodily and mental. It has its natural termination with years of discretion. But for protection against physical weakness and for protection against intellectual incapacity, the Romans looked to two different institutions, distinct both in theory and design. The ideas attendant on both are combined in the modern idea of guardianship.

The Law of Persons contains but one other chapter which can be usefully cited for our present purpose. The legal rules by which systems of mature jurisprudence regulate the connection of *Master and Slave*, present no very distinct traces of the original condition common to ancient societies. But there are reasons for this exception. There seems to be something in the institution of Slavery which has at all times either

shocked or perplexed mankind, however little
habituated to reflection, and however slightly
advanced in the cultivation of its moral instincts.
The compunction which ancient communities
almost unconsciously experienced appears to have
always resulted in the adoption of some imaginary
principle upon which a defence, or at least a
rationale, of slavery could be plausibly founded.
Very early in their history the Greeks explained
the institution as grounded on the intellectual
inferiority of certain races and their consequent
natural aptitude for the servile condition. The
Romans, in a spirit equally characteristic, derived
it from a supposed agreement between the victor
and the vanquished in which the first stipulated
for the perpetual services of his foe; and the other
gained in consideration the life which he had legi-
timately forfeited. Such theories were not only
unsound but plainly unequal to the case for which
they affected to account. Still they exercised
powerful influence in many ways. They satisfied
the conscience of the Master. They perpetuated
and probably increased the debasement of the
Slave. And they naturally tended to put out of
sight the relation in which servitude had originally
stood to the rest of the domestic system. The
relation, though not clearly exhibited, is casually
indicated in many parts of primitive law, and
more particularly in the typical system—that of
ancient Rome.

Much industry and some learning have been
bestowed in the United States of America on the
question whether the Slave was in the early stages
of society a recognised member of the Family.
There is a sense in which an affirmative answer
must certainly be given. It is clear, from the

testimony both of ancient law and of many
primeval histories, that the Slave might under
certain conditions be made the Heir, or Universal
Successor, of the Master, and this significant
faculty, as I shall explain in the Chapter on Succession, implies that the government and representation of the Family might, in a particular
state of circumstances, devolve on the bondman.
It seems, however, to be assumed in the American arguments on the subject that, if we allow
Slavery to have been a primitive Family institution, the acknowledgment is pregnant with an
admission of the moral defensibility of Negro-ser-
vitude at the present moment. What then is
meant by saying that the Slave was originally
included in the Family? Not that his situation
may not have been the fruit of the coarsest
motives which can actuate man. The simple wish
to use the bodily powers of another person as a
means of ministering to one's own ease or
pleasure is doubtless the foundation of Slavery,
and as old as human nature. When we speak of
the Slave as anciently included in the Family, we
intend to assert nothing as to the motives of those
who brought him into it or kept him there; we
merely imply that the tie which bound him to his
master was regarded as one of the same general
character with that which united every other
member of the group to its chieftain. This consequence is, in fact, carried in the general assertion already made that the primitive ideas of
mankind were unequal to comprehending any
basis of the connection *inter se* of individuals,
apart from the relations of family. The Family
consisted primarily of those who belonged to it
by consanguinity and next of those who had been

engrafted on it by adoption; but there was still a third class of persons who were only joined to it by common subjection to its head, and these were the Slaves. The born and the adopted subjects of the chief were raised above the Slave by the certainty that in the ordinary course of events they would be relieved from bondage and entitled tc exercise powers of their own; but that the inferiority of the Slave was not such as to place him outside the pale of the Family, or such as to degrade him to the footing of inanimate property, is clearly proved, I think, by the many traces which remain of his ancient capacity for inheritance in the last resort. It would, of course, be unsafe in the highest degree to hazard conjectures how far the lot of the Slave was mitigated, in the beginnings of society, by having a definite place reserved to him in the empire of the Father. It is, perhaps, more probable that the son was practically assimilated to the Slave, than that the Slave shared any of the tenderness which in later times was shown to the son. But it may be asserted with some confidence of advanced and matured codes that, wherever servitude is sanctioned, the Slave has uniformly greater advantages under systems which preserve some memento of his earlier condition than under those which have adopted some other theory of his civil degradation. The point of view from which jurisprudence regards the Slave is always of great importance to him. The Roman law was arrested in its growing tendency to look upon him more and more as an article of property by the theory of the Law of Nature; and hence it is that, wherever servitude is sanctioned by institutions which have been deeply affected by Roman juris-

prudence, the servile condition is never intoler-
ably wretched.   There is a great deal of evidence
that in those American States which have taken
the highly Romanised code of Louisiana as the
basis of their jurisprudence, the lot and prospects
of the negro-population are better in many
material respects than under institutions founded
on the English Common Law, which, as recently
interpreted, has no true place for the Slave, and
can only therefore regard him as a chattel.

We have now examined all parts of the ancient
Law of Persons which fall within the scope of this
treatise, and the result of the inquiry is, I trust,
to give additional definiteness and precision to our
view of the infancy of jurisprudence.   The Civil
laws of States first make their appearance as the
Themistes of a patriarchal sovereign, and we can
now see that these Themistes are probably only a
developed form of the irresponsible commands
which, in a still earlier condition of the race, the
head of each isolated household may have addressed to his wives, his children, and his slaves.
But, even after the State has been organised, the
laws have still an extremely limited application.
Whether they retain their primitive character as
Themistes, or whether they advance to the condition of Customs or Codified Texts, they are binding not on individuals, but on Families.   Ancient
jurisprudence, if a perhaps deceptive comparison
may be employed, may be likened to International
Law, filling nothing, as it were, excepting the
interstices between the great groups which are
the atoms of society.   In a community so situated,
the legislation of assemblies and the jurisdiction
of Courts reaches only to the heads of families,
and to every other individual the rule of conduct

is the law of his home, of which his Parent is the
legislator. But the sphere of civil law, small at
first, tends steadily to enlarge itself. The agents
of legal change, Fictions, Equity, and Legislation, are brought in turn to bear on the primeval
institutions, and at every point of the progress, a
greater number of personal rights and a larger
amount of property are removed from the domestic forum to the cognizance of the public
tribunals. The ordinances of the government
obtain gradually the same efficacy in private concerns as in matters of state, and are no longer
liable to be overridden by the behests of a despot
enthroned by each hearthstone. We have in the
annals of Roman law a nearly complete history of
the crumbling away of an archaic system, and of
the formation of new institutions from the recombined materials, institutions some of which
descended unimpaired to the modern world, while
others, destroyed or corrupted by contact with
barbarism in the dark ages, had again to be re-
covered by mankind. When we leave this jurisprudence at the epoch of its final reconstruction
by Justinian, few traces of archaism can be discovered in any part of it except in the single
article of the extensive powers still reserved to
the living Parent. Everywhere else principles of
convenience, or of symmetry, or of simplifica-
tion—new principles at any rate—have usurped
the authority of the jejune considerations which
satisfied the conscience of ancient times. Everywhere a new morality has displaced the canons of
conduct and the reasons of acquiescence which
were in unison with the ancient usages, because
in fact they were born of them.

The movement of the progressive societies has

been uniform in one respect. Through all its
course it has been distinguished by the gradual
dissolution of family dependency and the growth
of individual obligation in its place. The Individual is steadily substituted for the Family, as
the unit of which civil laws take account. The
advance has been accomplished at varying rates
of celerity, and there are societies not absolutely
stationary in which the collapse of the ancient
organisation can only be perceived by careful
study of the phenomena they present. But,
whatever its pace, the change has not been subject to reaction or recoil, and apparent retarda-
tions will be found to have been occasioned
through the absorption of archaic ideas and customs from some entirely foreign source. Nor is
it difficult to see what is the tie between man and
man which replaces by degrees those forms of
reciprocity in rights and duties which have their
origin in the Family. It is Contract. Starting,
as from one terminus of history, from a condition of society in which all the relations of
Persons are summed up in the relations of
Family, we seem to have steadily moved towards
a phase of social order in which all these relations
arise from the free agreement of Individuals. In
Western Europe the progress achieved in this
direction has been considerable. Thus the status
of the Slave has disappeared—it has been superseded by the contractual relation of the servant
to his master. The status of the Female under
Tutelage, if the tutelage be understood of persons
other than her husband, has also ceased to exist;
from her coming of age to her marriage all the
relations she may form are relations of contract.
So too the status of the Son under Power has no

true place in the law of modern European societies. If any civil obligation binds together the Parent and the child of full age, it is one to which only contract gives its legal validity. The apparent exceptions are exceptions of that stamp which illustrate the rule. The child before years of discretion, the orphan under guardianship, the adjudged lunatic, have all their capacities and incapacities regulated by the Law of Persons. But why? The reason is differently expressed in the conventional language of different systems, but in substance it is stated to the same effect by all. The great majority of Jurists are constant to the principle that the classes of persons just mentioned are subject to extrinsic control on the single ground that they do not possess the faculty of forming a judgment on their own interests; in other words, that they are wanting in the first essential of an engagement by Contract.

The word Status may be usefully employed to construct a formula expressing the law of progress thus indicated, which, whatever be its value, seems to me to be sufficiently ascertained. All the forms of Status taken notice of in the Law of Persons were derived from, and to some extent are still coloured by, the powers and privileges anciently residing in the Family. If then we employ Status, agreeably with the usage of the best writers, to signify these personal conditions only, and avoid applying the term to such conditions as are the immediate or remote result of agreement, we may say that the movement of the progressive societies has hitherto been a movement *from Status to Contract.*

CHAPTER VI

THE EARLY HISTORY OF TESTAMENTARY SUCCESSION

If an attempt were made to demonstrate in England the superiority of the historical method of investigation to the modes of inquiry concerning Jurisprudence which are in fashion among us, no department of Law would better serve as an example than Testaments or Wills. Its capabilities it owes to its great length and great continuity. At the beginning of its history we find ourselves in the very infancy of the social state, surrounded by conceptions which it requires some effort of mind to realise in their ancient form; while here, at the other extremity of its line of progress, we are in the midst of legal notions which are nothing more than those same conceptions disguised by the phraseology and by the habits of thought which belong to modern times, and exhibiting therefore a difficulty of another kind, the difficulty of believing that ideas which form part of our everyday mental stock can really stand in need of analysis and examination. The growth of the Law of Wills between these extreme points can be traced with remarkable distinctness. It was much less interrupted at the epoch of the birth of feudalism, than the history of most other branches of law. It is, indeed, true that, as regards all provinces of jurisprudence, the break caused by the division between ancient and modern history, or in other words by the dissolution of the Roman empire, has been very greatly exaggerated. Indolence has disinclined

many writers to be at the pains of looking for
threads of connection entangled and obscured by
the confusions of six troubled centuries, while
other inquirers, not naturally deficient in patience
and industry, have been misled by idle pride in
the legal system of their country, and by consequent unwillingness to confess its obligations
to the jurisprudence of Rome. But these un-
favourable influences have had comparatively
little effect on the province of Testamentary Law.
The barbarians were confessedly strangers to any
such conception as that of a Will. The best
authorities agree that there is no trace of it in
those parts of their written codes which comprise
the customs practised by them in their original
seats, and in their subsequent settlements on the
edge of the Roman empire. But soon after they
became mixed with the population of the Roman
provinces they appropriated from the Imperial
jurisprudence the conception of a Will, at first in
part, and afterwards in all its integrity. The influence of the Church had much to do with this
rapid assimilation. The ecclesiastical power had
very early succeeded to those privileges of custody and registration of Testaments which several
of the heathen temples had enjoyed; and even
thus early it was almost excusively to private
bequests that the religious foundations owed their
temporal possessions. Hence it is that the
decrees of the earliest Provincial Councils perpetually contain anathemas against those who
deny the sanctity of Wills. Here, in England,
Church influence was certainly chief among the
causes which by universal acknowledgment have
prevented that discontinuity in the history of
Testamentary Law, which is sometimes believed

to exist in the history of other provinces of Jurisprudence. The jurisdiction over one class of Wills was delegated to the Ecclesiastical Courts, which applied to them, though not always intelligently, the principles of Roman jurisprudence; and, though neither the courts of Common Law nor the Court of Chancery owned any positive obligation to follow the Ecclesiastical tribunals, they could not escape the potent influence of a system of settled rules in course of application by their side. The English law of testamentary succession to personalty has become a modified form of the dispensation under which the inheritances of Roman citizens were administered.

It is not difficult to point out the extreme difference of the conclusions forced on us by the historical treatment of the subject from those to which we are conducted when, without the help of history, we merely strive to analyse our *primâ facie* impressions. I suppose there is nobody who, starting from the popular or even the legal conception of a Will, would not imagine that certain qualities are necessarily attached to it. He would say, for example, that a Will necessarily takes effect *at death only*—that it is *secret*, not known as a matter of course to persons taking interests under its provisions—that it is *revocable*, i.e. always capable of being superseded by a new act of testation. Yet I shall be able to show that there was a time when none of these characteristics belonged to a Will. The Testaments from which our Wills are directly descended at first took effect immediately on their execution; they were not secret; they were not revocable. Few legal agencies are, in fact, the fruit of more complex historical agencies than that by which a man's written intentions control the posthumous disposition of his goods. Testaments very slowly and gradually gathered round them the qualities I have mentioned; and they did this from causes and under pressure of events which may be called casual, or which at any rate have no interest for us at present, except so far as they have affec'ed the history of law.

At a time when legal theories were more abundant than at present—theories which, it is true, were for the most part gratuitous and premature enough, but which nevertheless rescued jurisprudence from that worse and more ignoble condition, not unknown to ourselves, in which nothing like a generalisation is aspired to, and law is regarded as a mere empirical pursuit—it was the fashion to explain the ready and apparently intuitive perception which we have of certain qualities in a Will, by saying that they were natural to it, or, as the phrase would run in full, attached to it by the Law of Nature. Nobody, I imagine, would affect to maintain such a doctrine, when once it was ascertained that all these characteristics had their origin within historical memory; at the same time, vestiges of the theory of which the doctrine is an offshoot, linger in forms of expression which we all of us use and perhaps scarcely know how to dispense with. I may illustrate this by mentioning a position common in the legal literature of the 17th century. The jurists of that period very commonly assert that the power of Testation itself is of Natural Law, that it is a right conferred by the Law of Nature. Their teaching, though all persons may not at once see the connection, is in substance followed by those who affirm that the right of dictating or controlling the posthumous disposal of property is a necessary or natural consequence of the proprietary rights themselves. And every student of technical jurisprudence must have come across the same view, clothed in the language of a rather different school, which, in its rationale of this department of law, treats succession *ex testamento* as the mode of devolution which the property of deceased persons ought primarily to follow, and then proceeds to account for succession *ab intestato* as the incidental provision of the lawgiver for the discharge of a function which was only left unperformed through the neglect or misfortune of the deceased proprietor. These opinions are only expanded forms of the more compendious doctrine that Testamentary disposition is an institution of the Law of Nature. It is certainly never quite safe to pronounce dogmatically as to the range of association embraced by modern minds, when they reflect on Nature and her Law; but I believe that most persons, who affirm that the Testamentary Power is of Natural Law, may be taken to imply either that, as a matter of fact, it is universal, or that nations are prompted to sanction it by an original instinct and impulse. With respect to the first of these positions, I think that, when explicitly set forth, it can never be seriously contended for in an age which has seen the severe restraints imposed on the Testamentary Power by the *Code Napoléon*, and has witnessed the steady multiplication of systems for which the French codes have served as a model. To the second assertion we must object that it is contrary to the best-ascertained facts in the early history of law, and I venture to affirm generally that, in all indigenous societies, a condition of jurisprudence in which Testamentary privileges are *not* allowed, or rather not contemplated, has preceded that later stage of legal development in which the mere will of the proprietor is permitted under more or less of restriction to override the claims of his kindred in blood.

The conception of a Will or Testament cannot be considered by itself. It is a member, and not the first, of a series of conceptions. In itself a Will is simply the instrument by which the intention of the testator is declared. It must be clear, I think, that before such an instrument takes its turn for discussion, there are several preliminary points to be examined—as, for example, what is it, what sort of right or interest, which passes from a dead man on his decease? to whom and in what form does it pass? and how came it that the dead were allowed to control the posthumous disposition of their property? Thrown into technical language, the dependence of the various conceptions which contribute to the notion of a Will is thus expressed. A Will or Testament is an instrument by which the devolution of an inheritance is prescribed. Inheritance is a form of universal succession. A universal succession is a succession to a *universitas juris*, or university of rights and duties. Inverting this order we have therefore to inquire what is a *universitas juris;* what is a universal succession; what is the form of universal succession which is called an inheritance. And there are also two further questions, independent to some extent of the points I have mooted, but demanding solution before the subject of Wills can be exhausted. These are, how came an inheritance to be controlled in any case

by the testator's volition, and what is the nature
of the instrument by which it came to be controlled?

The first question relates to the *universitas
juris;* that is, a university (or bundle) of rights
and duties. A *universitas juris* is a collection of
rights and duties united by the single circumstance of their having belonged at one time to
some one person. It is, as it were, the legal
clothing of some given individual. It is not
formed by grouping together *any* rights and *any*
duties. It can only be constituted by taking all
the rights and all the duties of a particular person.
The tie which so connects a number of rights of
property, rights of way, rights to legacies, duties
of specific performance, debts, obligations to com-
pensate wrongs—which so connects all these legal
privileges and duties together as to constitute
them a *universitas juris*, is the *fact* of their having
attached to some individual capable of exercising
them. Without this *fact* there is no university of
rights and duties. The expression *universitas
juris* is not classical, but for the notion jurisprudence is exclusively indebted to Roman law;
nor is it at all difficult to seize. We must endeavour to collect under one conception the whole set
of legal relations in which each one of us stands to
the rest of the world. These, whatever be their
character and composition, make up together a
universitas juris; and there is but little danger of
mistake in forming the notion, if we are only
careful to remember that duties enter into it quite
as much as rights. Our duties may overbalance
our rights. A man may owe more than he is
worth, and therefore if a money value is set on
his collective legal relations he may be what is

called insolvent. But for all that the entire group of rights and duties which centres in him is not the less a 'juris universitas.'

We come next to a 'universal succession.' A universal succession is a succession to a *universitas juris*. It occurs when one man is invested with the legal clothing of another, becoming at the same moment subject to all his liabilities and entitled to all his rights. In order that the universal succession may be true and perfect, the devolution must take place *uno ictu*, as the jurists phrase it. It is of course possible to conceive one man acquiring the whole of the rights and duties of another at different periods, as for example by successive purchases; or he might acquire them in different capacities, part as heir, part as purchaser, part as legatee. But though the group of rights and duties thus made up should in fact amount to the whole legal personality of ·a particular individual, the acquisition would not be a universal succession. In order that there may be a true universal succession, the transmission must be such as to pass the whole aggregate of rights and duties at the *same* moment and in virtue of the *same* legal capacity in the recipient. The notion of a universal succession, like that of a juris universitas, is permanent in jurisprudence, though in the English legal system it is obscured by the great variety of capacities in which rights are acquired, and, above all, by the distinction between the two great provinces of English property, 'realty' and 'personalty.' The succession of an assignee in bankruptcy to the entire property of the bankrupt is, however, a universal succession, though as the assignee only pays debts to the extent of the assets, this is only a modified form of the primary notion. Were it common among us for persons to take assignments of *all* a man's property on condition of paying *all* his debts, such transfers would exactly resemble the universal successions known to the oldest Roman Law. When a Roman citizen *adrogated* a son, i.e. took a man not already under Patria Potestas, as his adoptive child, he succeeded *universally* to the adoptive child's estate, i.e. he took all the property and became liable for all the obligations. Several other forms of universal succession appear in the primitive Roman Law, but infinitely the most important and the most durable of all was that one with which we are more immediately concerned, Hæreditas or Inheritance. Inheritance was a universal succession occurring at a death. The universal successor was Hæres or Heir. He stepped at once into all the rights and all the duties of the dead man. He was instantly clothed with his entire legal person, and I need scarcely add that the special character of the Hæres remained the same, whether he was named by a Will or whether he took on an Intestacy. The term Hæres is no more emphatically used of the Intestate than of the Testamentary Heir, for the manner in which a man became Hæres had nothing to do with the legal character he sustained. The dead man's universal successor, however he became so, whether by Will or by Intestacy, was his Heir. But the Heir was not necessarily a single person. A group of persons considered in law as a single unit, might succeed as *co-heirs* to the Inheritance.

Let me now quote the usual Roman definition of an Inheritance. The reader will be in a position to appreciate the full force of the separate terms.

*Hæreditas est successio in universum jus quod
defunctus habuit* (' an inheritance is a succession
to the entire legal position of a deceased man ').
The notion was that, though the physical person
of the deceased had perished, his legal personality
survived and descended unimpaired on his Heir
or Co-heirs, in whom his identity (so far as the
law was concerned) was continued. Our own
law, in constituting the Executor or Administrator the representative of the deceased to the
extent of his personal assets, may serve as an
illustration of the theory from which it emanated,
but, although it illustrates, it does not explain it.
The view of even the later Roman Law required
a closeness of correspondence between the position
of the deceased and of his Heir which is no
feature of an English representation; and in the
primitive jurisprudence everything turned on the
continuity of succession. Unless provision was
made in the will for the instant devolution of the
testator's rights and duties on the Heir or Co-
heirs, the testament lost all its effect.

In modern Testamentary jurisprudence, as in
the later Roman law, the object of first importance is the execution of the testator's intentions.
In the ancient law of Rome the subject of corresponding carefulness was the bestowal of the
Universal Succession. One of these rules seems
to our eyes a principle dictated by common sense,
while the other looks very much like an idle
crotchet. Yet that without the second of them the
first would never have come into being is as
certain as any proposition of the kind can be.

In order to solve this apparent paradox, and to
bring into greater clearness the train of ideas
which I have been endeavouring to indicate, I

must borrow the results of the inquiry which was attempted in the earlier portion of the preceding chapter. We saw one peculiarity invariably distinguishing the infancy of society. Men are regarded and treated, not as individuals, but always as members of a particular group. Everybody is first a citizen, and then, as a citizen, he is a member of his order—of an aristocracy or a democracy, of an order of patricians or plebeians; or, in those societies which an unhappy fate has afflicted with a special perversion in their course of development, of a caste. Next, he is a member of a gens, house, or clan; and lastly, he is a member of his *family*. This last was the narrowest and most personal relation in which he stood; nor, paradoxical as it may seen, was he ever regarded as *himself*, as a distinct individual. His individuality was swallowed up in his family. I repeat the definition of a primitive society given before. It has for its units, not individuals, but groups of men united by the reality or the fiction of blood-relationship.

It is in the peculiarities of an undeveloped society that we seize the first trace of a universal succession. Contrasted with the organisation of a modern state, the commonwealths of primitive times may be fairly described as consisting of a number of little despotic governments, each perfectly distinct from the rest, each absolutely controlled by the prerogative of a single monarch. But though the Patriarch, for we must not yet call him the Pater-familias, had rights thus extensive, it is impossible to doubt that he lay under an equal amplitude of obligations. If he governed the family, it was for its behoof. If he was lord of its possessions, he held them as trustee for his children and kindred. He had no privilege or position distinct from that conferred on him by his relation to the petty commonwealth which he governed. The Family, in fact, was a Corporation; and he was its representative or, we might almost say, its Public officer. He enjoyed rights and stood under duties, but the rights and the duties were, in the contemplation of his fellow-citizens and in the eye of the law, quite as much those of the collective body as his own. Let us consider for a moment the effect which would be produced by the death of such a representative. In the eye of the law, in the view of the civil magistrate, the demise of the domestic authority would be a perfectly immaterial event. The person representing the collective body of the family and primarily responsible to municipal jurisdiction would bear a different name; and that would be all. The rights and obligations which attached to the deceased head of the house would attach, without breach of continuity, to his successor; for, in point of fact, they would be the rights and obligations of the family, and the family had the distinctive characteristic of a corporation—that it never died. Creditors would have the same remedies against the new chieftain as against the old, for the liability being that of the still existing family would be absolutely unchanged. All rights available to the family would be as available after the demise of the headship as before it—except that the Corporation would be obliged—if indeed language so precise and technical can be properly used of these early times—would be obliged to *sue* under a slightly modified name.

The history of jurisprudence must be followed in its whole course, if we are to understand how

gradually and tardily society dissolved itself into
the component atoms of which it is now constituted—by what insensible gradations the relation
of man to man substituted itself for the relation of
the individual to his family and of families to
each other. The point now to be attended to is
that even when the revolution had apparently
quite accomplished itself, even when the magistrate had in great measure assumed the place of
the Pater-familias, and the civil tribunal substituted itself for the domestic forum, nevertheless
the whole scheme of rights and duties administered by the judicial authorities remained shaped
by the influence of the obsolete privileges and
coloured in every part by their reflection. There
seems little question that the devolution of the
Universitas Juris, so strenuously insisted upon by
the Roman Law as the first condition of a testamentary or intestate succession, was a feature
of the older form of society which men's minds
had been unable to dissociate from the new,
though with that newer phase it had no true or
proper connection. It seems, in truth, that the
prolongation of a man's legal existence in his heir,
or in a group of co-heirs, is neither more nor less
than a characteristic of *the family* transferred by a
fiction to *the individual.* Succession in corporations is necessarily universal, and the family was
a corporation. Corporations never die. The decease
of individual members makes no difference to the
collective existence of the aggregate body, and
does not in any way affect its legal incidents, its
faculties or liabilities. Now in the idea of a
Roman universal succession all these qualities of
a corporation seem to have been transferred to
the individual citizen. His physical death is

allowed to exercise no effect on the legal position which he filled, apparently on the principle that that position is to be adjusted as closely as possible to the analogies of a family, which, in its corporate character, was not of course liable to physical extinction.

I observe that not a few continental jurists have much difficulty in comprehending the nature of the connection between the conceptions blended in a universal succession, and there is perhaps no topic in the philosophy of jurisprudence on which their speculations, as a general rule, possess so little value. But the student of English law ought to be in no danger of stumbling at the analysis of the idea which we are examining. Much light is cast upon it by a fiction in our own system with which all lawyers are familiar. English lawyers classify corporations as Corporations aggregate and Corporations sole. A Corporation aggregate is a true Corporation, but a Corporation sole is an individual, being a member of a series of individuals, who is invested by a fiction with the qualities of a Corporation. I need hardly cite the King or the Parson of a Parish as instances of Corporations sole. The capacity or office is here considered apart from the particular person who from time to time may occupy it, and, this capacity being perpetual, the series of individuals who fill it are clothed with the leading attribute of Corporations—Perpetuity. Now in the older theory of Roman Law the individual bore to the family precisely the same relation which in the rationale of English jurisprudence a Corporation sole bears to a Corporation aggregate. The derivation and association of ideas are exactly the same. In fact, if we say to ourselves

that for purposes of Roman Testamentary Jurisprudence each individual citizen was a Corporation sole, we shall not only realise the full conception of an inheritance, but have constantly at
command the clue to the assumption in which it
originated. It is an axiom with us that the King
never dies, being a Corporation sole. His capacities are instantly filled by his successor, and
the continuity of dominion is not deemed to have
been interrupted. With the Romans it seemed an
equally simple and natural process, to eliminate
the fact of death from the devolution of rights
and obligations. The testator lived on in his heir
or in the group of his co-heirs. He was in law
the same person with them, and if any one in his
testamentary dispositions had even constructively
violated the principle which united his actual and
his posthumous existence, the law rejected the
defective instrument, and gave the inheritance to
the kindred in blood, whose capacity to fulfil the
conditions of heirship was conferred on them by
the law itself, and not by any document which by
possibility might be erroneously framed.

When a Roman citizen died intestate or leaving
no valid Will, his descendants or kindred became
his heirs according to a scale which will be presently described. The person or class of persons
who succeeded did not simply *represent* the
deceased, but, in conformity with the theory just
delineated, they *continued* his civil life, his legal
existence. The same results followed when the
order of succession was determined by a Will,
but the theory of the identity between the dead
man and his heirs was certainly much older than
any form of Testament or phase of Testamentary
jurisprudence. This indeed is the proper moment

for suggesting a doubt which will press on us with greater force the further we plumb the depths of this subject,—whether *wills* would ever have come into being at all if it had not been for these remarkable ideas connected with universal succession. Testamentary law is the application of a principle which may be explained on a variety of philosophical hypotheses as plausible as they are gratuitous; it is interwoven with every part of modern society, and it is defensible on the broadest grounds of general expediency. But the warning can never be too often repeated, that the grand source of mistake in questions of jurisprudence is the impression that those reasons which actuate us at the present moment, in the maintenance of an existing institution, have necessarily anything in common with the sentiment in which the institution originated. It is certain that, in the old Roman Law of Inheritance, the notion of a will or testament is inextricably mixed up, I might almost say confounded, with the theory of a man's posthumous existence in the person of his heir.

The conception of a universal succession, firmly as it has taken root in jurisprudence, has not occurred spontaneously to the framers of every body of laws. Wherever it is now found, it may be shown to have descended from Roman law; and with it have come down a host of legal rules on the subject of Testaments and Testamentary gifts, which modern practitioners apply without discerning their relation to the parent theory. But, in the pure Roman jurisprudence, the principle that a man lives on in his Heir—the elimination, if we may so speak, of the fact of death—is, too obviously for mistake, the centre round which

the whole Law of Testamentary and Intestate
succession is circling. The unflinching sternness
of the Roman law in enforcing compliance with
the governing theory would in itself suggest that
the theory grew out of something in the primitive
constitution of Roman society; but we may push
the proof a good way beyond the presumption. It
happens that several technical expressions, dating
from the earliest institution of Wills at Rome,
have been accidentally preserved to us. We have
in Gaius the formula of investiture by which the
universal successor was created. We have the
ancient name by which the person afterwards
called Heir was at first designated. We have
further the text of the celebrated clause in the
Twelve Tables by which the Testamentary power
was expressly recognised, and the clauses regulating Intestate Succession have also been preserved. All these archaic phrases have one salient
peculiarity. They indicate that what passed from
the Testator to the Heir was the *Family*, that is,
the aggregate of rights and duties contained in
the Patria Potestas and growing out of it. The
material property is in three instances not mentioned at all; in two others, it is visibly named
as an adjunct or appendage of the Family. The
original Will or Testament was therefore an instrument, or (for it was probably not at first in
writing) a proceeding, by which the devolution of
the *Family* was regulated. It was a mode of
declaring who was to have the chieftainship, in
succession to the Testator. When Wills are
understood to have this for their original object,
we see at once how it is that they came to be
connected with one of the most curious relics of
ancient religion and law, the *sacra*, or Family

Rites. These *sacra* were the Roman form of an institution which shows itself wherever society has not wholly shaken itself free from its primitive clothing. They are the sacrifices and ceremonies by which the brotherhood of the family is commemorated, the pledge and the witness of its perpetuity. Whatever be their nature,—whether it be true or not that in all cases they are the worship of some mythical ancestor,—they are everywhere employed to attest the sacredness of the family-relation; and therefore they acquire prominent significance and importance, whenever the continuous existence of the Family is endangered by a change in the person of its chief. Accordingly, we hear most about them in connection with demises of domestic sovereignty. Among the Hindoos, the right to inherit a dead man's property is exactly co-extensive with the duty of performing his obsequies. If the rites are not properly performed or not performed by the proper person, no relation is considered as established between the deceased and anybody surviving him; the Law of Succession does not apply, and nobody can inherit the property. Every great event in the life of a Hindoo seems to be regarded as leading up to and bearing upon these solemnities. If he marries, it is to have children who may celebrate them after his death; if he has no children, he lies under the strongest obligation to adopt them from another family, "with a view," writes the Hindoo doctor, "to the funeral cake, the water, and the solemn sacrifice." The sphere preserved to the Roman *sacra* in the time of Cicero, was not less in extent. It embraced Inheritances and Adoptions. No Adoption was allowed to take place without due pro-

vision for the *sacra* of the family from which the
adoptive son was transferred, and no Testament
was allowed to distribute an Inheritance without a
strict apportionment of the expenses of these ceremonies among the different co-heirs. The differences between the Roman law at this epoch, when
we obtain our last glimpse of the *sacra*, and the
existing Hindoo system, are most instructive.
Among the Hindoos, the religious element in law
has acquired a complete predominance. Family
sacrifices have become the keystone of all the
Law of Persons and much of the Law of Things.
They have even received a monstrous extension,
for it is a plausible opinion that the self-immola-
tion of the widow at her husband's funeral, a
practice continued to historical times by the
Hindoos, and commemorated in the traditions of
several Indo-European races, was an addition
grafted on the primitive *sacra*, under the influence
of the impression, which always accompanies the
idea of sacrifice, that human blood is the most
precious of all oblations. With the Romans, on
the contrary, the legal obligation and the religious
duty have ceased to be blended. The necessity of
solemnising the *sacra* forms no part of the theory
of civil law, but they are under the separate jurisdiction of the College of Pontiffs. The letters of
Cicero to Atticus, which are full of allusions to
them, leave no doubt that they constituted an
intolerable burden on Inheritances; but the point
of development at which law breaks away from
religion has been passed, and we are prepared
for their entire disappearance from the later jurisprudence.

In Hindoo law there is no such thing as a true
Will. The place filled by Wills is occupied by

Adoptions. We can now see the relation of the Testamentary Power to the Faculty of Adoption, and the reason why the exercise of either of them could call up a peculiar solicitude for the performance of the *sacra*. Both a Will and an Adoption threaten a distortion of the ordinary course of Family descent, but they are obviously contrivances for preventing the descent being wholly interrupted, when there is no succession of kindred to carry it on. Of the two expedients Adoption, the factitious creation of blood-relationship, is the only one which has suggested itself to the greater part of archaic societies. The Hindoos have indeed advanced one point on what was doubtless the antique practice, by allowing the widow to adopt when the father has neglected to do so, and there are in the local customs of Bengal some faint traces of the Testamentary powers. But to the Romans belongs pre-eminently the credit of inventing the Will, the institution which, next to the Contract, has exercised the greatest influence in transforming human society. We must be careful not to attribute to it in its earliest shape the functions which have attended it in more recent times. It was at first, not a mode of distributing a dead man's goods, but one among several ways of transferring the representation of the household to a new chief. The goods descend no doubt to the Heir, but that is only because the government of the family carries with it in its devolution the power of disposing of the common stock. We are very far as yet from that stage in the history of Wills in which they become powerful instruments in modifying society through the stimulus they give to the circulation of property and the plasticity they produce in proprietary rights. No such consequences as these appear in fact to have been associated with the Testamentary power even by the latest Roman lawyers. It will be found that Wills were never looked upon in the Roman community as a contrivance for parting Property and the Family, or for creating a variety of miscellaneous interests, but rather as a means of making a better provision for the members of a household than could be secured through the rules of Intestate succession. We may suspect indeed that the associations of a Roman with the practice of will-making were extremely different from those familiar to us nowadays. The habit of regarding Adoption and Testation as modes of continuing the Family cannot but have had something to do with the singular laxity of Roman notions as to the inheritance of sovereignty. It is impossible not to see that the succession of the early Roman Emperors to each other was considered reasonably regular, and that, in spite of all that had occurred, no absurdity attached to the pretension of such Princes as Theodosius or Justinian to style themselves Cæsar and Augustus.

When the phenomena of primitive societies emerge into light, it seems impossible to dispute a proposition which the jurists of the 17th century considered doubtful, that Intestate Inheritance is a more ancient institution than Testamentary Succession. As soon as this is settled, a question of much interest suggests itself, how and under what conditions were the directions of a will first allowed to regulate the devolution of authority over the household, and consequently the posthumous distribution of property. The difficulty of deciding the point arises from the rarity of Testamentary power in archaic communities. It is doubtful whether a true power of testation was known to any original society except the Roman. Rudimentary forms of it occur here and there, but most of them are not exempt from the suspicion of a Roman origin. The Athenian will was, no doubt, indigenous, but then, as will appear presently, it was only an inchoate Testament. As to the Wills which are sanctioned by the bodies of law which have descended to us as the codes of the barbarian conquerors of Imperial Rome, they are almost certainly Roman. The most penetrating German criticism has recently been directed to these *leges Barbarorum*, the great object of investigation being to detach those portions of each system which formed the customs of the tribe in its original home from the adventitious ingredients which were borrowed from the laws of the Romans. In the course of this process, one result has invariably disclosed itself, that the ancient nucleus of the code contains no trace of a Will. Whatever testamentary law exists, has been taken from Roman jurisprudence. Similarly, the rudimentary Testament which (as I am informed) the Rabbinical Jewish law provides for, has been attributed to contact with the Romans. The only form of testament, not belonging to a Roman or Hellenic society, which can reasonably be supposed indigenous, is that recognised by the usages of the province of Bengal; and the testament of Bengal is only a rudimentary Will.

The evidence, however, such as it is, seems to point to the conclusion that Testaments are at first only allowed to take effect on failure of the persons entitled to have the inheritance by right

of blood genuine or fictitious. Thus, when
Athenian citizens were empowered for the first
time by the Laws of Solon to execute Testaments,
they were forbidden to disinherit their direct male
descendants. So, too, the Will of Bengal is only
permitted to govern the succession so far as it
is consistent with certain overriding claims of the
family. Again, the original institutions of the
Jews having provided nowhere for the privileges
of Testatorship, the later Rabbinical jurisprudence, which pretends to supply the *casus
omissi* of the Mosaic law, allows the Power of
Testation to attach when all the kindred entitled
under the Mosaic system to succeed have failed
or are undiscoverable. The limitations by which
the ancient German codes hedge in the testamentary jurisprudence which has been incorporated with them are also significant, and point
in the same direction. It is the peculiarity of
most of these German laws, in the only shape in
which we know them, that, besides the *allod* or
domain of each household, they recognise several
subordinate kinds or orders of property, each of
which probably represents a separate transfusion
of Roman principles into the primitive body of
Teutonic usage. The primitive German or
allodial property is strictly reserved to the
kindred. Not only is it incapable of being disposed of by testament but it is scarcely capable
of being alienated by conveyance *inter vivos*. The
ancient German law, like the Hindoo jurisprudence, makes the male children co-proprietors
with their father, and the endowment of the
family cannot be parted with except by the consent of all its members. But the other sorts of
property, of more modern origin and lower dignity

than the allodial possessions, are much more easily alienated than they, and follow much more lenient rules of devolution. Women and the descendants of women succeed to them, obviously on the principle that they lie outside the sacred precinct of the Agnatic brotherhood. Now, it is on these last descriptions of property, and on these only, that the Testaments borrowed from Rome were at first allowed to operate.

These few indications may serve to lend additional plausibility to that which in itself appears to be the most probable explanation of an ascertained fact in the early history of Roman Wills. We have it stated on abundant authority that Testaments, during the primitive period of the Roman State, were executed in the Comitia Calata, that is, in the Comitia Curiata, or Parliament of the Patrician Burghers of Rome, when assembled for Private Business. This mode of execution has been the source of the assertion, handed down by one generation of civilians to another, that every Will at one era of Roman history was a solemn legislative enactment. But there is no necessity whatever for resorting to an explanation which has the defect of attributing far too much precision to the proceedings of the ancient assembly. The proper key to the story concerning the execution of Wills in the Comitia Calata must no doubt be sought in the oldest Roman Law of *intestate* succession. The canons of primitive Roman jurisprudence regulating the inheritance of relations from each other were, so long as they remained unmodified by the Edictal Law of the Prætor, to the following effect :— First, the *sui* or direct descendants who had never been emancipated succeeded. On the failure of the *sui*, the Nearest Agnate came into their place, that is, the nearest person or class of the kindred who was or might have been under the same Patria Potestas with the deceased. The third and last degree came next, in which the inheritance devolved on the *gentiles*, that is on the collective members of the dead man's *gens* or *House*. The House, I have explained already, was a fictitious extension of the family, consisting of all Roman Patrician citizens who bore the same name, and who, on the ground of bearing the same name, were supposed to be descended from a common ancestor. Now the Patrician Assembly called the Comitia Curiata was a Legislature in which Gentes or Houses were exclusively represented. It was a representative assembly of the Roman people, constituted on the assumption that the constituent unit of the state was the Gens. This being so, the inference seems inevitable, that the congnizance of Wills by the Comitia was connected with the rights of the Gentiles, and was intended to secure them in their privilege of ultimate inheritance. The whole apparent anomaly is removed, if we suppose that a Testament could only be made when the testator had no *gentiles* discoverable, or when they waived their claims, and that every Testament was submitted to the General Assembly of the Roman Gentes, in order that those aggrieved by its dispositions might put their veto upon it if they pleased, or by allowing it to pass might be presumed to have renounced their reversion. It is possible that on the eve of the publication of the Twelve Tables this vetoing power may have been greatly curtailed or only occasionally and capriciously exercised. It is much easier, however,

to indicate the meaning and origin of the jurisdiction confided to the Comitia Calata, than to
trace its gradual development or progressive
decay.

The Testament to which the pedigree of all
modern Wills may be traced is not, however, the
Testament executed in the Calata Comitia, but
another Testament designed to compete with it
and destined to supersede it. The historical importance of this early Roman Will, and the light
it casts on much of ancient thought, will excuse
me for describing it at some length.

When the Testamentary power first discloses
itself to us in legal history, there are signs that,
like almost all the great Roman institutions, it
was the subject of contention between the Patricians and the Plebeians. The effect of the political maxim, *Plebs Gentem non habet*, ' a
Plebeian cannot be a member of a House ', was
entirely to exclude the Plebeians from the Comitia
Curiata. Some critics have accordingly supposed
that a Plebeian could not have his Will read or
recited to the Patrician Assembly, and was thus
deprived of Testamentary privileges altogether.
Others have been satisfied to point out the hard-
ships of having to submit a proposed Will to the
unfriendly jurisdiction of an assembly in which
the Testator was not represented. Whatever be
the true view, a form of Testament came into
use, which has all the characteristics of a contrivance intended to evade some distasteful obligation. The Will in question was a conveyance
inter vivos, a complete and irrevocable alienation
of the Testator's family and substance to the
person whom he meant to be his heir. The strict
rules of Roman law must always have permitted

such an alienation, but, when the transaction was intended to have a posthumous effect, there may have been disputes whether it was valid for Testamentary purposes without the formal assent of the Patrician Parliament. If a difference of opinion existed on the point between the two classes of the Roman population, it was extinguished, with many other sources of heartburning, by the great Decemviral compromise. The text of the Twelve Tables is still extant which says, ' *Pater familias uti de pecuniâ tutelâve rei suæ legâssit, ita jus esto* '—a law which can hardly have had any other object than the legalisation of the Plebeian Will.

It is well known to scholars that, centuries after the Patrician Assembly had ceased to be the legislature of the Roman State, it still continued to hold formal sittings for the convenience of private business. Consequently, at a period long subsequent to the publication of the Decemviral Law, there is reason to believe that the Comitia Calata still assembled for the validation of Testaments. Its probable functions may be best indicated by saying that it was a Court of Registration, with the understanding however that the Wills exhibited were not *enrolled*, but simply recited to the members, who were supposed to take note of their tenor and to commit them to memory. It is very likely that this form of Testament was never reduced to writing at all, but at all events if the Will had been originally written, the office of the Comitia was certainly confined to hearing it read aloud, the document being retained afterwards in the custody of the Testator, or deposited under the safeguard of some religious corporation. This publicity may have been one

of the incidents of the Testament executed in the
Comitia Calata which brought it into popular disfavour. In the early years of the Empire the
Comitia still held its meetings, but they seem
to have lapsed into the merest form, and few
Wills, or none, were probably presented at the
periodical sitting.

It is the ancient Plebeian Will—the alternative
of the Testament just described—which in its
remote effects has deeply modified the civilisation of the modern world. It acquired at Rome
all the popularity which the Testament submitted
to the Comitia Calata appears to have lost. The
key to all its characteristics lies in its descent
from the *mancipium*, or ancient Roman conveyance, a proceeding to which we may unhesitatingly assign the parentage of two great institutions without which modern society can scarcely
be supposed capable of holding together, the Contract and the Will. The *mancipium*, or as the
word would exhibit itself in later Latinity, the
Mancipation, carries us back by its incidents to
the infancy of civil society. As it sprang from
times long anterior, if not to the invention, at all
events to the popularisation, of the art of writing,
gestures, symbolical acts, and solemn phrases
take the place of documentary forms, and a
lengthy and intricate ceremonial is intended to
call the attention of the parties to the importance
of the transaction, and to impress it on the
memory of the witnesses. The imperfection too
of oral, as compared with written, testimony
necessitates the multiplication of the witnesses
and assistants beyond what in later times would
be reasonable or intelligible limits.

The Roman Mancipation required the presence

first of all of the parties, the vendor and vendee, or we should perhaps rather say, if we are to use modern legal language, the grantor and grantee. There were also no less than *five* witnesses; and an anomalous personage, the Libripens, who brought with him a pair of scales to weigh the uncoined copper money of ancient Rome. The Testament we are considering—the Testament *per æs et libram*, ' with the copper and the scales ', as it long continued to be technically called—was an ordinary Mancipation with no change in the form and hardly any in words. The testator was the grantor; the five witnesses and the libripens were present; and the place of grantee was taken by a person known technically as the *familiæ emptor*, the Purchaser of the Family. The ordinary ceremony of a Mancipation was then proceeded with. Certain formal gestures were made and sentences pronounced. The *Emptor familiæ* simulated the payment of a price by striking the scales with a piece of money, and finally the Testator ratified what had been done in a set form of words called the " Nuncupatio " or publication of the transaction, a phrase which, I need scarcely remind the lawyer, has had a long history in Testamentary jurisprudence. It is necessary to attend particularly to the character of the person called *familiæ emptor*. There is no doubt that at first he was the Heir himself. The testator conveyed to him outright his whole ' familia ', that is, all the rights he enjoyed over and through the family; his property, his slaves, and all his ancestral privileges, together, on the other hand, with all his duties and obligations.

With these data before us, we are able to note

several remarkable points in which the Mancipatory Testament, as it may be called, differed in its primitive form from a modern will. As it amounted to a conveyance *out-and-out* of the Testator's estate, it was not *revocable*. There could be no new exercise of a power which had been exhausted.

Again, it was not secret. The Familiæ Emptor, being himself the Heir, knew exactly what his rights were, and was aware that he was irreversibly entitled to the inheritance; a knowledge which the violences inseparable from the best-ordered ancient society rendered extremely dangerous. But perhaps the most surprising consequence of this relation of Testaments to Conveyances was the immediate vesting of the inheritance in the Heir. This has seemed so incredible to not a few civilians, that they have spoken of the Testator's estate as vesting conditionally on the Testator's death, or as granted to him from a time uncertain, i.e. the death of the grantor. But down to the latest period of Roman jurisprudence there was a certain class of transactions which never admitted of being directly modified by a condition, or of being limited to or from a point of time. In technical language they did not admit *conditio* or *dies*. Mancipation was one of them, and therefore, strange as it may seem, we are forced to conclude that the primitive Roman Will took effect at once, even though the Testator survived his act of Testation. It is indeed likely that Roman citizens originally made their Wills only in the article of death, and that a provision for the continuance of the Family effected by a man in the flower of life would take the form rather of an Adoption than of a Will. Still we

must believe that, if the Testator did recover, he
could only continue to govern his household by
the sufferance of his Heir.

Two or three remarks should be made before
I explain how these inconveniences were
remedied, and how Testaments came to be invested with the characteristics now universally
associated with them. The Testament was not
necessarily written: at first, it seems to have
been invariably oral, and, even in later times, the
instrument declaratory of the bequests was only
incidentally connected with the Will and formed
no essential part of it. It bore in fact exactly
the same relation to the Testament, as the
deed leading the uses bore to the Fines and
Recoveries of old English law, or as the
charter of feoffment bore to the feoffment itself.
Previously, indeed, to the Twelve Tables, no
writing would have been of the slightest use, for
the Testator had no power of giving legacies, and
the only persons who could be advantaged by a
will were the Heir or Co-heirs. But the extreme
generality of the clause in the Twelve Tables soon
produced the doctrine that the Heir must take
the inheritance burdened by any directions which
the Testator might give him, or, in other words,
take it subject to legacies. Written testamentary
instruments assumed thereupon a new value, as a
security against the fraudulent refusal of the heir
to satisfy the legatees; but to the last it was at
the Testator's pleasure to rely exclusively on the
testimony of the witnesses, and to declare by
word of mouth the legacies which the *familiæ
emptor* was commissioned to pay.

The terms of the expression *Emptor familiæ*
demand notice. 'Emptor' indicates that the

Will was literally a sale, and the word ' familiæ ', when compared with the phraseology in the Testamentary clause in the Twelve Tables, leads us to some instructive conclusions. ' Familia ', in classical Latinity, means always a man's slaves. Here, however, and generally in the language of ancient Roman law, it includes all persons under his Potestas, and the Testator's material property or substance is understood to pass as an adjunct or appendage of his household. Turning to the law of the Twelve Tables, it will be seen that it speaks of *tutela rei suæ*, ' the guardianship of his substance ', a form of expression which is the exact reverse of the phrase just examined. There does not therefore appear to be any mode of escaping from the conclusion, that, even at an era so comparatively recent as that of the Decemviral compromise, terms denoting ' household ' and ' property ' were blended in the current phraseology. If a man's household had been spoken of as his property we might have explained the expression as pointing to the extent of the Patria Potestas, but, as the interchange is reciprocal, we must allow that the form of speech carries us back to that primeval period in which property is owned by the family, and the family is governed by the citizen, so that the members of the community do not own their property *and* their family, but rather own their property *through* their family.

At an epoch not easy to settle with precision, the Roman Prætors fell into the habit of acting upon Testaments solemnised in closer conformity with the spirit than the letter of the law. Casual dispensations became insensibly the established practice, till at length a wholly new form of Will was matured and regularly engrafted on the Edictal Jurisprudence. The new or *Prætorian* Testament derived the whole of its impregnability from the *Jus Honorarium* or Equity of Rome. The Prætor of some particular year must have inserted a clause in his Inaugural Proclamation declaratory of his intention to sustain all Testaments which should have been executed with such and such solemnities; and, the reform having been found advantageous, the article relating to it must have been again introduced by the Prætor's successor, and repeated by the next in office, till at length it formed a recognised portion of that body of jurisprudence which from these successive incorporations was styled the Perpetual or Continuous Edict. On examining the conditions of a valid Prætorian Will they will be plainly seen to have been determined by the requirements of the Mancipatory Testament, the innovating Prætor having obviously prescribed to himself the retention of the old formalities just so far as they were warrants of genuineness or securities against fraud. At the execution of the Mancipatory Testament seven persons had been present besides the Testator. Seven witnesses were accordingly essential to the Prætorian Will : two of them corresponding to the *libripens* and *familiæ emptor*, who were now stripped of their symbolical character, and were merely present for the purpose of supplying their testimony. No emblematic ceremony was gone through; the Will was merely recited; but then it is probable (though not absolutely certain) that a written instrument was necessary to perpetuate the evidence of the Testator's dispositions. At all events, whenever a writing was read or exhibited as a person's last

Will, we know certainly that the Prætorian Court would not sustain it by special intervention, unless each of the seven witnesses had severally affixed his seal to the outside. This is the first appearance of *sealing* in the history of jurisprudence, considered as a mode of authentication. It is to be observed that the seals of Roman Wills, and other documents of importance, did not simply serve as the index of the presence or assent of the signatory, but were literally fastenings which had to be broken before the writing could be inspected.

The Edictal Law would therefore enforce the dispositions of a Testator, when, instead of being symbolised through the forms of mancipation, they were simply evidenced by the seals of seven witnesses. But it may be laid down as a general proposition, that the principal qualities of Roman property were incommunicable except through processes which were supposed to be coeval with the origin of the Civil Law. The Prætor therefore could not confer an *Inheritance* on anybody. He could not place the Heir or Co-heirs in that very relation in which the Testator had himself stood to his own rights and obligations. All he could do was to confer on the person designated as Heir the practical enjoyment of the property bequeathed, and to give the force of legal acquittances to his payments of the Testator's debts. When he exerted his powers to these ends, the Prætor was technically said to communicate the *Bonorum Possessio*. The Heir specially inducted under these circumstances, or *Bonorum Possessor*, had every proprietary privilege of the Heir by the Civil Law. He took the profits and he could alienate, but then, for all his remedies for

redress against wrong, he must go, as we should
phrase it, not to the Common Law, but to the
Equity side of the Prætorian Court. No great
chance of error would be incurred by describing
him as having an *equitable* estate in the inheritance; but then, to secure ourselves against being
deluded by the analogy, we must always recollect
that in one year the *Bonorum Possessio* was
operated upon by a principle of Roman Law
known as Usucapion, and the Possessor became
Quiritarian owner of all the property comprised in
the inheritance.

We know too little of the older law of Civil
Process to be able to strike the balance of advantage and disadvantage between the different
classes of remedies supplied by the Prætorian
Tribunal. It is certain, however, that, in spite of
its many defects, the Mancipatory Testament by
which the *universitas juris* devolved at once and
unimpaired was never entirely superseded by the
new Will; and at a period less bigoted to anti-
quarian forms, and perhaps not quite alive to
their significance, all the ingenuity of the Jurisconsults seems to have been expended on the improvement of the more venerable instrument. At
the era of Gaius, which is that of the Antonine
Cæsars, the great blemishes of the Mancipatory
Will had been removed. Originally, as we have
seen, the essential character of the formalities
had required that the Heir himself should be the
Purchaser of the Family, and the consequence
was that he not only instantly acquired a vested
interest in the Testator's Property, but was
formally made aware of his rights. But the age
of Gaius permitted some unconcerned person to
officiate as Purchaser of the Family. The Heir,

therefore, was not necessarily informed of the succession to which he was destined; and Wills thenceforward acquired the property of *secrecy*. The substitution of a stranger for the actual Heir in the functions of ' Familiæ Emptor ' had other ulterior consequences. As soon as it was legalised, a Roman Testament came to consist of two parts or stages—a Conveyance, which was a pure form, and a Nuncupatio, or Publication. In this latter passage of the proceeding, the Testator either orally declared to the assistants the wishes which were to be executed after his death, or produced a written document in which his wishes were embodied. It was not probably till attention had been quite drawn off from the imaginary Conveyance, and concentrated on the Nuncupation as the essential part of the transaction, that Wills were allowed to become *revocable*.

I have thus carried the pedigree of Wills some way down in legal history. The root of it is the old Testament ' with the copper and the scales ', founded on a Mancipation or Conveyance. This ancient Will has, however, manifold defects, which are remedied, though only indirectly, by the Prætorian law. Meantime the ingenuity of the Jurisconsults effects, in the Common-Law Will or Mancipatory Testament, the very improvements which the Prætor may have concurrently carried out in Equity. These last ameliorations depend, however, on mere legal dexterity, and we see accordingly that the Testamentary Law of the day of Gaius or Ulpian is only transitional. What changes next ensued we know not; but at length, just before the reconstruction of the jurisprudence by Justinian, we find the subjects of the Eastern Roman Empire employing a form of

Will of which the pedigree is traceable to the
Prætorian Testament on one side, and to the
Testament ' with the copper and the scales ' on
the other. Like the Testament of the Prætor, it
required no Mancipation, and was invalid unless
sealed by seven witnesses. Like the Mancipatory Will, it passed the Inheritance and not
merely a *Bonorum Possessio*. Several, however,
of its most important features were annexed by
positive enactments, and it is out of regard to
this threefold derivation from the Prætorian
Edict, from the Civil Law, and from the Imperial
Constitutions, that Justinian speaks of the law
of Wills in his own day as *Jus Tripertitum*. The
new Testament thus described is the one generally known as the Roman Will. But it was the
Will of the Eastern Empire only; and the researches of Savigny have shown that in Western
Europe the old Mancipatory Testament, with all
its apparatus of conveyance, copper, and scales,
continued to be the form in use far down in the
Middle Ages.

CHAPTER VII

ANCIENT AND MODERN IDEAS RESPECTING WILLS AND SUCCESSIONS

ALTHOUGH there is much in the modern European
Law of Wills which is intimately connected with
the oldest rules of Testamentary disposition practised mong men, there are nevertheless some important differences between ancient and modern
ideas on the subject of Wills and Successions.

Some of the points of difference I shall endeavour to illustrate in this chapter.

At a period, removed several centuries from the era of the Twelve Tables, we find a variety of rules engrafted on the Roman Civil Law with the view of limiting the disinherison of children; we have the jurisdiction of the Prætor very actively exerted in the same interest; and we are also presented with a new remedy, very anomalous in character and of uncertain origin, called the Querela Inofficiosi Testamenti, ' the Plaint of an Unduteous Will ', directed to the reinstatement of the issue in inheritances from which they had been unjustifiably excluded by a father's Testament. Comparing this condition of the law with the text of the Twelve Tables which concedes in terms the utmost liberty of Testation, several writers have been tempted to interweave a good deal of dramatic incident into their history of the Law Testamentary. They tell us of the boundless license of disinherison in which the heads of families instantly began to indulge, of the scandal and injury to public morals which the new practices engendered, and of the applause of all good men which hailed the courage of the Prætor in arresting the progress of paternal depravity. This story, which is not without some foundation for the principal fact it relates, is often so told as to disclose very serious misconceptions of the principles of legal history. The Law of the Twelve Tables is to be explained by the character of the age in which it was enacted. It does not license a tendency which a later era thought itself bound to counteract, but it proceeds on the assumption that no such tendency exists, or, perhaps we should say, in ignorance of the possibility of its existence. There is no likelihood that Roman citizens began immediately to avail themselves freely of the power to disinherit. It is against all reason and sound appreciation of history to suppose that the yoke of family bondage, still patiently submitted to, as we know, where its pressure galled most cruelly, would be cast off in the very particular in which its incidence in our own day is not otherwise than welcome. The Law of the Twelve Tables permitted the execution of Testaments in the only case in which it was thought possible that they could be executed, viz., on failure of children and proximate kindred. It did not forbid the disinherison of direct descendants, inasmuch as it did not legislate against a contingency which no Roman lawgiver of that era could have contemplated. No doubt, as the offices of family affection progressively lost the aspect of primary personal duties, the disinherison of children was occasionally attempted. But the interference of the Prætor, so far from being called for by the universality of the abuse, was doubtless first prompted by the fact that such instances of unnatural caprice were few and exceptional, and at conflict with the current morality.

The indications furnished by this part of Roman Testamentary Law are of a very different kind. It is remarkable that a Will never seems to have been regarded by the Romans as a means of *disinheriting* a Family, or of effecting the unequal distribution of a patrimony. The rules of law preventing its being turned to such a purpose, increase in number and stringency as the jurisprudence unfolds itself; and these rules correspond doubtless with the abiding sentiment of Roman society, as distinguished from occasional variations of feeling in individuals. It would rather seem as if the Testamentary Power were chiefly valued for the assistance it gave in *making provision* for a Family, and in dividing the inheritance more evenly and fairly than the Law of Intestate Succession would have divided it. If this be the true reading of the general sentiment on the point, it explains to some extent the singular horror of Intestacy which always characterised the Roman. No evil seems to have been considered a heavier visitation than the forfeiture of Testamentary privileges; no curse appears to have been bitterer than that which imprecated on an enemy that he might die without a Will. The feeling has no counterpart, or none that is easily recognisable, in the forms of opinion which exist at the present day. All men at all times will doubtless prefer chalking out the destination of their substance to having that office performed for them by the law; but the Roman passion for Testacy is distinguished from the mere desire to indulge caprice by its intensity; and it has of course nothing whatever in common with that pride of family, exclusively the creation of feudalism, which accumulates one description of property in the hands of a single representative. It is probable, *à priori*, that it was something in the rules of Intestate Succession which caused this vehement preference for the distribution of property under a Testament over its distribution by law. The difficulty, however, is, that on glancing at the Roman law of Intestate Succession, in the form which it wore for many centuries before Justinian shaped it into that scheme of inheritance which has been almost universally adopted by modern lawgivers, it by no means strikes one

as remarkably unreasonable or inequitable. On the contrary, the distribution it prescribes is so fair and rational, and differs so little from that with which modern society has been generally contented, that no reason suggests itself why it should have been regarded with extraordinary distaste, especially under a jurisprudence which pared down to a narrow compass the testamentary privileges of persons who had children to provide for. We should rather have expected that, as in France at this moment, the heads of families would generally save themselves the trouble of executing a Will, and allow the Law to do as it pleased with their assets. I think, however, if we look a little closely at the pre-Justinianean scale of Intestate Succession, we shall discover the key to the mystery. The texture of the law consists of two distinct parts. One department of rules comes from the Jus Civile, the Common-Law of Rome; the other from the Edict of the Prætor. The Civil Law, as I have already stated for another purpose, calls to the inheritance only three orders of successors in their turn; the Unemancipated children, the nearest class of Agnatic kindred, and the Gentiles. Between these three orders, the Prætor interpolates various classes of relatives, of whom the Civil Law took no notice whatever. Ultimately, the combination of the Edict and of the Civil Law forms a table of succession not materially different from that which has descended to the generality of modern codes.

The point for recollection is that there must anciently have been a time at which the rules of the Civil Law determined the scheme of Intestate Succession exclusively, and at which the arrangements of the Edict were non-existent, or not consistently carried out. We cannot doubt that, in its infancy, the Prætorian jurisprudence had to contend with formidable obstructions, and it is more than probable that, long after popular sentiment and legal opinion had acquiesced in it, the modifications which it periodically introduced were governed by no certain principles, and fluctuated with the varying bias of successive magistrates. The rules of Intestate Succession, which the Romans must at this period have practised, account, I think—and more than account—for that vehement distaste for an Intestacy to which Roman society during so many ages remained constant. The order of succession was this : on the death of a citizen, having no will or no valid will, his Unemancipated children became his Heirs. His *emancipated* sons had no share in the inheritance. If he left no direct descendants living at his death, the nearest grade of the Agnatic kindred succeeded, but no part of the inheritance was given to any relative united (however closely) with the dead man through female descents. All the other branches of the family were excluded, and the inheritance escheated to the *Gentiles*, or entire body of Roman citizens bearing the same name with the deceased. So that on failing to execute an operative Testament, a Roman of the era under examination left his emancipated children absolutely without provision, while, on the assumption that he died childless, there was imminent risk that his possessions would escape from the family altogether, and devolve on a number of persons with whom he was merely connected by the sacerdotal fiction that assumed all members of the

same *gens* to be descended from a common ancestor. The prospect of such an issue is in itself a
nearly sufficient explanation of the popular sentiment; but, in point of fact, we shall only half
understand it, if we forget that the state of things
I have been describing is likely to have existed
at the very moment when Roman society was in
the first stage of its transition from its primitive
organisation in detached families. The empire of
the father had indeed received one of the earliest
blows directed at it through the recognition of
Emancipation as a legitimate usage, but the law,
still considering the Patria Potestas to be the
root of family connection, persevered in looking
on the emancipated children as strangers to the
rights of Kinship and aliens from the blood. We
cannot, however, for a moment suppose that the
limitations of the family imposed by legal
pedantry had their counterpart in the natural
affection of parents. Family attachments must
still have retained that nearly inconceivable
sanctity and intensity which belonged to them
under the Patriarchal system; and, so little are
they likely to have been extinguished by the act
of emancipation, that the probabilities are altogether the other way. It may be unhesitatingly
taken for granted that enfranchisement from the
father's power was a demonstration, rather than
a severance, of affection—a mark of grace and
favour accorded to the best-beloved and most
esteemed of the children. If sons thus honoured
above the rest were absolutely deprived of their
heritage by an Intestacy, the reluctance to incur
it requires no farther explanation. We might have
assumed *à priori* that the passion for Testacy was
generated by some moral injustice entailed by the

rules of Intestate succession; and here we find
them at variance with the very instinct by which
early society was cemented together. It is
possible to put all that has been urged in a very
succinct form. Every dominant sentiment of the
primitive Romans was entwined with relations of
the family. But what was the Family? The Law
defined it one way—natural affection another. In
the conflict between the two, the feeling we would
analyse grew up, taking the form of an enthusiasm for the institution by which the dictates
of affection were permitted to determine the fortunes of its objects.

I regard, therefore, the Roman horror of Intestacy as a monument of a very early conflict between ancient law and slowly changing ancient
sentiment on the subject of the Family. Some
passages in the Roman Statute-Law, and one
statute in particular which limited the capacity
for inheritance possessed by women, must have
contributed to keep alive the feeling; and it is
the general belief that the system of creating
Fidei-Commissa, or bequests in trust, was devised
to evade the disabilities imposed by those
statutes. But the feeling itself, in its remarkable
intensity, seems to point back to some deeper
antagonism between law and opinion; nor is it
at all wonderful that the improvements of jurisprudence by the Prætor should not have extinguished it. Everybody conversant with the philosophy of opinion is aware that a sentiment by no
means dies out, of necessity, with the passing
away of the circumstances which produced it. It
may long survive them; nay, it may afterwards
attain to a pitch and climax of intensity which it
never attained during their actual continuance.

The view of a Will which regards it as conferring the power of diverting property from the
Family, or of distributing it in such uneven proportions as the fancy or good sense of the Testator may dictate, is not older than that later
portion of the Middle Ages in which Feudalism
had completely consolidated itself. When
modern jurisprudence first shows itself in the
rough, Wills are rarely allowed to dispose with
absolute freedom of a dead man's assets.
Wherever at this period the descent of property
was regulated by Will—and over the greater part
of Europe moveable or personal property was the
subject of Testamentary disposition—the exercise
of the Testamentary power was seldom allowed to
interfere with the right of the widow to a definite
share, and of the children to certain fixed proportions, of the devolving inheritance. The shares of
the children, as their amount shows, were determined by the authority of Roman law. The provision for the widow was attributable to the
exertions of the Church, which never relaxed its
solicitude for the interest of wives surviving their
husbands—winning, perhaps, one of the most
arduous of its triumphs when, after exacting for
two or three centuries an express promise from
the husband at marriage to endow his wife, it at
length succeeded in engrafting the principle of
Dower on the Customary Law of all Western
Europe. Curiously enough, the dower of lands
proved a more stable institution than the analogous and more ancient reservation of certain
shares of the personal property to the widow and
children. A few local customs in France maintained the right down to the Revolution, and
there are traces of similar usages in England;

but on the whole the doctrine prevailed that moveables might be freely disposed of by Will, and, even when the claims of the widow continued to be respected, the privileges of the children were obliterated from jurisprudence. We need not hesitate to attribute the change to the influence of Primogeniture. As the Feudal law of land practically disinherited all the children in favour of one, the equal distribution even of those sorts of property which might have been equally divided ceased to be viewed as a duty. Testaments were the principal instruments employed in producing inequality, and in this condition of things originated the shade of difference which shows itself between the ancient and the modern conception of a Will. But, though the liberty of bequest, enjoyed through Testaments, was thus an accidental fruit of Feudalism, there is no broader distinction than that which exists between a system of free Testamentary disposition and a system, like that of the Feudal land-law, under which property descends compulsorily in prescribed lines of devolution. This truth appears to have been lost sight of by the authors of the French Codes. In the social fabric which they determined to destroy, they saw Primogeniture resting chiefly on Family settlements, but they also perceived that Testaments were frequently employed to give the eldest son precisely the same preference which was reserved to him under the strictest of entails. In order, therefore, to make sure of their work, they not only rendered it impossible to prefer the eldest son to the rest in marriage-arrangements, but they almost expelled Testamentary succession from the law, lest it should be used to defeat their fundamental principle of an equal distribution of property among children at the parent's death. The result is that they have established a system of small perpetual entails, which is infinitely nearer akin to the system of feudal Europe than would be a perfect liberty of bequest. The land-law of England, ' the Herculaneum of Feudalism ', is certainly much more closely allied to the land-law of the Middle Ages than that of any Continental country, and Wills with us are frequently used to aid or imitate that preference of the eldest son and his line which is a nearly universal feature in marriage settlements of real property. But nevertheless feeling and opinion in this country have been profoundly affected by the practice of free Testamentary disposition; and it appears to me that the state of sentiment in a great part of French society, on the subject of the conservation of property in families, is much liker that which prevailed through Europe two or three centuries ago than are the current opinions of Englishmen.

The mention of Primogeniture introduces one of the most difficult problems of historical jurisprudence. Though I have not paused to explain my expressions, it may have been noticed that I have frequently spoken of a number of ' co-heirs ' as placed by the Roman Law of Succession on the same footing with a single Heir. In point of fact, we know of no period of Roman jurisprudence at which the place of the Heir, or Universal Successor, might not have been taken by a group of co-heirs. This group succeeded as a single unit, and the assets were afterwards divided among them in a separate legal proceeding. When the Succession was *ab intestato*, and the group consisted of the children of the

deceased, they each took an equal share of the
property; nor, though males had at one time
some advantages over females, is there the
faintest trace of Primogeniture. The mode of
distribution is the same throughout archaic jurisprudence. It certainly seems that, when civil
society begins and families cease to hold together
through a series of generations, the idea which
spontaneously suggests itself is to divide the
domain equally among the members of each successive generation, and to reserve no privilege to
the eldest son or stock. Some peculiarly significant hints as to the close relation of this phenomenon to primitive thought are furnished by
systems yet more archaic than the Roman.
Among the Hindoos, the instant a son is born,
he acquires a vested right in his father's property,
which cannot be sold without recognition of his
joint ownership. On the son's attaining full age,
he can sometimes compel a partition of the estate
even against the consent of the parent; and,
should the parent acquiesce, one son can always
have a partition even against the will of the
others. On such partition taking place, the father
has no advantage over his children, except that
he has two of the shares instead of one. The
ancient law of the German tribes was exceedingly
similar. The *allod* or domain of the family was
the joint-property of the father and his sons.
It does not, however, appear to have been
habitually divided even at the death of the parent,
and in the same way the possessions of a Hindoo,
however divisible theoretically, are so rarely distributed in fact, that many generations constantly
succeed each other without a partition taking
place, and thus the Family in India has a per-

petual tendency to expand into the Village Community, under conditions which I shall hereafter attempt to elucidate. All this points very clearly to the absolutely equal division of assets among the male children at death as the practice most usual with society at the period when family-dependency is in the first stages of disintegration. Here then emerges the historical difficulty of Primogeniture. The mere clearly we perceive that, when the Feudal institutions were in process of formation, there was no source in the world whence they could derive their elements but the Roman law of the provincials on the one hand and the archaic customs of the barbarians on the other, the more are we perplexed at first sight by our knowledge that neither Roman nor barbarian was accustomed to give any preference to the eldest son or his line in the succession to property.

Primogeniture did not belong to the Customs which the barbarians practised on their first establishment within the Roman Empire. It is known to have had its origin in the *benefices* or beneficiary gifts of the invading chieftains. These benefices, which were occasionally conferred by the earlier immigrant kings, but were distributed on a great scale by Charlemagne, were grants of Roman provincial land to be holden by the beneficiary on condition of military service. The *allodial* proprietors do not seem to have followed their sovereign on distant or difficult enterprises, and all the grander expeditions of the Frankish chiefs and of Charlemagne were accomplished with forces composed of soldiers either personally dependent on the royal house or compelled to serve it by the tenure of their land. The benefices,

however, were not at first in any sense hereditary.
They were held at the pleasure of the grantor, or
at most for the life of the grantee; but still, from
the very outset, no effort seems to have been
spared by the beneficiaries to enlarge the tenure,
and to continue their lands in their family after
death. Through the feebleness of Charlemagne's
successors these attempts were universally successful, and the Benefice gradually transformed
itself into the hereditary Fief. But, though the
fiefs were hereditary, they did not necessarily
descend to the eldest son. The rules of succession
which they followed were entirely determined by
the terms agreed upon between the grantor and
the beneficiary, or imposed by one of them on the
weakness of the other. The original tenures were
therefore extremely various; not indeed so capriciously various as is sometimes asserted, for all
which have hitherto been described present some
combination of the modes of succession familiar
to Romans and to barbarians, but still exceedingly miscellaneous. In some of them, the eldest
son and his stock undoubtedly succeeded to the
fief before the others, but such successions, so far
from being universal, do not even appear to have
been general. Precisely the same phenomena
recur during that more recent transmutation of
European society which entirely substituted the
feudal form of property for the domainial (or
Roman) and the allodial (or German). The allods
were wholly absorbed by the fiefs. The greater
allodial proprietors transformed themselves into
feudal lords by conditional alienations of portions
of their land to dependants; the smaller sought
an escape from the oppressions of that terrible
time by surrendering their property to some

powerful chieftain, and receiving it back at his hands on condition of service in his wars. Meantime, that vast mass of the population of Western Europe whose condition was servile or semi-servile—the Roman and German personal slaves, the Roman *coloni* and the German *lidi*—were concurrently absorbed by the feudal organisation, a few of them assuming a menial relation to the lords, but the greater part receiving land on terms which in those centuries were considered degrading. The tenures created during this era of universal infeudation were as various as the conditions which the tenants made with their new chiefs or were forced to accept from them. As in the case of the benefices, the succession to some, but by no means to all, of the estates followed the rule of Primogeniture. No sooner, however, has the feudal system prevailed throughout the West, than it becomes evident that Primogeniture has some great advantage over every other mode of succession. It spread over Europe with remarkable rapidity, the principal instrument of diffusion being Family Settlements, the Pactes de Famille of France and Haus-Gesetze of Germany, which universally stipulated that lands held by knightly service should descend to the eldest son. Ultimately the law resigned itself to follow inveterate practice, and we find that in all the bodies of Customary Law, which were gradually built up, the eldest son and stock are preferred in the succession to estates of which the tenure is free and military. As to lands held by servile tenures (and originally all tenures were servile which bound the tenant to pay money or bestow manual labour), the system of succession prescribed by custom differed greatly in different countries and

different provinces. The more general rule was
that such lands were divided equally at death
among all the children, but still in some instances
the eldest son was preferred, in some the
youngest. But Primogeniture usually governed
the inheritance of that class of estates, in some
respects the most important of all, which were
held by tenures that, like the English Socage,
were of later origin than the rest, and were
neither altogether free nor altogether servile.

The diffusion of Primogeniture is usually
accounted for by assigning what are called Feudal
reasons for it. It is asserted that the feudal
superior had a better security for the military
service he required when the fief descended to a
single person, instead of being distributed among
a number on the decease of the last holder. Without denying that this consideration may partially
explain the favour gradually acquired by Primogeniture, I must point out that Primogeniture
became a custom of Europe much more through
its popularity with the tenants than through any
advantage it conferred on the lords. For its
origin, moreover, the reason given does not
account at all. Nothing in law springs entirely
from a sense of convenience. There are always
certain ideas existing antecedently on which the
sense of convenience works, and of which it can
do no more than form some new combination;
and to find these ideas in the present case is
exactly the problem.

A valuable hint is furnished to us from a quarter
fruitful of such indications. Although in India the
possessions of a parent are divisible at his death,
and may be divisible during his life, among all his
male children in equal shares, and though this

principle of the equal distribution of *property* extends to every part of the Hindoo institutions, yet wherever *public office* or *political power* devolves at the decease of the last Incumbent, the succession is nearly universally according to the rules of Primogeniture. Sovereignties descend theref)re to the eldest son, and where the affairs of the Village Community, the corporate unit of Hindoo society, are confided to a single manager, it is generally the eldest son who takes up the administration at his parent's death. All offices, indeed, in India, tend to become hereditary, and, when their nature permits it, to vest in the eldest member of the oldest stock. Comparing these Indian successions with some of the ruder social organisations which have survived in Europe almost to our own day, the conclusion suggests itself that, when Patriarchal power is not only *domestic* but *political*, it is not distributed among all the issue at the parent's death, but is the birthright of the eldest son. The chieftainship of a Highland clan, for example, followed the order of Primogeniture. There seems, in truth, to be a form of family-dependency still more archaic than any of those which we know from the primitive records of organised civil societies. The Agnatic Union of the kindred in ancient Roman law, and a multitude of similar indications, point to a period at which all the ramifying branches of the family tree held together in one organic whole; and it is no presumptuous conjecture, that, when the corporation thus formed by the kindred was in itself an independent society, it was governed by the eldest male of the oldest line. It is true that we have no actual knowledge of any such society. Even in the most elementary communi-

ties, family-organisations, as we know them, are
at most *imperia in imperio*. But the position of
some of them, of the Celtic clans in particular,
was sufficiently near independence within historical times to force on us the conviction that they
were once separate *imperia*, and that Primogeniture regulated the succession to the chieftainship.
It is, however, necessary to be on our guard
against modern associations with the term of
law. We are speaking of a family-connection
still closer and more stringent than any with
which we are made acquainted by Hindoo society
or ancient Roman law. If the Roman Pater-
familias was visibly steward of the family possessions, if the Hindoo father is only joint-sharer
with his sons, still more emphatically must the
true patriarchal chieftain be merely the administrator of a common fund.

The examples of succession by Primogeniture
which were found among the Benefices may,
therefore, have been imitated from a system of
family-government known to the invading races,
though not in general use. Some ruder tribes
may have still practised it, or, what is still more
probable, society may have been so slightly removed from its more archaic condition that the
minds of some men spontaneously recurred to it,
when they were called upon to settle the rules of
inheritance for a new form of property. But
there is still the question, Why did Primogeniture gradually supersede every other principle
of succession? The answer, I think, is, that
European society decidedly retrograded during
the dissolution of the Carlovingian empire. It
sank a point or two back even from the miserably
low degree which it had marked during the early

barbarian monarchies. The great characteristic
of the period was the feebleness, or rather the
abeyance, of kingly and therefore of civil
authority; and hence it seems as if, civil society
no longer cohering, men universally flung themselves back on a social organisation older than the
beginnings of civil communities. The lord with
his vassals, during the ninth and tenth centuries,
may be considered as a patriarchal household,
recruited, not as in the primitive times by Adoption, but by Infeudation; and to such a con-
federacy, succession by Primogeniture was a
source of strength and durability. So long as the
land was kept together on which the entire
organisation rested, it was powerful for defence
and attack; to divide the land was to divide the
little society, and voluntarily to invite aggression
in an era of universal violence. We may be
perfectly certain that into this preference for
Primogeniture there entered no idea of disinheriting the bulk of the children in favour of one.
Everybody would have suffered by the division
of the fief. Everybody was a gainer by its consolidation. The Family grew stronger by the
concentration of power in the same hands; nor
is it likely that the lord who was invested with
the inheritance had any advantage over his
brethren and kinsfolk in occupations, interests,
or indulgences. It would be a singular anachron-
ism to estimate the privileges succeeded to by
the heir of a fief, by the situation in which the
eldest son is placed under an English strict settlement.

I have said that I regard the early feudal con-
federacies as descended from an archaic form of
the Family, and as wearing a strong resemblance

to it. But then in the ancient world, and in the societies which have not passed through the crucible of feudalism, the Primogeniture which seems to have prevailed never transformed itself into the Primogeniture of the later feudal Europe. When the group of kinsmen ceased to be governed through a series of generations by a hereditary chief, the domain which had been managed for all appears to have been equally divided among all. Why did this not occur in the feudal world? If during the confusions of the first feudal period the eldest son held the land for the behoof of the whole family, why was it that when feudal Europe had consolidated itself, and regular communities were again established, the whole family did not resume that capacity for equal inheritance which had belonged to Roman and German alike? The key which unlocks this difficulty has rarely been seized by the writers who occupy themselves in tracing the genealogy of Feudalism. They perceive the materials of the feudal institutions, but they miss the cement. The ideas and social forms which contributed to the formation of the system were unquestionably barbarian and archaic, but, as soon as Courts and lawyers were called in to interpret and define it, the principles of interpretation which they applied to it were those of the latest Roman jurisprudence, and were therefore excessively refined and matured. In a patriarchally governed society, the eldest son may succeed to the government of the Agnatic group, and to the absolute disposal of its property. But he is not therefore a true proprietor. He has correlative duties not involved in the conception of proprietorship, but quite undefined and quite

incapable of definition. The later Roman
jurisprudence, however, like our own law, looked
upon uncontrolled power over property as equivalent to ownership, and did not, and, in fact, could
not, take notice of liabilities of such a kind, that
the very conception of them belonged to a period
anterior to regular law. The contact of the refined and the barbarous notion had inevitably for
its effect the conversion of the eldest son into
legal proprietor of the inheritance. The clerical
and secular lawyers so defined his position from
the first; but it was only by insensible degrees
that the younger brother, from participating on
equal terms in all the dangers and enjoyments
of his kinsman, sank into the priest, the soldier
of fortune, or the hanger-on of the mansion.
The legal revolution was identical with that which
occurred on a smaller scale, and in quite recent
times, through the greater part of the Highlands
of Scotland. When called in to determine the
legal powers of the chieftain over the domains
which gave sustenance to the clan, Scottish jurisprudence had long since passed the point at which
it could take notice of the vague limitations on
completeness of dominion imposed by the claims
of the clansmen, and it was inevitable therefore
that it should convert the patrimony of many
into the estate of one.

For the sake of simplicity I have called the
mode of succession Primogeniture whenever a
single son or descendant succeeds to the authority
over a household or society. It is remarkable,
however, that in the few very ancient examples
which remain to us of this sort of succession, it
is not always the eldest son, in the sense familiar
to us, who takes up the representation. The form

of Primogeniture which has spread over Western Europe has also been perpetuated among the Hindoos, and there is every reason to believe that it is the normal form. Under it, not only the eldest son, but the eldest line is always preferred. If the eldest son fails, his eldest son has precedence not only over brothers but over uncles; and, if he too fails, the same rule is followed in the next generation. But when the succession is not merely to *civil* but to *political* power, a difficulty may present itself which will appear of greater magnitude according as the cohesion of society is less perfect. The chieftain who last exercised authority may have outlived his eldest son, and the grandson who is primarily entitled to succeed may be too young and immature to undertake the actual guidance of the community, and the administration of its affairs. In such an event, the expedient which suggests itself to the more settled societies is to place the infant heir under guardianship till he reaches the age of fitness for government. The guardianship is generally that of the male Agnates; but it is remarkable that the contingency supposed is one of the rare cases in which ancient societies have consented to the exercise of power by women, doubtless out of respect to the overshadowing claims of the mother. In India, the widow of a Hindoo sovereign governs in the name of her infant son, and we cannot but remember that the custom regulating succession to the throne of France—which, whatever be its origin, is doubtless of the highest antiquity—preferred the queen-mother to all other claimants for the Regency, at the same time that it rigorously excluded all females from the throne. There is, however, another mode of

obviating the inconvenience attending the devolution of sovereignty on an infant heir, and it is
one which would doubtless occur spontaneously to
rudely organised communities. This is to set
aside the infant heir altogether, and confer the
chieftainship on the eldest surviving male of the
first generation. The Celtic clan-associations,
among the many phenomena which they have
preserved of an age in which civil and political
society were not yet even rudimentarily separated, have brought down this rule of succession
to historical times. With them, it seems to have
existed in the form of a positive canon, that,
failing the eldest son, his next brother succeeds
in priority to all grandsons, whatever be their
age at the moment when the sovereignty devolves. Some writers have explained the principle by assuming that the Celtic customs took
the last chieftain as a sort of root or stock, and
then gave the succession to the descendant who
should be least remote from him; the uncle thus
being preferred to the grandson as being nearer to
the common root. No objection can be taken to
this statement if it be merely intended as a
description of the system of succession; but it
would be a serious error to conceive the men who
first adopted the rule as applying a course of
reasoning which evidently dates from the time
when feudal schemes of succession begun to be
debated among lawyers. The true origin of the
preference of the uncle to the grandson is doubtless a simple calculation on the part of rude men
in a rude society that it is better to be governed
by a grown chieftain than by a child, and that
the younger son is more likely to have come to
maturity than any of the eldest son's descendants.

At the same time, we have some evidence that the form of Primogeniture with which we are best acquainted is the primary form, in the tradition that the assent of the clan was asked when an infant heir was passed over in favour of his uncle. There is a tolerably well authenticated instance of this ceremony in the annals of the Macdonalds.

Under Mahometan law, which has probably preserved an ancient Arabian custom, inheritances of property are divided equally among sons, the daughters taking a half share; but if any of the children die before the division of the inheritance, leaving issue behind, these grandchildren are entirely excluded by their uncles and aunts. Consistently with this principle, the succession, when political authority devolves, is according to the form of Primogeniture which appears to have obtained among the Celtic societies. In the two great Mahometan families of the West, the rule is believed to be, that the uncle succeeds to the throne in preference to the nephew, though the latter be the son of an elder brother; but though this rule has been followed quite recently in Egypt, I am informed that there is some doubt as to its governing the devolution of the Turkish sovereignty. The policy of the Sultans has in fact hitherto prevented cases for its application from occurring, and it is possible that their wholesale massacres of their younger brothers may have been perpetuated quite as much in the interest of their children as for the sake of making away with dangerous competitors for the throne. It is evident, however, that in polygamous societies the form of Primogeniture will always tend to vary. Many considerations may constitute a claim on the succession, the rank of the mother, for example, or her degree in the affections of the father. Accordingly, some of the Indian Mahometan sovereigns, without pretending to any distinct testamentary power, claim the right of nominating the son who is to succeed. The *blessing* mentioned in the Scriptural history of Isaac and his sons has sometimes been spoken of as a will, but it seems rather to have been a mode of naming an eldest son.

CHAPTER VIII

THE EARLY HISTORY OF PROPERTY

THE Roman Institutional Treatises, after giving their definition of the various forms and modifications of ownership, proceed to discuss the Natural Modes of Acquiring Property. Those who are unfamiliar with the history of jurisprudence are not likely to look upon these " natural modes " of acquisition as possessing, at first sight, either much speculative or much practical interest. The wild animal which is snared or killed by the hunter, the soil which is added to our field by the imperceptible deposits of a river, the tree which strikes its roots into our ground, are each said by the Roman lawyers to be acquired by us *naturally*. The older jurisconsults had doubtless observed that such acquisitions were universally sanctioned by the usages of the little societies around them, and thus the lawyers of a later age, finding them classed in the ancient Jus Gentium, and perceiving them to be of the simplest description,

allotted them a place among the ordinances of
Nature. The dignity with which they were invested has gone on increasing in modern times
till it is quite out of proportion to their original
importance. Theory has made them its favourite
food, and has enabled them to exercise the most
serious influence on practice.

It will be necessary for us to attend to one
only among these ' natural modes of acquisition ', Occupatio or Occupancy. Occupancy is
the advisedly taking possession of that which at
the moment is the property of no man, with the
view (adds the technical definition) of acquiring
property in it for yourself. The objects which
the Roman lawyers called *res nullius*—things
which have not or have never had an owner—
can only be ascertained by enumerating them.
Among things which *never had* an owner are wild
animals, fishes, wild fowl, jewels disinterred for
the first time, and lands newly discovered or
never before cultivated. Among things which
have not an owner are moveables which have
been abandoned, lands which have been deserted,
and (an anomalous but most formidable item)
the property of an enemy. In all these objects
the full rights of dominion were acquired by the
Occupant, who first took possession of them with
the intention of keeping them as his own—an
intention which, in certain cases, had to be mani-
fested by specific acts. It is not difficult, I think,
to understand the universality which caused the
practice of Occupancy to be placed by one generation of Roman lawyers in the Law common to all
Nations, and the simplicity which occasioned its
being attributed by another to the Law of Nature.
But for its fortunes in modern legal history **we**

are less prepared by *à priori* considerations. The
Roman principle of Occupancy, and the rules into
which the jurisconsults expanded it, are the
source of all modern International Law on the
subject of Capture in War and of the acquisition
of sovereign rights in newly discovered countries.
They have also supplied a theory of the Origin of
Property, which is at once the popular theory,
and the theory which, in one form or another,
is acquiesced in by the great majority of speculative jurists.

I have said that the Roman principle of Occupancy has determined the tenor of that chapter
of International Law which is concerned with
Capture in War. The Law of Warlike Capture
derives its rules from the assumption that communities are remitted to a state of nature by the
outbreak of hostilities, and that, in the artificial
natural condition thus produced, the institution
of private property falls into abeyance so far as
concerns the belligerents. As the later writers
on the Law of Nature have always been anxious
to maintain that private property was in some
sense sanctioned by the system which they were
expounding, the hypothesis that an enemy's property is *res nullius* has seemed to them perverse
and shocking, and they are careful to stigmatise
it as a mere fiction of jurisprudence. But, as
soon as the Law of Nature is traced to its source
in the Jus Gentium, we see at once how the
goods of an enemy came to be looked upon as
nobody's property, and therefore as capable of
being acquired by the first occupant. The idea
would occur spontaneously to persons practising
the ancient forms of Warfare, when victory dissolved the organisation of the conquering army and

dismissed the soldiers to indiscriminate plunder. It is probable, however, that originally it was only moveable property which was thus permitted to be acquired by the Captor. We know on independent authority that a very different rule prevailed in ancient Italy as to the acquisition of ownership in the soil of a conquered country, and we may therefore suspect that the application of the principle of occupancy to land (always a matter of difficulty) dates from the period when the Jus Gentium was becoming the Code of Nature, and that it is the result of a generalisation effected by the jurisconsults of the golden age. Their dogmas on the point are preserved in the Pandects of Justinian, and amount to an unqualified assertion that enemy's property of every sort is *res nullius* to the other belligerent, and that Occupancy, by which the Captor makes them his own, is an institution of Natural Law. The rules which International jurisprudence derives from these positions have sometimes been stigmatised as needlessly indulgent to the ferocity and cupidity of combatants, but the charge has been made, I think, by persons who are unacquainted with the history of wars, and who are consequently ignorant how great an exploit it is to command obedience for a rule of any kind. The Roman principle of Occupancy, when it was admitted into the modern law of Capture in War, drew with it a number of subordinate canons, limiting and giving precision to its operation, and if the contests which have been waged since the treatise of Grotius became an authority, are compared with those of an earlier date, it will be seen that, as soon as the Roman maxims were received, Warfare instantly assumed a more tolerable complexion. If the Roman law of Occupancy is to be taxed with having had pernicious influence on any part of the modern Law of Nations, there is another chapter in it which may be said, with some reason, to have been injuriously affected. In applying to the discovery of new countries the same principles which the Romans had applied to the finding of a jewel, the Publicists forced into their service a doctrine altogether unequal to the task expected from it. Elevated into extreme importance by the discoveries of the great navigators of the 15th and 16th centuries, it raised more disputes than it solved. The greatest uncertainty was very shortly found to exist on the very two points on which certainty was most required, the extent of the territory which was acquired for his sovereign by the discoverer, and the nature of the acts which were necessary to complete the *adprehensio* or assumption of sovereign possession. Moreover, the principle itself, conferring as it did such enormous advantages as the consequence of a piece of good luck, was instinctively mutinied against by some of the most adventurous nations in Europe, the Dutch, the English, and the Portuguese. Our own countrymen, without expressly denying the rule of International Law, never did, in practice, admit the claim of the Spaniards to engross the whole of America south of the Gulf of Mexico, or that of the King of France to monopolise the valleys of the Ohio and the Mississippi. From the accession of Elizabeth to the accession of Charles the Second, it cannot be said that there was at any time thorough peace in the American waters, and the encroachments of the New England Colonists on the territory of the

French King continued for almost a century longer. Bentham was so struck with the confusion attending the application of the legal principle, that he went out of his way to eulogise the famous Bull of Pope Alexander the Sixth, dividing the undiscovered countries of the world between the Spaniards and Portuguese by a line drawn one hundred leagues West of the Azores; and, grotesque as his praises may appear at first sight, it may be doubted whether the arrangement of Pope Alexander is absurder in principle than the rule of Public law, which gave half a continent to the monarch whose servants had fulfilled the conditions required by Roman jurisprudence for the acquisition of property in a valuable object which could be covered by the hand.

To all who pursue the inquiries which are the subject of this volume Occupancy is pre-eminently interesting on the score of the service it has been made to perform for speculative jurisprudence, in furnishing a supposed explanation of the origin of private property. It was once universally believed that the proceeding implied in Occupancy was identical with the process by which the earth and its fruits, which were at first in common, became the allowed property of individuals. The course of thought which led to this assumption is not difficult to understand, if we seize the shade of difference which separates the ancient from the modern conception of Natural Law. The Roman lawyers had laid down that Occupancy was one of the Natural modes of acquiring property, and they undoubtedly believed that, were mankind living under the institutions of Nature, Occupancy would be one of their practices. How far they persuaded themselves that such a condition of the race had ever existed, is a point, as I have already stated, which their language leaves in much uncertainty; but they certainly do seem to have made the conjecture, which has at all times possessed much plausibility, that the institution of property was not so old as the existence of mankind. Modern jurisprudence, accepting all their dogmas without reservation, went far beyond them in the eager curiosity with which it dwelt on the supposed state of Nature. Since then it had received the position that the earth and its fruits were once *res nullius*, and since its peculiar view of Nature led it to assume without hesitation that the human race had actually practised the Occupancy of *res nullius* long before the organisation of civil societies, the inference immediately suggested itself that Occupancy was the process by which the ' no man's goods ' of the primitive world became the private property of individuals in the world of history. It would be wearisome to enumerate the jurists who have subscribed to this theory in one shape or another, and it is the less necessary to attempt it because Blackstone, who is always a faithful index of the average opinions of his day, has summed them up in his 2nd book and 1st chapter.

' The earth,' he writes, ' and all things therein were the general property of mankind from the immediate gift of the Creator. Not that the communion of goods seems ever to have been applicable, even in the earliest ages, to aught but the substance of the thing; nor could be extended to the use of it. For, by the law of nature and reason he who first began to use it acquired therein a kind of transient property that lasted so long as he was using it, and no longer; or to speak with greater precision, the right of possession continued for the same time only that the act of possession lasted. Thus the ground was in common, and no part was the permanent property of any man in particular; yet whoever was in the occupation of any determined spot of it, for rest, for shade, or the like, acquired for the time a sort of ownership, from which it would have been unjust and contrary to the law of nature to have driven him by force, but the instant that he quitted the use of occupation of it, another might seize it without injustice.' He then proceeds to argue that " when mankind increased in number, it became necessary to entertain conceptions of more permanent dominion, and to appropriate to individuals not the immediate use only, but the very substance of the thing to be used."

Some ambiguities of expression in this passage lead to the suspicion that Blackstone did not quite understand the meaning of the proposition which he found in his authorities, that property in the earth's surface was first acquired, under the law of Nature, by the *occupant;* but the limitation which designedly or through misapprehension he has imposed on the theory brings it into a form which it has not infrequently assumed. Many writers more famous than Blackstone for precision of language have laid down that, in the beginning of things, Occupancy first gave a right against the world to an exclusive but temporary enjoyment, and that afterwards this right, while it remained exclusive, became perpetual. Their object in so stating their theory was to reconcile the doctrine that in the state of Nature *res nullius* became property through Occupancy, with the inference which they drew from the Scriptural history that the Patriarchs did not at first permanently appropriate the soil which had been grazed over by their flocks and herds.

The only criticism which could be directly applied to the theory of Blackstone would consist in inquiring whether the circumstances which make up his picture of a primitive society are more or less probable than other incidents which could be imagined with equal readiness. Pursuing this method of examination, we might fairly ask whether the man who had *occupied* (Blackstone evidently uses this word with its ordinary English meaning) a particular spot of ground for rest or shade would be permitted to retain it without disturbance. The chances surely are that his right to possession would be exactly coextensive with his power to keep it, and that he would be constantly liable to disturbance by the first comer who coveted the spot and thought himself strong enough to drive away the possessor. But the truth is that all such cavil at these positions is perfectly idle from the very baselessness of the positions themselves. What mankind did in the primitive state may not be a hopeless subject of inquiry, but of their motives for doing it it is impossible to know anything. These sketches of the plight of human beings in the first ages of the world are effected by first supposing mankind to be divested of a great part of the circumstances by which they are now surrounded, and by then assuming that, in the condition thus imagined, they would preserve the same sentiments and prejudices by which they are now actuated,— although, in fact, these sentiments may have been created and engendered by those very circumstances of which, by the hypothesis, they are to be stripped.

There is an aphorism of Savigny which has been sometimes thought to countenance a view of the origin of property somewhat similar to the theories epitomised by Blackstone. The great German jurist has laid down that all Property is founded on Adverse Possession ripened by Prescription. It is only with respect to Roman law that Savigny makes this statement, and before it can fully be appreciated much labour must be expended in explaining and defining the expressions employed. His meaning will, however, be indicated with sufficient accuracy if we consider him to assert that, how far soever we carry our inquiry into the ideas of property received among the Romans, however closely we approach in tracing them to the infancy of law, we can get no farther than a conception of ownership involving the three elements in the canon—Possession, Adverseness of Possession, that is a holding not permissive or subordinate, but exclusive against the world, and Prescription, or a period of time during which the Adverse Possession has uninterruptedly continued. It is exceedingly probable that this maxim might be enunciated with more generality than was allowed to it by its author, and that no sound or safe conclusion can be looked for from investigations into any system of laws which are pushed farther back than the point at which these combined ideas constitute the notion of proprietary right. Meantime, so far from bearing out the popular theory of the origin of property, Savigny's canon is particularly valuable as directing our attention to its weakest point. In the view of Blackstone and

those whom he follows, it was the mode of
assuming the exclusive enjoyment which mysteri-
ously affected the minds of the fathers of our race.
But the mystery does not reside here. It is not
wonderful that property began in adverse possession. It is not surprising that the first proprietor
should have been the strong man armed who kept
his goods in peace. But why it was that lapse
of time created a sentiment of respect for his
possession—which is the exact source of the
universal reverence of mankind for that which has
for a long period *de facto* existed—are questions
really deserving the profoundest examination, but
lying far beyond the boundary of our present
inquiries.

Before pointing out the quarter in which we
may hope to glean some information, scanty and
uncertain at best, concerning the early history of
proprietary right, I venture to state my opinion
that the popular impression in reference to the
part played by Occupancy in the first stages of
civilisation directly reverses the truth. Occupancy is the advised assumption of physical
possession; and the notion that an act of this
description confers a title to ' res nullius ', so
far from being characteristic of very early societies, is in all probability the growth of a refined
jurisprudence and of a settled condition of the
laws. It is only when the rights of property have
gained a sanction from long practical inviolability,
and when the vast majority of the objects of enjoyment have been subjected to private ownership, that mere possession is allowed to invest
the first possessor with dominion over commodities in which no prior proprietorship has been
asserted. The sentiment in which this doctrine

originated is absolutely irreconcilable with that
infrequency and uncertainty of proprietary rights
which distinguish the beginnings of civilisation.
Its true basis seems to be, not an instinctive bias
towards the institution of Property, but a presumption, arising out of the long continuance of
that institution, that *everything ought to have an
owner*. When possession is taken of a ' res
nullius ', that is, of an object which *is* not, or has
never been, reduced to dominion, the possessor is
permitted to become proprietor from a feeling that
all valuable things are naturally the subjects of an
exclusive enjoyment, and that in the given case
there is no one to invest with the right of property except the Occupant. The Occupant in
short, becomes the owner, because all things are
presumed to be somebody's property and because
no one can be pointed out as having a better right
than he to the proprietorship of this particular
thing.

Even were there no other objection to the descriptions of mankind in their natural state which
we have been discussing, there is one particular in
which they are fatally at variance with the authen-
tic evidence possessed by us. It will be observed,
that the acts and motives which these theories
suppose are the acts and motives of Individuals.
It is each Individual who for himself subscribes
the Social Compact. It is some shifting sandbank
in which the grains are Individual men, that
according to the theory of Hobbes is hardened
into the social rock by the wholesome discipline of
force. It is an Individual who, in the picture
drawn by Blackstone, " is in the occupation of a
determined spot of ground for rest, for shade, or
the like.' The vice is one which necessarily

afflicts all the theories descended from the Natural Law of the Romans, which differed principally from their Civil Law in the account which it took of Individuals, and which has rendered precisely its greatest service to civilisation in enfranchising the individual from the authority of archaic society. But Ancient Law, it must again be repeated, knows next to nothing of Individuals. It is concerned not with Individuals, but with Families, not with single human beings, but groups. Even when the law of the State has succeeded in permeating the small circles of kindred into which it had originally no means of penetrating, the view it takes of Individuals is curiously different from that taken by jurisprudence in its maturest stage. The life of each citizen is not regarded as limited by birth and death; it is but a continuation of the existence of his forefathers, and it will be prolonged in the existence of his descendants.

The Roman distinction between the Law of Persons and the Law of Things, which though extremely convenient is entirely artificial, has evidently done much to divert inquiry on the subject before us from the true direction. The lessons learned in discussing the Jus Personarum have been forgotten where the Jus Rerum is reached, and Property, Contract, and Delict, have been considered as if no hints concerning their original nature were to be gained from the facts ascertained respecting the original condition of Persons. The futility of this method would be manifest if a system of pure archaic law could be brought before us, and if the experiment could be tried of applying to it the Roman classifications. It would soon be seen that the separation of the Law of Persons from that of Things has no meaning in the infancy of law, that the rules belonging to the two departments are inextricably mingled together, and that the distinctions of the later jurists are appropriate only to the later jurisprudence. From what has been said in the earlier portions of this treatise, it will be gathered that there is a strong *à priori* improbability of our obtaining any clue to the early history of property, if we confine our notice to the proprietary right of individuals. It is more than likely that joint-ownership, and not separate ownership, is the really archaic institution, and that the forms of property which will afford us instruction will be those which are associated with the rights of families and of groups of kindred. The Roman jurisprudence will not here assist in enlightening us, for it is exactly the Roman jurisprudence which, transformed by the theory of Natural Law, has bequeathed to the moderns the impression that individual ownership is the normal state of proprietary right, and that ownership in common by groups of men is only the exception to a general rule. There is, however, one community which will always be carefully examined by the inquirer who is in quest of any lost institution of primeval society. How far soever any such institution may have undergone change among the branch of the Indo-European family which has been settled for ages in India, it will seldom be found to have entirely cast aside the shell in which it was originally reared. It happens that, among the Hindoos, we do find a form of ownership which ought at once to rivet our attention from its exactly fitting in with the ideas which our studies in the Law of Persons would lead us to entertain respecting the original condition of property. The Village Community of India is at once an organised patriarchal society and an assemblage of co-proprietors. The personal relations to each other of the men who compose it are indistinguishably confounded with their proprietary rights, and to the attempts of English functionaries to separate the two may be assigned some of the most formidable miscarriages of Anglo-Indian administration. The Village Community is known to be of immense antiquity. In whatever direction research has been pushed into Indian history, general or local, it has always found the Community in existence at the farthest point of its progress. A great number of intelligent and observant writers, most of whom had no theory of any sort to support concerning its nature and origin, agree in considering it the least destructible institution of a society which never willingly surrenders any one of its usages to innovation. Conquests and revolutions seem to have swept over it without disturbing or displacing it, and the most beneficent systems of government in India have always been those which have recognised it as the basis of administration.

The mature Roman law, and modern jurisprudence following in its wake, look upon co-ownership as an exceptional and momentary condition of the rights of property. This view is clearly indicated in the maxim which obtains universally in Western Europe, *Nemo in communione potest invitus detineri* (' No one can be kept in co-proprietorship against his will '). But in India this order of ideas is reversed, and it may be said that separate proprietorship is always on its way to become proprietorship in common. The process has been adverted to already. As soon as a son is born, he acquires a vested interest in his father's substance, and on attaining years of discretion he is even, in certain contingencies, permitted by the letter of the law to call for a partition of the family estate. As a fact, however, a division rarely takes place even at the death of the father, and the property constantly remains undivided for several generations, though every member of every generation has a legal right to an undivided share in it. The domain thus held in common is sometimes administered by an elected manager, but more generally, and in some provinces always, it is managed by the eldest agnate, by the eldest representative of the eldest line of the stock. Such an assemblage of joint proprietors, a body of kindred holding a domain in common, is the simplest form of an Indian Village Community, but the Community is more than a brotherhood of relatives and more than an association of partners. It is an organised society, and besides providing for the management of the common fund, it seldom fails to provide, by a complete staff of functionaries, for internal government, for police, for the administration of justice, and for the apportionment of taxes and public duties.

The process which I have described as that under which a Village Community is formed, may be regarded as typical. Yet it is not to be supposed that every Village Community in India drew together in so simple a manner. Although, in the North of India, the archives, as I am informed, almost invariably show that the Community was founded by a single assemblage of

blood-relations, they also supply information that
men of alien extraction have always, from time to
time, been engrafted on it, and a mere purchaser
of a share may generally, under certain conditions, be admitted to the brotherhood. In the
South of the Peninsula there are often Communities which appear to have sprung not from one
but from two or more families; and there are
some whose composition is known to be entirely
artificial; indeed, the occasional aggregation of
men of different castes in the same society is fatal
to the hypothesis of a common descent. Yet in
all these brotherhoods either the tradition is preserved, or the assumption made, of an original
common parentage. Mountstuart Elphinstone,
who writes more particularly of the Southern
Village Communities, observes of them (*History
of India*, i. 126) : ' The popular notion is that
the Village landholders are all descended from one
or more individuals who settled the village; and
that the only exceptions are formed by persons
who have derived their rights by purchase or
otherwise from members of the original stock. The
supposition is confirmed by the fact that, to this
day, there are only single families of landholders
in small villages and not many in large ones;
but each has branched out into so many
members that it is not uncommon for the whole
agricultural labour to be done by the landholders,
without the aid either of tenants or of labourers.
The rights of the landholders are theirs collectively
and, though they almost always have a more or
less perfect partition of them, they never have
an entire separation. A landholder, for instance,
can sell or mortgage his rights; but he must first
have the consent of the Village, and the pur-

chaser steps exactly into his place and takes up all his obligations. If a family becomes extinct, its share returns to the common stock.'

Some considerations which have been offered in the fifth chapter of this volume will assist the reader, I trust, in appreciating the significance of Elphinstone's language. No institution of the primitive world is likely to have been preserved to our day, unless it has acquired an elasticity foreign to its original nature through some vivifying legal fiction. The Village Community then is not necessarily an assemblage of blood-relations, but it is *either* such an assemblage *or* a body of co-proprietors formed on the model of an association of kinsmen. The type with which it should be compared is evidently not the Roman Family, but the Roman Gens or House. The Gens was also a group on the model of the family; it was the family extended by a variety of fictions of which the exact nature was lost in antiquity. In historical times, its leading characteristics were the very two which Elphinstone remarks in the Village Community. There was always the assumption of a common origin, an assumption sometimes notoriously at variance with fact; and, to repeat the historian's words, ' if a family became extinct, its share returned to the common stock.' In old Roman law, unclaimed inheritances escheated to the Gentiles. It is further suspected by all who have examined their history that the Communities, like the Gentes, have been very generally adulterated by the admission of strangers, but the exact mode of absorption cannot now be ascertained. At present, they are recruited, as Elphinstone tells us, by the admission of purchasers, with the consent of the brotherhood. The acquisition of the adopted member is, however, of the nature of a universal succession; together with the share he has bought, he succeeds to the liabilities which the vendor had incurred towards the aggregate group. He is an Emptor Familiæ, and inherits the legal clothing of the person whose place he begins to fill. The consent of the whole brotherhood required for his admission may remind us of the consent which the Comitia Curiata, the Parliament of that larger brotherhood of self-styled kinsmen, the ancient Roman commonwealth, so strenuously insisted on as essential to the legalization of an Adoption or the confirmation of a Will.

The tokens of an extreme antiquity are discoverable in almost every single feature of the Indian Village Communities. We have so many independent reasons for suspecting that the infancy of law is distinguished by the prevalence of co-ownership, by the intermixture of personal with proprietary rights, and by the confusion of public with private duties, that we should be justified in deducing many important conclusions from our observation of these proprietary brotherhoods, even if no similarly compounded societies could be detected in any other part of the world. It happens, however, that much earnest curiosity has been very recently attracted to a similar set of phenomena in those parts of Europe which have been most slightly affected by the feudal transformation of property, and which in many important particulars have as close an affinity with the Eastern as with the Western world. The researches of M. de Haxthausen, M. Tengoborski, and others, have shown us that the Russian villages are not fortuitous assemblages of men, nor are they unions founded on contract; they are naturally organised communities like those of India. It is true that these villages are always in theory the patrimony of some noble proprietor, and the peasants have within historical times been converted into the predial, and to a great extent into the personal, serfs of the seignior. But the pressure of this superior ownership has never crushed the ancient organization of the village, and it is probable that the enactment of the Czar of Russia, who is supposed to have introduced serfdom, was really intended to prevent the peasants from abandoning that co-operation without which the old social order could not long be maintained. In the assumption of an agnatic connection between the villagers, in the blending of personal rights with privileges of ownership, and in a variety of spontaneous provisions for internal administration, the Russian Village appears to be a nearly exact repetition of the Indian Community; but there is one important difference which we note with the greatest interest. The co-owners of an Indian village, though their property is blended, have their rights distinct, and this separation of rights is complete and continues indefinitely. The severance of rights is also theoretically complete in a Russian village, but there it is only temporary. After the expiration of a given, but not in all cases of the same, period, separate ownerships are extinguished, the land of the village is thrown into a mass, and then it is re-distributed among the families composing the community, according to their number. This repartition having been effected, the rights of families and of individuals are again allowed to branch out into various lines, which they continue to follow till another period of division comes round. An even more curious variation from this type of ownership occurs in some of those countries which long formed a debateable land between the Turkish empire and the possessions of the House of Austria. In Servia, in Croatia, and the Austrian Sclavonia, the villages are also brotherhoods of persons who are at once co-owners and kinsmen; but there the internal arrangements of the community differ from those adverted to in the last two examples. The substance of the common property is in this case neither divided in practice nor considered in theory as divisible, but the entire land is cultivated by the combined labour of all the villagers, and the produce is annually distributed among the households, sometimes according to their supposed wants, sometimes according to rules which give to particular persons a fixed share of the usufruct. All these practices are traced by the jurists of the East of Europe to a principle which is asserted to be found in the earliest Sclavonian laws, the principle that the property of families cannot be divided for a perpetuity.

The great interest of these phenomena in an inquiry like the present arises from the light they throw on the development of distinct proprietary rights *inside* the groups by which property seems to have been originally held. We have the strongest reason for thinking that property once belonged not to individuals nor even to isolated families, but to larger societies composed on the patriarchal model; but the mode of transition from ancient to modern ownerships, obscure at best, would have been infinitely obscurer if several distinguishable forms of Village Communities had not been discovered and examined. It is worth while to attend to the varieties of internal arrangement within the patriarchal groups which are, or were till recently, observable among races of Indo-European blood. The chiefs of the ruder Highland clans used, it is said, to dole out food to the heads of the households under their juris-diction at the very shortest intervals, and some-times day by day. A periodical distribution is also made to the Sclavonian villagers of the Aus-trian and Turkish provinces by the elders of their body, but then it is a distribution once for all of the total produce of the year. In the Russian villages, however, the substance of the property ceases to be looked upon as indivisible, and separate proprietary claims are allowed freely to grow up, but then the progress of separation is per-emptorily arrested after it has continued a certain time. In India, not only is there no indivisibility of the common fund, but separate proprietorship in parts of it may be indefinitely prolonged and may branch out into any number of derivative ownerships, the *de facto* partition of the stock being, however, checked by inveterate usage, and by the rule against the admission of strangers without the consent of the brotherhood. It is not of course intended to insist that these different forms of the Village Community represent distinct stages in a process of transmutation which has been everywhere accomplished in the same manner. But, though the evidence does not war-rant our going so far as this, it renders less pre-sumptuous the conjecture that private property, in the shape in which we know it, was chiefly formed by the gradual disentanglement of the separate rights of individuals from the blended rights of a community. Our studies in the Law of Persons seemed to show us the Family expanding into the Agnatic group of kinsmen, then the Agnatic group dissolving into separate households; lastly the household supplanted by the individual; and it is now suggested that each step in the change corresponds to an analogous alteration in the nature of Ownership. If there be any truth in the suggestion, it is to be observed that it materially affects the problem which theorists on the origin of Property have generally proposed to themselves. The question—perhaps an insoluble one—which they have mostly agitated is, what were the motives which first induced men to respect each other's possessions? It may still be put, without much hope of finding an answer to it, in the form of any inquiry into the reasons which led one composite group to keep aloof from the domain of another. But, if it be true that far the most important passage in the history of Private Property is its gradual elimination from the coownership of kinsmen, then the great point of inquiry is identical with that which lies on the threshold of all historical law—what were the motives which originally prompted men to hold together in the family union? To such a question, Jurisprudence, unassisted by other sciences, is not competent to give a reply. The fact can only be noted.

The undivided state of property in ancient societies is consistent with a peculiar sharpness of division, which shows itself as soon as any single share is completely separated from the patrimony of the group. This phenomenon springs, doubtless, from the circumstance that the property is supposed to become the domain of a new group,

so that any dealing with it, in its divided state,
is a transaction between two highly complex
bodies. I have already compared Ancient Law to
Modern International Law, in respect of the size
and complexity of the corporate associations,
whose rights and duties it settles. As the contracts and conveyances known to ancient law are
contracts and conveyances to which not single individuals, but organised companies of men, are
parties, they are in the highest degree ceremonious; they require a variety of symbolical acts
and words intended to impress the business on
the memory of all who take part in it; and they
demand the presence of an inordinate number of
witnesses. From these peculiarities, and others
allied to them, springs the universally unmalle-
able character of the ancient forms of property.
Sometimes the patrimony of the family is absolutely inalienable, as was the case with the
Sclavonians, and still oftener, though alienations
may not be entirely illegitimate, they are virtually impracticable, as among most of the Germanic tribes, from the necessity of having the
consent of a large number of persons to the transfer. Where these impediments do not exist, or
can be surmounted, the act of conveyance itself
is generally burdened with a perfect load of
ceremony, in which not one iota can be safely
neglected. Ancient law uniformly refuses to dispense with a single gesture, however grotesque;
with a single syllable, however its meaning may
have been forgotten; with a single witness, however superfluous may be his testimony. The
entire solemnities must be scrupulously completed
by persons legally entitled to take part in them, or
else the conveyance is null, and the seller is

re-established in the rights of which he had vainly attempted to divest himself.

These various obstacles to the free circulation of the objects of use and enjoyment, begin of course to make themselves felt as soon as society has acquired even a slight degree of activity, and the expedients by which advancing communities endeavour to overcome them form the staple of the history of Property. Of such expedients there is one which takes precedence of the rest from its antiquity and universality. The idea seems to have spontaneously suggested itself to a great number of early societies, to classify property into kinds. One kind or sort of property is placed on a lower footing of dignity than the others, but at the same time is relieved from the fetters which antiquity has imposed on them. Subsequently, the superior convenience of the rules governing the transfer and descent of the lower order of property becomes generally recognized, and by a gradual course of innovation the plasticity of the less dignified class of valuable objects is communicated to the classes which stand conventionally higher. The history of Roman Property Law is the history of the assimilation of Res Mancipi to Res Nec Mancipi. The history of Property on the European Continent is the history of the subversion of the feudalized law of land by the Romanized law of moveables; and, though the history of ownership in England is not nearly completed, it is visibly the law of personalty which threatens to absorb and annihilate the law of realty.

The only *natural* classification of the objects of enjoyment, the only classification which corresponds with an essential difference in the subject-

matter, is that which divides them into Moveables
and Immoveables. Familiar as is this classification to jurisprudence, it was very slowly
developed by Roman law, from which we inherit
it, and was only finally adopted by it in its latest
stage. The classifications of Ancient Law have
sometimes a superficial resemblance to this. They
occasionally divide property into categories, and
place immoveables in one of them; but then it
is found that they either class along with immoveables a number of objects which have no sort
of relation with them, or else divorce them from
various rights to which they have a close affinity.
Thus, the Res Mancipi of Roman Law included
not only land, but slaves, horses, and oxen.
Scottish law ranks with land a certain class of
securities, and Hindoo law associates it with
slaves. English law, on the other hand, parts
leases of land for years from other interests in the
soil, and joins them to personalty under the name
of chattels real. Moreover, the classifications of
Ancient Law are classifications implying superiority and inferiority; while the distinction between
moveables and immoveables, so long at least as it
was confined to Roman jurisprudence, carried
with it no suggestion whatever of a difference in
dignity. The Res Mancipi, however, did certainly
at first enjoy a precedence over the Res Nec Mancipi, as did heritable property in Scotland and
realty in England, over the personalty to which
they were opposed. The lawyers of all systems
have spared no pains in striving to refer these
classifications to some intelligible principle; but
the reasons of the severance must ever be vainly
sought for in the philosophy of law : they belong
not to its philosophy, but to its history. The

explanation which appears to cover the greatest
number of instances is, that the objects of enjoyment honoured above the rest were the forms of
property known first and earliest to each particular community, and dignified therefore emphatically with the designation of *Property*. On
the other hand, the articles not enumerated
among the favoured objects seem to have been
placed on a lower standing, because the knowledge of their value was posterior to the epoch at
which the catalogue of superior property was
settled. They were at first unknown, rare,
limited in their uses, or else regarded as mere
appendages to the privileged objects. Thus,
though the Roman Res Mancipi included a number of moveable articles of great value, still the
most costly jewels were never allowed to take
rank as Res Mancipi, because they were unknown
to the early Romans. In the same way chattels
real in England are said to have been degraded
to the footing of personalty, from the infrequency
and valuelessness of such estates under the feudal
land-law. But the grand point of interest is, the
continued degradation of these commodities when
their importance had increased and their number
had multiplied. Why were they not successively
included among the favoured objects of enjoyment? One reason is found in the stubbornness
with which Ancient Law adheres to its classifications. It is a characteristic both of uneducated
minds and of early societies, that they are little
able to conceive a general rule apart from the
particular applications of it with which they are
practically familiar. They cannot dissociate a
general term or maxim from the special examples
which meet them in daily experience; and in this

way the designation covering the best-known forms of property is denied to articles which exactly resemble them in being objects of enjoyment and subjects of right. But to these influences, which exert peculiar force in a subject-matter so stable as that of law, are afterwards added others more consistent with progress in enlightenment and in the conceptions of general expediency. Courts and lawyers become at last alive to the inconvenience of the embarrassing formalities required for the transfer, recovery, or devolution of the favoured commodities, and grow unwilling to fetter the newer descriptions of property with the technical trammels which characterized the infancy of law. Hence arises a disposition to keep these last on a lower grade in the arrangements of Jurisprudence, and to permit their transfer by simpler processes than those which, in archaic conveyances, serve as stumbling-blocks to good faith and stepping-stones to fraud. We are perhaps in some danger of under-rating the inconveniences of the ancient modes of transfer. Our instruments of conveyance are written, so that their language, well pondered by the professional draftsman, is rarely defective in accuracy. But an ancient conveyance was not written, but *acted*. Gestures and words took the place of written technical phraseology, and any formula mispronounced, or symbolical act omitted, would have vitiated the proceeding as fatally as a material mistake in stating the uses or setting out the remainders would, two hundred years ago, have vitiated an English deed. Indeed, the mischiefs of the archaic ceremonial are even thus only half stated. So long as elaborate conveyances, written or acted, are required for the alienation of *land* alone, the chances of mistake are not considerable in the transfer of a description of property which is seldom got rid of with much precipitation. But the higher class of property in the ancient world comprised not only land but several of the commonest and several of the most valuable moveables. When once the wheels of society had begun to move quickly, there must have been immense inconvenience in demanding a highly intricate form of transfer for a horse or an ox, or for the most costly chattel of the old world—the Slave. Such commodities must have been constantly and even ordinarily conveyed with incomplete forms, and held, therefore, under imperfect titles.

The Res Mancipi of old Roman law were. land—in historical times, land on Italian soil,— slaves and beasts of burden, such as horses and oxen. It is impossible to doubt that the objects which make up the class are the instruments of agricultural labour, the commodities of first consequence to a primitive people. Such commodities were at first, I imagine, called emphatically Things or Property, and the mode of conveyance by which they were transferred was called a Mancipium or Mancipation; but it was not probably till much later that they received the distinctive appellation of Res Mancipi, ' Things which require a Mancipation.' By their side there may have existed or grown up a class of objects, for which it was not worth while to insist upon the full ceremony of Mancipation. It would be enough if, in transferring these last from owner to owner, a part only of the ordinary formalities were proceeded with, namely, that actual delivery, physical transfer, or *tradition*, which is

the most obvious index of a change of proprietorship. Such commodities were the Res Nec Mancipi of the ancient jurisprudence, ' things which
did not require a Mancipation ', little prized probably at first, and not often passed from one
group of proprietors to another. While, however,
the list of the Res Mancipi was irrevocably closed,
that of the Res Nec Mancipi admitted of indefinite
expansion; and hence every fresh conquest of
man over material nature added an item to the
Res Nec Mancipi, or effected an improvement in
those already recognised. Insensibly, therefore,
they mounted to an equality with the Res Mancipi, and the impression of an intrinsic inferiority
being thus dissipated, men began to observe the
manifold advantages of the simple formality
which accompanied their transfer over the more
intricate and more venerable ceremonial. Two
of the agents of legal amelioration, Fictions and
Equity, were assiduously employed by the Roman
lawyers to give the practical effects of a Mancipation to a Tradition: and, though Roman legislators long shrank from enacting that the right
of property in a Res Mancipi should be immediately transferred by bare delivery of the article,
yet even this step was at last ventured upon by
Justinian, in whose jurisprudence the difference
between Res Mancipi and Res Nec Mancipi disappears, and Tradition or Delivery becomes the
one great conveyance known to the law. The
marked preference which the Roman lawyers very
early gave to Tradition caused them to assign
it a place in their theory which has helped to
blind their modern disciples to its true history.
It was classed among the ' natural ' modes of
acquisition, both because it was generally prac-

tised among the Italian tribes, and because it
was a process which attained its object by the
simplest mechanism. If the expressions of the
jurisconsults be pressed, they undoubtedly imply
that Tradition, which belongs to the Law Natural,
is more ancient than Mancipation, which is an institution of Civil Society; and this, I need not
say, is the exact reverse of the truth.

The distinction between Res Mancipi and Res
Nec Mancipi is the type of a class of distinctions
to which civilization is much indebted, distinctions which run through the whole mass of commodities, placing a few of them in a class by
themselves, and relegating the others to a lower
category. The inferior kinds of property are first,
from disdain and disregard, released from the
perplexed ceremonies in which primitive law de-
lights, and thus afterwards, in another state of
intellectual progress, the simple methods of transfer and recovery which have been allowed to come
into use serve as a model which condemns by
its convenience and simplicity the cumbrous
solemnities inherited from ancient days. But, in
some societies, the trammels in which Property
is tied up are much too complicated and stringent
to be relaxed in so easy a manner. Whenever
male children have been born to a Hindoo, the
law of India, as I have stated, gives them all an
interest in his property, and makes their consent
a necessary condition of its alienation. In the
same spirit, the general usage of the old Germanic peoples—it is remarkable that the Anglo-
Saxon customs seem to have been an exception—
forbade alienations without the consent of the
male children; and the primitive law of the
Sclavonians even prohibited them altogether. It

is evident that such impediments as these cannot be overcome by a distinction between kinds of property, inasmuch as the difficulty extends to commodities of all sorts; and accordingly, Ancient Law, when once launched on a course of improvement, encounters them with a distinction of another character, a distinction classifying property, not according to its nature but according to its origin. In India, where there are traces of both systems of classification, the one which we are considering is exemplified in the difference which Hindoo law establishes between Inheritances and Acquisitions. The inherited property of the father is shared by the children as soon as they are born; but according to the custom of most provinces, the acquisitions made by him during his lifetime are wholly his own, and can be transferred by him at pleasure. A similar distinction was not unknown to Roman law, in which the earliest innovation on the Parental Powers took the form of a permission given to the son to keep for himself whatever he might have acquired in military service. But the most extensive use ever made of this mode of classification appears to have been among the Germans. I have repeatedly stated that the *allod*, though not inalienable, was commonly transferable with the greatest difficulty; and moreover, it descended exclusively to the agnatic kindred. Hence an extraordinary variety of distinctions came to be recognized, all intended to diminish the inconveniences inseparable from allodial property. The *wehrgeld*, for example, or composition for the homicide of a relative, which occupies so large a space in German jurisprudence, formed no part of the family domain, and descended accord-

ing to rules of succession altogether different.
Similarly, the *reipus*, or fine leviable on the re-
marriage of a widow, did not enter into the *allod*
of the person to whom it was paid, and followed
a line of devolution in which the privileges of the
agnates were neglected. The law, too, as among
the Hindoos, distinguished the Acquisitions of the
chief of the household from his Inherited property, and permitted him to deal with them under
much more liberal conditions. Classifications of
the other sort were also admitted, and the familiar
distinction drawn between land and moveables;
but moveable property was divided into several
subordinate categories, to each of which different
rules applied. This exuberance of classification,
which may strike us as strange in so rude a
people as the German conquerors of the Empire,
is doubtless to be explained by the presence in
their systems of a considerable element of Roman
law, absorbed by them during their long sojourn
on the confines of the Roman dominion. It is
not difficult to trace a great number of the rules
governing the transfer and devolution of the commodities which lay outside the *allod*, to their
source in Roman jurisprudence, from which they
were probably borrowed at widely distant epochs,
and in fragmentary importations. How far the
obstacles to the free circulation of property were
surmounted by such contrivances, we have not
the means even of conjecturing, for the distinctions adverted to have no modern history. As I
before explained, the allodial form of property
was entirely lost in the feudal, and when the consolidation of feudalism was once completed, there
was practically but one distinction left standing
of all those which had been known to the western

world—the distinction between land and goods, immoveables and moveables. Externally this distinction was the same with that which Roman law had finally accepted, but the law of the middle ages differed from that of Rome in distinctly considering immoveable property to be more dignified than moveable. Yet this one sample is enough to show the importance of the class of expedients to which it belongs. In all the countries governed by systems based on the French codes, that is, through much the greatest part of the Continent of Europe, the law of moveables, which was always Roman law, has superseded and annulled the feudal law of land. England is the only country of importance in which this transmutation, though it has gone some way, is not nearly accomplished. Our own, too, it may be added, is the only considerable European country in which the separation of moveables from immoveables has been somewhat disturbed by the same influences which caused the ancient classifications to depart from the only one which is countenanced by nature. In the main, the English distinction has been between land and goods; but a certain class of goods have gone as heir-looms with the land, and a certain description of interests in land have from historical causes been ranked with personalty. This is not the only instance in which English jurisprudence, standing apart from the main current of legal modification, has reproduced phenomena of archaic law.

I proceed to notice one or two more contrivances by which the ancient trammels of proprietary right were more or less successfully relaxed, premising that the scheme of this treatise only permits me to mention those which are of great antiquity. On one of them in particular it is necessary to dwell for a moment or two, because persons unacquainted with the early history of law will not be easily persuaded that a principle, of which modern jurisprudence has very slowly and with the greatest difficulty obtained the recognition, was really familiar to the very infancy of legal science. There is no principle in all law which the moderns, in spite of its beneficial character, have been so loath to adopt and to carry to its legitimate consequences as that which was known to the Romans as Usucapion, and which has descended to modern jurisprudence under the name of Prescription. It was a positive rule of the oldest Roman law, a rule older than the Twelve Tables, that commodities which had been uninterruptedly possessed for a certain period became the property of the possessor. The period of possession was exceedingly short—one or two years according to the nature of the commodities—and in historical times Usucapion was only allowed to operate when possession had commenced in a particular way; but I think it likely that at a less advanced epoch possession was converted into ownership under conditions even less severe than we read of in our authorities. As I have said before, I am far from asserting that the respect of men for *de facto* possession is a phenomenon which jurisprudence can account for by itself, but it is very necessary to remark that primitive societies, in adopting the principle of Usucapion, were not beset with any of the speculative doubts and hesitations which have impeded its reception among the moderns. Prescriptions were viewed by the modern lawyers, first with repugnance, afterwards with reluctant approval.

In several countries, including our own, legislation long declined to advance beyond the rude device of barring all actions based on a wrong which had been suffered earlier than a fixed point of time in the past, generally the first year of some preceding reign; nor was it till the middle ages had finally closed, and James the First had ascended the throne of England, that we obtained a true statute of limitation of a very imperfect kind. This tardiness in copying one of the most famous chapters of Roman law, which was no doubt constantly read by the majority of European lawyers, the modern world owes to the influence of the Canon Law. The ecclesiastical customs out of which the Canon Law grew, concerned as they were with sacred or quasi-sacred interests, very naturally regarded the privileges which they conferred as incapable of being lost through disuse however prolonged; and in accordance with this view, the spiritual jurisprudence, when afterwards consolidated, was distinguished by a marked leaning against Prescriptions. It was the fate of the Canon Law, when held up by the clerical lawyers as a pattern to secular legislation, to have a peculiar influence on first principles. It gave to the bodies of custom which were formed throughout Europe far fewer express rules than did the Roman law, but then it seems to have communicated a bias to professional opinion on a surprising number of fundamental points, and the tendencies thus produced progressively gained strength as each system was developed. One of the dispositions it produced was a disrelish for Prescriptions; but I do not know that this prejudice would have operated as powerfully as it has done, if it had not fallen in with

the doctrine of the scholastic jurists of the realist
sect, who taught that, whatever turn actual legislation might take, a *right*, how long soever neglected, was in point of fact indestructible. The
remains of this state of feeling still exist.
Wherever the philosophy of law is earnestly discussed, questions repecting the speculative basis
of Prescription are always hotly disputed; and it
is still a point of the greatest interest in France
and Germany, whether a person who has been
out of possession for a series of years is deprived
of his ownership as a penalty for his neglect, or
loses it through the summary interposition of
the law in its desire to have a *finis litium*. But
no such scruples troubled the mind of early
Roman society. Their ancient usages directly
took away the ownership of everybody who had
been out of possession, under certain circumstances, during one or two years. What was the
exact tenor of the rule of Usucapion in its earliest
shape, it is not easy to say; but, taken with the
limitations which we find attending it in the
books, it was a most useful security against the
mischiefs of a too cumbrous system of conveyance. In order to have the benefit of Usucapion,
it was necessary that the adverse possession
should have begun in good faith, that is, with
belief on the part of the possessor that he was
lawfully acquiring the property, and it was farther
required that the commodity should have been
transferred to him by some mode of alienation
which, however unequal to conferring a complete
title in the particular case, was at least recognised
by the law. In the case therefore of a Mancipation, however slovenly the performance might
have been, yet if it had been carried so far as to

involve a Tradition or Delivery, the vice of the title would be cured by Usucapion in two years at most. I know nothing in the practice of the Romans which testifies so strongly to their legal genius as the use which they made of Usucapion. The difficulties which beset them were nearly the same with those which embarrassed and still embarrass the lawyers of England. Owing to the complexity of their system, which as yet they had neither the courage nor the power to reconstruct, actual right was constantly getting divorced from technical right, the equitable ownership from the legal. But Usucapion, as manipulated by the jurisconsults, supplied a self-acting machinery, by which the defects of titles to property were always in course of being cured, and by which the ownerships that were temporarily separated were again rapidly cemented together with the briefest possible delay. Usucapion did not lose its advantages till the reforms of Justinian. But as soon as law and equity had been completely fused, and when Mancipation ceased to be the Roman conveyance, there was no further necessity for the ancient contrivance, and Usucapion, with its periods of time considerably lengthened, became the Prescription which has at length been adopted by nearly all systems of modern law.

I pass by with brief mention another expedient having the same object with the last, which, though it did not immediately make its appearance in English legal history, was of immemorial antiquity in Roman law; such indeed is its apparent age that some German civilians, not sufficiently aware of the light thrown on the subject by the analogies of English law, have thought it

even older than the Mancipation. I speak of the
Cessio in Jure, a collusive recovery, in a Court
of law, of property sought to be conveyed. The
plaintiff claimed the subject of this proceeding
with the ordinary forms of a litigation; the defendant made default; and the commodity was of
course adjudged to the plaintiff. I need scarcely
remind the English lawyer that this expedient
suggested itself to our forefathers, and produced
those famous Fines and Recoveries which did so
much to undo the harshest trammels of the feudal
land-law. The Roman and English contrivances
have very much in common and illustrate each
other most instructively, but there is this difference between them, that the object of the English lawyers was to remove complications already
introduced into the title, while the Roman jurisconsults sought to prevent them by substituting
a mode of transfer necessarily unimpeachable for
one which too often miscarried. The device is, in
fact, one which suggests itself as soon as Courts
of Law are in steady operation, but are nevertheless still under the empire of primitive notions. In
an advanced state of legal opinion, tribunals regard collusive litigation as an abuse of their procedure; but there has always been a time when,
if their forms were scrupulously complied with,
they never dreamed of looking further.

The influence of Courts of Law and of their
procedure upon Property has been most extensive,
but the subject is too large for the dimensions of
this treatise, and would carry us further down
the course of legal history than is consistent with
its scheme. It is desirable, however, to mention,
that to this influence we must attribute the importance of the distinction between Property and

Possession—not, indeed, the distinction itself,
which (in the language of an eminent English
civilian) is the same thing as the distinction
between the legal right to act upon a thing and
the physical power to do so—but the extraordinary
importance which the distinction has obtained in
the philosophy of law. Few educated persons are
so little versed in legal literature as not to have
heard that the language of the Roman jurscon-
sults on the subject of Possession long occasioned
the greatest possible perplexity, and that the
genius of Savigny is supposed to have chiefly
proved itself by the solution which he discovered
for the enigma. Possession, in fact, when employed by the Roman lawyers, appears to have
contracted a shade of meaning not easily
accounted for. The word, as appears from its
etymology, must have originally denoted physical
contact or physical contact resumeable at
pleasure; but, as actually used without any
qualifying epithet, it signifies not simply physical
detention, but physical detention coupled with
the intention to hold the thing detained as one's
own. Savigny, following Niebuhr, perceived that
for this anomaly there could only be a historical
origin. He pointed out that the Patrician
burghers of Rome, who had become tenants of the
greatest part of the public domain at nominal
rents, were, in the view of the old Roman law,
mere possessors, but then they were possessors
intending to keep their land against all comers.
They, in truth, put forward a claim almost identical with that which has recently been advanced
in England by the lessees of Church lands.
Admitting that in theory they were the tenants-
at-will of the state, they contended that time and

undisturbed enjoyment had ripened their holding into a species of ownership, and that it would be unjust to eject them for the purpose of redistributing the domain. The association of this claim with the Patrician tenancies, permanently influenced the sense of ' possession.' Meanwhile the only legal remedies of which the tenants could avail themselves, if ejected or threatened with disturbance, were the Possessory Interdicts, summary processes of Roman law which were either expressly devised by the Prætor for their protection, or else, according to another theory, had in older times been employed for the provisional maintenance of possessions pending the settlement of questions of legal right. It came, therefore, to be understood that everybody who possessed property *as his own* had the power of demanding the Interdicts, and, by a system of highly artificial pleading, the Interdictal process was moulded into a shape fitted for the trial of conflicting claims to a disputed possession. Then commenced a movement which, as Mr. John Austin pointed out, exactly reproduced itself in English law. Proprietors, *domini*, began to prefer the simpler forms or speedier course of the Interdict to the lagging and intricate formalities of the Real Action, and for the purpose of availing themselves of the possessory remedy fell back upon the possession which was supposed to be involved in their proprietorship. The liberty conceded to persons who were not true Possessors, but Owners, to vindicate their rights by possessory remedies, though it may have been at first a boon, had ultimately the effect of seriously deteriorating both English and Roman jurisprudence. The Roman law owes to it those subtleties on the subject of Possession which have done so much to discredit it, while English law, after the actions which it appropriated to the recovery of real property had fallen into the most hopeless confusion, got rid at last of the whole tangled mass by a heroic remedy. No one can doubt that the virtual abolition of the English real actions which took place nearly thirty years since was a public benefit, but still persons sensitive to the harmonies of jurisprudence will lament that, instead of cleansing, improving, and simplifying the true proprietary actions, we sacrificed them all to the possessory action of ejectment, thus basing our whole system of land recovery upon a legal fiction.

Legal tribunals have also powerfully assisted to shape and modify conceptions of proprietary right by means of the distinction between Law and Equity, which always makes its first appearance as a distinction between jurisdictions. Equitable property in England is simply property held under the jurisdiction of the Court of Chancery. At Rome, the Prætor's Edict introduced its novel principles in the guise of a promise that under certain circumstances a particular action or a particular plea would be granted; and, accordingly, the property *in bonis*, or Equitable Property, of Roman law was property exclusively protected by remedies which had their source in the Edict. The mechanism by which equitable rights were saved from being overridden by the claims of the legal owner was somewhat different in the two systems. With us their independence is secured by the Injunction of the Court of Chancery. Since however Law and Equity, while not as yet consolidated, were administered under the

Roman system by the same Court, nothing like the Injunction was required, and the Magistrate took the simpler course of refusing to grant to the Civil Law Owner those actions and pleas by which alone he could obtain the property that belonged in equity to another. But the practical operation of both systems was nearly the same. Both, by means of a distinction in procedure, were able to preserve new forms of property in a sort of provisional existence, until the time should come when they were recognized by the whole law. In this way, the Roman Prætor gave an immediate right of property to the person who had acquired a Res Mancipi by mere delivery, without waiting for the ripening of Usucapion. Similarly he in time recognized an ownership in the Mortgagee who had at first been a mere ' bailee ' or depositary, and in the Emphyteuta, or tenant of land which was subject to a fixed perpetual rent. Following a parallel line of progress, the English Court of Chancery created a special proprietorship for the Mortgagor, for the Cestui que Trust, for the Married Woman who had the advantage of a particular kind of settlement, and for the Purchaser who had not yet acquired a complete legal ownership. All these are examples in which forms of proprietary right, distinctly new, were recognized and preserved. But indirectly Property has been affected in a thousand ways by equity both in England and at Rome. Into whatever corner of jurisprudence its authors pushed the powerful instrument in their command, they were sure to meet, and touch, and more or less materially modify the law of property. When in the preceding pages I have spoken of certain ancient legal distinctions and expedients as having powerfully affected the history of ownership, I must be understood to mean that the greatest part of their influence has arisen from the hints and suggestions of improvement infused by them into the mental atmosphere which was breathed by the fabricators of equitable systems.

But to describe the influence of Equity on Ownership would be to write its history down to our own days. I have alluded to it principally because several esteemed contemporary writers have thought that in the Roman severance of Equitable from Legal property we have the clue to that difference in the conception of Ownership, which apparently distinguishes the law of the middle ages from the law of the Roman Empire. The leading characteristic of the feudal conception is its recognition of a double proprietorship, the superior ownership of the lord of the fief co-existing with the inferior property or estate of the tenant. Now, this duplication of proprietary right looks, it is urged, extremely like a generalized form of the Roman distribution of rights over property into *Quiritarian* or legal, and (to use a word of late origin) *Bonitarian* or equitable. Gaius himself observes upon the splitting of *dominion* into two parts as a singularity of Roman law, and expressly contrasts it with the entire or allodial ownership to which other nations were accustomed. Justinian, it is true, re-consolidated dominion into one, but then it was the partially reformed system of the Western Empire, and not Justinian's jurisprudence, with which the barbarians were in contact during so many centuries. While they remained poised on the edge of the Empire, it may well be that they learned this distinction, which afterwards bore remarkable fruit. In favour of this theory, it must at all events be admitted that the element of Roman law in the various bodies of barbarian custom has been very imperfectly examined. The erroneous or insufficient theories which have served to explain Feudalism resemble each other in their tendency to draw off attention from this particular ingredient in its texture. The older investigators, who have been mostly followed in this country, attached an exclusive importance to the circumstances of the turbulent period during which the Feudal system grew to maturity; and in later times a new source of error has been added to those already existing, in that pride of nationality which has led German writers to exaggerate the completeness of the social fabric which their forefathers had built up before their appearance in the Roman world. One or two English inquirers who looked in the right quarter for the foundations of the feudal system, failed nevertheless to conduct their investigations to any satisfactory result, either from searching too exclusively for analogies in the compilations of Justinian, or from confining their attention to the compendia of Roman law which are found appended to some of the extant barbarian codes. But, if Roman jurisprudence had any influence on the barbarous societies, it had probably produced the greatest part of its effects before the legislation of Justinian. and before the preparation of these compendia. It was not the reformed and purified jurisprudence of Justinian, but the undigested system which prevailed in the Western Empire, and which the Eastern *Corpus Juris* never succeeded in displacing, that I conceive to have clothed with flesh and muscle the scanty skeleton of barbarous usage. The change must be supposed to have taken place before the Germanic tribes had distinctly appropriated, as conquerors, any portion of the Roman dominions, and therefore long before Germanic monarchs had ordered breviaries of Roman law to be drawn up for the use of their Roman subjects. The necessity for some such hypothesis will be felt by everybody who can appreciate the difference between archaic and developed law. Rude as are the *Leges Barbarorum* which remain to us, they are not rude enough to satisfy the theory of their purely barbarous origin; nor have we any reason for believing that we have received, in written records, more than a fraction of the fixed rules which were practised among themselves by the members of the conquering tribes. If we can once persuade ourselves that a considerable element of debased Roman law already existed in the barbarian systems, we shall have done something to remove a grave difficulty. The German law of the conquerors and the Roman law of their subjects would not have combined if they had not possessed more affinity for each other than refined jurisprudence has usually for the customs of savages. It is extremely likely that the codes of the barbarians, archaic as they seem, are only a compound of true primitive usage with half-understood Roman rules, and that it was the foreign ingredient which enabled them to coalesce with a Roman jurisprudence that had already receded somewhat from the comparative finish which it had acquired under the Western Emperors.

But, though all this must be allowed, there are several considerations which render it unlikely that the feudal form of ownership was directly

suggested by the Roman duplication of domainial
rights. The distinction between legal and equitable property strikes one as a subtlety little likely
to be appreciated by barbarians; and, moreover,
it can scarcely be understood unless Courts of
Law are contemplated in regular operation. But
the strongest reason against this theory is the
existence in Roman Law of a form of property—a
creation of Equity, it is true—which supplies a
much simpler explanation of the transition from
one set of ideas to the other. This is the Emphyteusis, upon which the Fief of the middle ages
has often been fathered, though without much
knowledge of the exact share which it had in
bringing feudal ownership into the world. The
truth is that the Emphyteusis, not probably as
yet known by its Greek designation, marks one
stage in a current of ideas which led ultimately
to feudalism. The first mention in Roman history
of estates larger than could be farmed by a Pater-
familias, with his household of sons and slaves,
occurs when we come to the holdings of the
Roman patricians. These great proprietors appear
to have had no idea of any system of farming by
free tenants. Their *latifundia* seem to have been
universally cultivated by slave-gangs, under
bailiffs who were themselves slaves or freedmen;
and the only organization attempted appears to
have consisted in dividing the inferior slaves into
small bodies, and making them the *peculium* of
the better and trustier sort, who thus acquired
a kind of interest in the efficiency of their labour.
This system was, however, especially disadvan-
tageous to one class of estated proprietors, the
Municipalities.   Functionaries in Italy were
changed with the rapidity which often surprises

us in the administration of Rome herself; so that
the superintendence of a large landed domain by
an Italian corporation must have been excessively
imperfect. Accordingly, we are told that with
the municipalities began the practice of letting
out *agri vectigules*, that is, of leasing land for a
perpetuity to a free tenant, at a fixed rent, and
under certain conditions. The plan was afterwards extensively imitated by individual proprietors, and the tenant, whose relation to the
owner had originally been determined by his contract, was subsequently recognized by the Prætor
as having himself a qualified proprietorship, which
in time became known as an Emphyteusis. From
this point the history of tenure parts into two
branches. In the course of that long period
during which our records of the Roman Empire
are most incomplete, the slave-gangs of the great
Roman families became transformed into the
coloni, whose origin and situation constitute one
of the obscurest questions in all history. We
may suspect that they were formed partly by the
elevation of the slaves, and partly by the degradation of the free farmers; and that they prove the
richer classes of the Roman Empire to have
become aware of the increased value which landed
property obtains when the cultivator has an interest in the produce of the land. We know that
their servitude was predial; that it wanted many
of the characteristics of absolute slavery, and that
they acquitted their service to the landlord in
rendering to him a fixed portion of the annual
crop. We know further that they survived all
the mutations of society in the ancient and
modern worlds. Though included in the lower
courses of the feudal structure, they continued

in many countries to render to the landlord precisely the same dues which they had paid to the Roman *dominus*, and from a particular class among them, the *coloni medietarii* who reserved half the produce for the owner, are descended the *metayer* tenantry, who still conduct the cultivation of the soil in almost all the South of Europe. On the other hand, the Emphyteusis, if we may so interpret the allusions to it in the *Corpus Juris*, became a favourite and beneficial modification of property; and it may be conjectured that wherever free farmers existed, it was this tenure which regulated their interest in the land. The Prætor, as has been said, treated the Emphyteuta as a true proprietor When ejected, he was allowed to reinstate himself by a Real Action, the distinctive badge of proprietary right, and he was protected from disturbance by the author of his lease so long as the *canon*, or quit-rent, was punctually paid But at the same time it must not be supposed that the ownership of the author of the lease was either extinct or dormant. It was kept alive by a power of re-entry on non-payment of the rent, a right of pre-emption in case of sale, and a certain control over the mode of cultivation. We have, therefore, in the Emphyteusis a striking example of the double ownership which characterized feudal property, and one, moreover, which is much simpler and much more easily imitated than the juxtaposition of legal and equitable rights. The history of the Roman tenure does not end, however, at this point. We have clear evidence that between the great fortresses which, disposed along the line of the Rhine and Danube, long secured the frontier of the Empire against its barbarian neighbours,

there extended a succession of strips of land, the
agri limitrophi, which were occupied by veteran
soldiers of the Roman army on the terms of an
Emphyteusis. There was a double ownership.
The Roman State was landlord of the soil, but
the soldiers cultivated it without disturbance so
long as they held themselves ready to be called
out for military service whenever the state of the
border should require it. In fact, a sort of gar-
rison-duty, under a system closely resembling
that of the military colonies on the Austro-
Turkish border, had taken the place of the quit-
rent which was the service of the ordinary Emphyteuta. It seems impossible to doubt that this
was the precedent copied by the barbarian
monarchs who founded feudalism. It had been
within their view for some hundred years, and
many of the veterans who guarded the border
were, it is to be remembered, themselves of barbarian extraction, who probably spoke the Germanic tongues. Not only does the proximity of
so easily followed a model explain whence the
Frankish and Lombard Sovereigns got the idea of
securing the military service of their followers
by granting away portions of their public domain;
but it perhaps explains the tendency which immediately showed itself in the Benefices to become
hereditary, for an Emphyteusis, though capable of
being moulded to the terms of the original contract, nevertheless descended as a general rule
to the heirs of the grantee. It is true that the
holder of a benefice, and more recently the lord
of one of those fiefs into which the benefices were
transformed, appears to have owed certain services
which were not likely to have been rendered by
the military colonist, and were certainly not ren-

dered by the Emphyteuta. The duty of respect and gratitude to the feudal superior, the obligation to assist in endowing his daughter and equipping his son, the liability to his guardianship in minority, and many other similar incidents of tenure, must have been literally borrowed from the relations of Patron and Freedman under Roman law, that is, of quondam-master and quondam-slave. But then it is known that the earliest beneficiaries were the personal companions of the sovereign, and it is indisputable that this position, brilliant as it seems, was at first attended by some shade of servile debasement. The person who ministered to the Sovereign in his Court had given up something of that absolute personal freedom which was the proudest privilege of the allodial proprietor.

CHAPTER IX

THE EARLY HISTORY OF CONTRACT

THERE are few general propositions concerning the age to which we belong which seem at first sight likely to be received with readier concurrence than the assertion that the society of our day is mainly distinguished from that of preceding generations by the largeness of the sphere which is occupied in it by Contract. Some of the phenomena on which this proposition rests are among those most frequently singled out for notice, for comment, and for eulogy. Not many of us are so unobservant as not to perceive that in innumerable cases where old law fixed a man's

social position irreversibly at his birth, modern
law allows him to create it for himself by convention; and indeed several of the few exceptions
which remain to this rule are constantly de-
nounced with passionate indignation. The point,
for instance, which is really debated in the vigorous controversy still carried on upon the subject
of negro servitude, is whether the status of the
slave does not belong to bygone institutions, and
whether the only relation between employer and
labourer which commends itself to modern
morality be not a relation determined exclusively
by contract. The recognition of this difference
between past ages and the present enters into the
very essence of the most famous contemporary
speculations. It is certain that the science of
Political Economy, the only department of moral
inquiry which has made any considerable progress
in our day, would fail to correspond with the
facts of life if it were not true that Imperative
Law had abandoned the largest part of the field
which it once occupied, and had left men to
settle rules of conduct for themselves with a
liberty never allowed to them till recently. The
bias indeed of most persons trained in political
economy is to consider the general truth on which
their science reposes as entitled to become universal, and, when they apply it as an art, their
efforts are ordinarily directed to enlarging the
province of Contract and to curtailing that of
Imperative Law, except so far as law is necessary
to enforce the performance of Contracts. The
impulse given by thinkers who are under the influence of these ideas is beginning to be very
strongly felt in the Western world. Legislation
has nearly confessed its inability to keep pace

with the activity of man in discovery, in invention, and in the manipulation of accumulated
wealth; and the law even of the least advanced
communities tends more and more to become a
mere surface-stratum having under it an ever-
changing assemblage of contractual rules with
which it rarely interferes except to compel compliance with a few fundamental principles or unless it be called in to punish the violation of good
faith.

Social inquiries, so far as they depend on the
consideration of legal phenomena, are in so backward a condition that we need not be surprised at
not finding these truths recognised in the commonplaces which pass current concerning the
progress of society. These commonplaces answer
much more to our prejudices than to our con-
victions. The strong disinclination of most men
to regard morality as advancing seems to be
especially powerful when the virtues on which
Contract depends are in question, and many of
us have an almost instinctive reluctance to admitting that good faith and trust in our fellows
are more widely diffused than of old, or that
there is anything in contemporary manners
which parallels the loyalty of the antique world.
From time to time, these prepossessions are
greatly strengthened by the spectacle of frauds,
unheard of before the period at which they were
observed, and astonishing from their complication
as well as shocking from criminality. But the
very character of these frauds shows clearly that,
before they became possible, the moral obligations of which they are the breach must have
been more than proportionately developed. It
is the confidence reposed and deserved by the

many which affords facilities for the bad faith of
the few, so that, if colossal examples of dishonesty occur, there is no surer conclusion than
that scrupulous honesty is displayed in the
average of the transactions which, in the particular case, have supplied the delinquent with his
opportunity. If we insist on reading the history
of morality as reflected in jurisprudence, by turning our eyes not on the law of Contract but on
the law of Crime, we must be careful that we
read it aright. The only form of dishonesty
treated of in the most ancient Roman law is
Theft. At the moment at which I write, the
newest chapter in the English criminal law is one
which attempts to prescribe punishment for the
frauds of Trustees. The proper inference from
this contrast is not that the primitive Romans
practised a higher morality than ourselves. We
should rather say that, in the interval between
their days and ours, morality has advanced from
a very rude to a highly refined conception—from
viewing the rights of property as exclusively
sacred, to looking upon the rights growing out of
the mere unilateral reposal of confidence as entitled to the protection of the penal law.

The definite theories of jurists are scarcely
nearer the truth in this point than the opinions
of the multitude. To begin with the views of the
Roman lawyers, we find them inconsistent with
the true history of moral and legal progress. One
class of contracts, in which the plighted faith of
the contracting parties was the only material ingredient, they specifically denominated Contracts
juris gentium, and though these contracts were
undoubtedly the latest born into the Roman
system, the expression employed implies, if a

definite meaning be extracted from it, that they
were more ancient than certain other forms of
engagement treated of in Roman law, in which
the neglect of a mere technical formality was as
fatal to the obligation as misunderstanding or
deceit. But then the antiquity to which they were
referred was vague, shadowy, and only capable
of being understood through the Present; nor
was it until the language of the Roman lawyers
became the language of an age which had lost
the key to their mode of thought that a ' Contract of the Law of Nations ' came to be distinctly looked upon as a Contract known to man
in a State of Nature. Rousseau adopted both the
juridical and the popular error. In the Disserta-
tion on the effects of Art and Science upon
Morals, the first of his works which attracted
attention and the one in which he states most
unreservedly the opinions which made him the
founder of a sect, the veracity and good faith
attributed to the ancient Persians are repeatedly
pointed out as traits of primitive innocence which
have been gradually obliterated by civilization;
and at a later period he found a basis for all his
speculations in the doctrine of an original Social
Contract. The Social Contract or Compact is the
most systematic form which has ever been
assumed by the error we are discussing. It is a
theory which, though nursed into importance by
political passions, derived all its sap from the
speculations of lawyers. True it certainly is that
the famous Englishmen, for whom it had first
had attraction, valued it chiefly for its political
serviceableness, but, as I shall presently attempt
to explain, they would never have arived at it, if
politicians had not long conducted their contro-

versies in legal phraseology. Nor were the English authors of the theory blind to that speculative amplitude which recommended it so strongly to the Frenchmen who inherited it from them. Their writings show they perceived that it could be made to account for all social, quite as well as for all political, phenomena. They had observed the fact, already striking in their day, that of the positive rules obeyed by men, the greater part were created by Contract, the lesser by Imperative Law. But they were ignorant or careless of the historical relation of these two constituents of jurisprudence. It was for the purpose, therefore, of gratifying their speculative tastes by attributing all jurisprudence to a uniform source, as much as with the view of eluding the doctrines which claimed a divine parentage for Imperative Law, that they devised the theory that all Law had its origin in Contract. In another stage of thought, they would have been satisfied to leave their theory in the condition of an ingenious hypothesis or a convenient verbal formula. But that age was under the dominion of legal superstitions. The State of Nature had been talked about till it had ceased to be regarded as paradoxical, and hence it seemed easy to give a fallacious reality and definiteness to the contractual origin of Law by insisting on the Social Compact as a historical fact.

Our own generation has got rid of these erroneous juridical theories, partly by outgrowing the intellectual state to which they belong, and partly by almost ceasing to theorize on such subjects altogether. The favourite occupation of active minds at the present moment, and the

one which answers to the speculations of our
forefathers on the origin of the social state, is
the analysis of society as it exists and moves
before our eyes; but, through omitting to call
in the assistance of history, this analysis too
often degenerates into an idle exercise of
curiosity, and is especially apt to incapacitate
the inquirer for comprehending states of society
which differ considerably from that to which he
is accustomed. The mistake of judging the men
of other periods by the morality of our own day
has its parallel in the mistake of supposing that
every wheel and bolt in the modern social
machine had its counterpart in more rudimentary
societies. Such impressions ramify very widely,
and masque themselves very subtly, in historical
works written in the modern fashion; but I find
the trace of their presence in the domain of
jurisprudence in the praise which is frequently
bestowed on the little apologue of Montesquieu
concerning the Troglodytes, inserted in the *Lettres
Persanes*. The Troglodytes were a people who
systematically violated their Contracts, and so
perished utterly. If the story bears the moral
which its author intended, and is employed to
expose an anti-social heresy by which this century and the last have been threatened, it is
most unexceptionable; but if the inference be
obtained from it that society could not possibly
hold together without attaching a sacredness to
promises and agreements which should be on
something like a par with the respect that is
paid to them by a mature civilisation, it involves
an error so grave as to be fatal to all sound
understanding of legal history. The fact is that
the Troglodytes have flourished and founded

powerful states with very small attention to the obligations of Contract. The point which before all others has to be apprehended in the constitution of primitive societies is that the individual creates for himself few or no rights, and few or no duties. The rules which he obeys are derived first from the station into which he is born, and next from the imperative commands addressed to him by the chief of the household of which he forms part. Such a system leaves the very smallest room for Contract. The members of the same family (for so we may interpret the evidence) are wholly incapable of contracting with each other, and the family is entitled to disregard the engagements by which any one of its subordinate members has attempted to bind it. Family, it is true, may contract with family, chieftain with chieftain, but the transaction is one of the same nature, and encumbered by as many formalities, as the alienation of property, and the disregard of one iota of the performance is fatal to the obligation. The positive duty resulting from one man's reliance on the word of another is among the slowest conquests of advancing civilization.

Neither Ancient Law nor any other source of evidence discloses to us society entirely destitute of the conception of Contract. But the conception, when it first shows itself, is obviously rudimentary. No trustworthy primitive record can be read without perceiving that the habit of mind which induces us to make good a promise is as yet imperfectly developed, and that acts of flagrant perfidy are often mentioned without blame and sometimes described with approbation. In the Homeric literature, for instance, the deceitful cunning of Ulysses appears as a virtue of the same rank with the prudence of Nestor, the constancy of Hector, and the gallantry of Achilles. Ancient law is still more suggestive of the distance which separates the crude form of Contract from its maturity. At first, nothing is seen like the interposition of law to compel the performance of a promise. That which the law arms with its sanctions is not a promise, but a promise accompanied with a solemn ceremonial. Not only are formalities of equal importance with the promise itself, but they are, if anything, of greater importance; for that delicate analysis which mature jurisprudence applies to the conditions of mind under which a particular verbal assent is given appears, in ancient law, to be transferred to the words and gestures of the accompanying performance. No pledge is enforced if a single form be omitted or misplaced, but, on the other hand, if the forms can be shown to have been accurately proceeded with, it is of no avail to plead that the promise was made under duress or deception. The transmutation of this ancient view into the familiar notion of a Contract is plainly seen in the history of jurisprudence. First one or two steps in the ceremonial are dispensed with; then the others are simplified or permitted to be neglected on certain conditions; lastly, a few specific contracts are separated from the rest and allowed to be entered into without form, the selected contracts being those on which the activity and energy of social intercourse depends. Slowly, but most distinctly, the mental engagement isolates itself amid the technicalities, and gradually becomes the sole ingredient on which the interest of the jurisconsult is concentrated. Such a mental engagement, signified through external acts, the Romans called a Pact or Convention; and when the Convention has once been conceived as the nucleus of a Contract, it soon becomes the tendency of advancing jurisprudence to break away the external shell of form and ceremony. Forms are thenceforward only retained so far as they are guarantees of authenticity, and securities for caution and deliberation. The idea of a Contract is fully developed, or, to employ the Roman phrase, Contracts are absorbed in Pacts.

The history of this course of change in Roman law is exceedingly instructive. At the earliest dawn of the jurisprudence, the term in use for a Contract was one which is very familiar to the students of historical Latinity. It was *nexum*, and the parties to the contract were said to be *nexi*, expressions which must be carefully attended to on account of the singular durableness of the metaphor on which they are founded. The notion that persons under a contractual engagement are connected together by a strong *bond* or *chain*, continued till the last to influence the Roman jurisprudence of Contract; and flowing thence it has mixed itself with modern ideas. What then was involved in this nexum or bond? A definition which has descended to us from one of the Latin antiquarians describes *nexum* as *omne quod geritur per æs et libram*, ' every transaction with the copper and the balance ', and these words have occasioned a good deal of perplexity. The copper and the balance are the well-known accompaniments of the Mancipation, the ancient solemnity described in a former chapter, by which the right of ownership in the highest form of

Roman Property was transferred from one person
to another. Mancipation was a *conveyance*, and
hence has arisen the difficulty, for the definition
thus cited appears to confound Contracts and Conveyances, which in the philosophy of jurisprudence are not simply kept apart, but are actually
opposed to each other. The *jus in re*, right *in
rem*, right ' availing against all the world ', or
Proprietary Right, is sharply distinguished by the
analyst of mature jurisprudence from the *jus ad
rem*, right *in personam*, right ' availing a single
individual or group ', or Obligation. Now Conveyances transfer Proprietary Rights, Contracts
create Obligations—how then can the two be included under the same name or same general
conception? This, like many similar embarrass-
ments, has been occasioned by the error of ascrib-
ing to the mental condition of an unformed society
a faculty which pre-eminently belongs to an
advanced stage of intellectual development, the
faculty of distinguishing in speculation ideas
which are blended in practice. We have indications not to be mistaken of a state of social
affairs in which Conveyances and Contracts were
practically confounded; nor did the discrepance
of the conceptions become perceptible till men
had begun to adopt a distinct practice in contracting and conveying.

It may here be observed that we know enough
of ancient Roman law to give some idea of the
mode of transformation followed by legal conceptions and by legal phraseology in the infancy
of Jurisprudence. The change which they under-
go appears to be a change from general to special;
or, as we might otherwise express it, the ancient
conceptions and the ancient terms are subjected

to a process of gradual specialization. An ancient
legal conception corresponds not to one but to
several modern conceptions. An ancient technical expression serves to indicate a variety of
things which in modern law have separate names
allotted to them. If however we take up the
history of Jurisprudence at the next stage, we
find that the subordinate conceptions have
gradually disengaged themselves and that the old
general names are giving way to special appella-
tions. The old general conception is not obliterated, but it has ceased to cover more than one or
a few of the notions which it first included. So
too the old technical name remains, but it dis-
charges only one of the functions which it once
performed. We may exemplify this phenomenon
in various ways. Patriarchal Power of all sorts
appears, for instance, to have been once conceived as identical in character, and it was doubtless distinguished by one name. The Power
exercised by the ancestor was the same whether
it was exercised over the family or the material
property—over flocks, herds, slaves, children, or
wife. We cannot be absolutely certain of its old
Roman name, but there is very strong reason for
believing, from the number of expressions indica-
ting shades of the notion of *power* into which the
word *manus* enters, that the ancient general term
was *manus*. But, when Roman law has advanced
a little, both the name and the idea have become
specialised. Power is discriminated, both in word
and in conception, according to the object over
which it is exerted. Exercised over material
commodities or slaves, it has become *dominium*—
over children, it is *Potestas*—over free persons
whose services have been made away to another

by their own ancestor, it is *mancipium*—over a
wife, it is still *manus*. The old word, it will be
perceived, has not altogether fallen into desue-
tude, but is confined to one very special exercise
of the authority it had formerly denoted. This
example will enable us to comprehend the nature
of the historical alliance between Contracts and
Conveyances. There seems to have been one
solemn ceremonial at first for all solemn transactions, and its name at Rome appears to have
been *nexum*. Precisely the same forms which
were in use when a conveyance of property was
effected seem to have been employed in the
making of a contract. But we have not very
far to move onwards before we come to a period
at which the notion of a Contract has disengaged
itself from the notion of a Conveyance. A
double change has thus taken place. The transaction ' with the copper and the balance ', when
intended to have for its office the transfer of
property, is known by the new and special name
of Mancipation. The ancient Nexum still de-
signates the same ceremony, but only when it is
employed for the special purpose of solemnizing
a contract.

When two or three legal conceptions are spoken
of as anciently blended in one, it is not intended
to imply that some one of the included notions
may not be older than the others, or, when those
others have been formed, may not greatly pre-
dominate over and take precedence over them.
The reason why one legal conception continues
so long to cover several conceptions, and one
technical phrase to do instead of several, is doubtless that practical changes are accomplished in
the law of primitive societies long before men

see occasion to notice or name them. Though I have said that Patriarchal Power was not at first distinguished according to the objects over which it was exercised, I feel sure that Power over Children was the root of the old conception of Power; and I cannot doubt that the earliest use of the Nexum, and the one primarily regarded by those who resorted to it, was to give proper solemnity to the alienation of property. It is likely that a very slight perversion of the Nexum from its original functions first gave rise to its employment in Contracts, and that the very slightness of the change long prevented its being appreciated or noticed. The old name remained because men had not become conscious that they wanted a new one; the old notion clung to the mind because nobody had seen reason to be at the pains of examining it. We have had the process clearly exemplified in the history of Testaments. A Will was at first a simple conveyance of property. It was only the enormous practical difference that gradually showed itself between this particular conveyance and all others which caused it to be regarded separately, and even as it was, centuries elapsed before the ameliorators of law cleared away the useless encumbrance of the nominal mancipation, and consented to care for nothing in the Will but the expressed intentions of the Testator. It is unfortunate that we cannot track the early history of Contracts with the same absolute confidence as the early history of Wills, but we are not quite without hints that contracts first showed themselves through the *nexum* being put to a new use and afterwards obtained recognition as distinct transactions through the important practical consequences of the experiment. There is some, but not very violent, conjecture in the following delineation of the process. Let us conceive a sale for ready money as the normal type of the Nexum. The seller brought the property of which he intended to dispose—a slave, for example—the purchaser atended with the rough ingots of copper which served for money—and an indispensable assist-ant, the *libripens*, presented himself with a pair of scales. The slave with certain fixed formalities was handed over to the vendee—the copper was weighed by the *libripens* and passed to the vendor. So long as the business lasted it was a *nexum*, and the parties were *nexi;* but the moment it was completed, the *nexum* ended, and the vendor and purchaser ceased to bear the name derived from their momentary relation. But now, let us move a step onward in commercial history. Suppose the slave transferred, but the money not paid. In *that* case, the *nexum* is finished, so far as the seller is concerned, and when he has once handed over his property, he is no longer *nexus;* but, in regard to the purchaser, the *nexum* continues. The transaction, as to his part of it, is incomplete, and he is still considered to be *nexus*. It follows, therefore, that the same term described the Conveyance by which the right of property was transmitted, and the personal obligation of the debtor for the unpaid purchase-money. We may still go forward, and picture to ourselves a proceeding wholly formal, in which *nothing* is handed over and *nothing* paid; we are brought at once to a transaction indicative of much higher commercial activity, an *executory Contract of Sale*.

If it be true that, both in the popular and in

the professional view, a *Contract* was long regarded as an *incomplete Conveyance*, the truth
has importance for many reasons. The speculations of the last century concerning mankind in
a state of nature, are not unfairly summed up in
the doctrine that ' in the primitive society property was nothing, and obligation everything; '
and it will now be seen that, if the proposition
were reversed, it would be nearer the reality.
On the other hand, considered historically, the
primitive association of Conveyances and Contracts explains something which often strikes the
scholar and jurist as singularly enigmatical, I
mean the extraordinary and uniform severity of
very ancient systems of law to *debtors*, and the
extravagant powers which they lodge with
creditors. When once we understand that the
nexum was artificially prolonged to give time to
the debtor, we can better comprehend his
position in the eye of the public and of the law.
His indebtedness was doubtless regarded as an
anomaly, and suspense of payment in general
as an artifice and a distortion of strict rule. The
person who had duly consummated his part in
the transaction must, on the contrary, have
stood in peculiar favour; and nothing would
seem more natural than to arm him with
stringent facilities for enforcing the completion
of a proceeding which, of strict right, ought
never to have been extended or deferred.

Nexum, therefore, which originally signified a
Conveyance of property, came insensibly to
denote a Contract also, and ultimately so constant became the association between this word
and the notion of a Contract, that a special term,
Mancipium or Mancipatio, had to be used for

the purpose of designating the true nexum or transaction in which the property was really transferred. Contracts are therefore now severed from Conveyances, and the first stage in their history is accomplished, but still they are far enough from that epoch of their development when the promise of the contractor has a higher sacredness than the formalities with which it is coupled. In attempting to indicate the character of the changes passed through in this interval, it is necessary to trespass a little on a subject which lies properly beyond the range of these pages, the analysis of Agreement effected by the Roman jurisconsults. Of this analysis, the most beautiful monument of their sagacity, I need not say more than that it is based on the theoretical separation of the Obligation from the Convention or Pact. Bentham and Mr. Austin have laid down that the ' two main essentials of a contract are these : first, a signification by the promising party of his *intention* to do the acts or to observe the forbearances which he promises to do or to observe. Secondly, a signification by the promisee that he *expects* the promising party will fulfil the proffered promise.' This is virtually identical with the doctrine of the Roman lawyers, but then, in their view, the result of these ' significations ' was not a Contract, but a Convention or Pact. A Pact was the utmost product of the engagements of individuals agreeing among themselves, and it distinctly fell short of a Contract. Whether it ultimately became a Contract depended on the question whether the law annexed an Obligation to it. A Contract was a Pact (or Convention) *plus* an Obligation. So long as the Pact remained unclothed with the Obligation, it was called *nude* or *naked*.

What was an Obligation? It is defined by the Roman lawyers as ' Juris vinculum, quo necessitate adstringimur alicujus solvendæ rei '. This definition connects the Obligation with the Nexum through the common metaphor on which they are founded, and shows us with much clearness the pedigree of a peculiar conception. The Obligation is the ' bond ' or ' chain ' with which the law joins together persons or groups of persons, in consequence of certain voluntary acts. The acts which have the effect of attracting an Obligation are chiefly those classed under the heads of Contract and Delict, of Agreement and Wrong; but a variety of other acts have a similar consequence which are not capable of being comprised in an exact classification. It is to be remarked, however, that the act does not draw to itself the Obligation in consequence of any moral necessity; it is the law which annexes it in the plenitude of its power, a point the more necessary to be noted, because a different doctrine has sometimes been propounded by modern interpreters of the Civil Law who had moral or metaphysical theories of their own to support. The image of a *vinculum juris* colours and pervades every part of the Roman law of Contract and Delict. The law bound the parties together, and the *chain* could only be undone by the process called *solutio*, an expression still figurative, to which our word ' payment ' is only occasionally and incidentally equivalent. The consistency with which the figurative image was allowed to present itself, explains an otherwise puzzling peculiarity of Roman legal phraseology, the fact that ' Obligation ' signified rights as well as duties, the right, for example, to have a debt paid as well as the duty of paying it. The Romans kept in fact the entire picture of the ' legal chain ' before their eyes, and regarded one end of it no more and no less than the other.

In the developed Roman law, the Convention, as soon as it was completed, was, in almost all cases, at once crowned with the Obligation, and so became a Contract; and this was the result to which contract-law was surely tending. But for the purpose of this inquiry, we must attend particularly to the intermediate stage—that in which something more than a perfect agreement was required to attract the Obligation. This epoch is synchronous with the period at which the famous Roman classification of Contracts into four sorts— the Verbal, the Literal, the Real, and the Consensual—had come into use, and during which these four orders of Contracts constituted the only descriptions of engagement which the law would enforce. The meaning of the fourfold distribution is readily understood as soon as we apprehend the theory which severed the Obligation from the Convention. Each class of contracts was in fact named from certain formalities which were required over and above the mere agreement of the contracting parties. In the Verbal Contract, as soon as the Convention was effected, a form of words had to be gone through before the vinculum juris was attached to it. In the Literal Contract, an entry in a ledger or table-book had the effect of clothing the Convention with the Obligation, and the same result followed, in the case of the Real Contract, from the delivery of the Res or Thing which was the subject of the preliminary engagement. The contracting parties came, in short, to an understanding in each case; but, if they went no further, they were not *obliged* to one another, and could not compel performance or ask redress for a breach of faith. But let them comply with certain prescribed formalities, and the Contract was immediately complete, taking its name from the particular form which it had suited them to adopt. The exceptions to this practice will be noticed presently.

I have enumerated the four Contracts in their historical order, which order, however, the Roman Institutional writers did not invariably follow. There can be no doubt that the Verbal Contract was the most ancient of the four, and that it is the eldest known descendant of the primitive Nexum. Several species of Verbal Contract were anciently in use, but the most important of all, and the only one treated of by our authorities, was effected by means of a *stipulation*, that is, a Question and Answer; a question addressed by the person who exacted the promise, and an answer given by the person who made it. This question and answer constituted the additional ingredient which, as I have just explained, was demanded by the primitive notion over and above the mere agreement of the persons interested. They formed the agency by which the Obligation was annexed. The old Nexum has now bequeathed to maturer jurisprudence first of all the conception of a chain uniting the contracting parties, and this has become the Obligation. It has further transmitted the notion of a ceremonial accompanying and consecrating the engagement, and this ceremonial has been trans-

muted into the Stipulation. The conversion of
the solemn conveyance, which was the prominent
feature of the original Nexum, into a mere question and answer, would be more of a mystery
than it is if we had not the analogous history of
Roman Testaments to enlighten us. Looking to
that history, we can understand how the formal
Conveyance was first separated from the part of
the proceeding which had immediate reference
to the business in hand, and how afterwards it
was omitted altogether. As then the question
and answer of the Stipulation were unquestionably the Nexum in a simplified shape, we are
prepared to find that they long partook of the
nature of a technical form. It would be a mistake
to consider them as exclusively recommending
themselves to the older Roman lawyers through
their usefulness in furnishing persons meditating
an agreement with an opportunity for consideration and reflection. It is not to be disputed that
they had a value of this kind, which was gradually
recognized; but there is proof that their function
in respect to Contracts was at first formal and
ceremonial in the statement of our authorities,
that not every question and answer was of old
sufficient to constitute a Stipulation, but only a
question and answer couched in technical
phraseology specially appropriated to the particular occasion.

But although it is essential for the proper
appreciation of the history of contract-law that the
Stipulation should be understood to have been
looked upon as a solemn form before it was recognized as a useful security, it would be wrong on
the other hand to shut our eyes to its real usefulness. The Verbal Contract, though it had lost

much of its ancient importance, survived to the
latest period of Roman jurisprudence; and we
may take it for granted that no institution of
Roman law had so extended a longevity unless it
served some practical advantage. I observe in an
English writer some expressions of surprise that
the Romans even of the earliest times were con-
tent with so meagre a protection against haste and
irreflection. But on examining the Stipulation
closely, and remembering that we have to do with
a state of society in which written evidence was
not easily procurable, I think we must admit that
this Question and Answer, had it been expressly
devised to answer the purpose which it served,
would have been justly designated a highly ingenious expedient. It was the *promisee* who, in
the character of stipulator, put all the terms of
the contract into the form of a question, and the
answer was given by the *promisor*. ' Do you
promise that you will deliver me such and such a
slave, at such and such a place, on such and
such a day? ' ' I do promise.' Now, if we
reflect for a moment, we shall see that this obligation to put the promise interrogatively inverts the
natural position of the parties, and, by effectually
breaking the tenor of the conversation, prevents
the attention from gliding over a dangerous
pledge. With us, a verbal promise is, generally
speaking, to be gathered exclusively from the
words of the promisor. In an old Roman law,
another step was absolutely required; it was
necessary for the promisee, after the agreement
had been made, to sum up all its terms in a
solemn interrogation; and it was of this interrogation, of course, and of the assent to it, that proof
had to be given at the trial—*not* of the promise,

which was not in itself binding. How great a difference this seemingly insignificant peculiarity may make in the phraseology of contract-law is speedily realised by the beginner in Roman jurisprudence, one of whose first stumbling-blocks is almost universally created by it. When we in English have occasion, in mentioning a contract, to connect it for convenience' sake with one of the parties—for example, if we wished to speak generally of a contractor—it is always the promis*or* at whom our words are pointing. But the general language of Roman law takes a different turn; it always regards the contract, if we may so speak, from the point of view of the promis*ee;* in speaking of a party to a contract, it is always the Stipulator, the person who asks the question, who is primarily alluded to. But the serviceableness of the stipulation is most vividly illustrated by referring to the actual examples in the pages of the Latin comic dramatists. If the entire scenes are read down in which these passages occur (*e.g.* Plautus, *Pseudolus*, Act I, sc. 1; Act IV, sc. 6; *Trinummus*, Act V, sc. 2), it will be perceived how effectually the attention of the person meditating the promise must have been arrested by the question, and how ample was the opportunity for withdrawal from an improvident undertaking.

In the Literal or Written Contract, the formal act, by which an Obligation was superinduced on the Convention, was an entry of the sum due, where it could be specifically ascertained, on the debit side of a ledger. The explanation of this Contract turns on a point of Roman domestic manners, the systematic character and exceeding regularity of book-keeping in ancient times.

There are several minor difficulties of old
Roman law, as, for example, the nature of the.
Slave's Peculium, which are only cleared up when
we recollect that a Roman household consisted
of a number of persons strictly accountable to its
head, and that every single item of domestic
receipt and expenditure, after being entered in
waste books, was transferred at stated periods to
a general household ledger. There are some
obscurities, however, in the descriptions we have
received of the Literal Contract, the fact being
that the habit of keeping books ceased to be
universal in later times, and the expression
' Literal Contract ' came to signify a form of
engagement entirely different from that originally
understood. We are not, therefore, in a position
to say, with respect to the primitive Literal Contract, whether the obligation was created by a
simple entry on the part of the creditor, or
whether the consent of the debtor or a corresponding entry in his own books was necessary
to give it legal effect. The essential point is
however established that, in the case of this Contract, all formalities were dispensed with on a
condition being complied with. This is another
step downwards in the history of contract-law.

The Contract which stands next in historical
succession, the Real Contract, shows a great
advance in ethical conceptions. Whenever any
agreement had for its object the delivery of a
specific thing—and this is the case with the large
majority of simple engagements—the Obligation
was drawn down as soon as the delivery had
actually taken place. Such a result must have
involved a serious innovation on the oldest ideas
of Contract; for doubtless, in the primitive times,

when a contracting party had neglected to clothe his agreement in a stipulation, nothing done in pursuance of the agreement would be recognised by the law. A person who had paid over money on loan would be unable to sue for its repayment unless he had formally *stipulated* for it. But, in the Real Contract, performance on one side is allowed to impose a legal duty on the other— evidently on ethical grounds. For the first time then moral considerations appear as an ingredient in Contract-law, and the Real Contract differs from its two predecessors in being founded on these, rather than on respect for technical forms or on deference to Roman domestic habits.

We now reach the fourth class, or Consensual Contracts, the most interesting and important of all. Four specified Contracts were distinguished by this name : Mandatum, *i.e.* Commission or Agency; Societas or Partnership; Emtio Venditio or Sale; and Locatio Conductio or Letting and Hiring. A few pages ago, after stating that a Contract consisted of a Pact or Convention to which an Obligation had been superadded, I spoke of certain acts or formalities by which the law permitted the Obligation to be attracted to the Pact. I used this language on account of the advantage of a general expression, but it is not strictly correct unless it be understood to include the negative as well as the positive. For, in truth, the peculiarity of these Consensual Contracts is that *no* formalities are required to create them out of the Pact. Much that is indefensible, and much more that is obscure, has been written about the Consensual Contracts, and it has even been asserted that in them the *consent* of the Parties is more emphatically given than in any other species of agreement. But the term Consensual merely indicates that the Obligation is here annexed at once to the *Consensus*. The Consensus, or mutual assent of the parties, is the final and crowning ingredient in the Convention, and it is the special characteristic of agreements falling under one of the four heads of Sale, Partnership, Agency, and Hiring, that, as soon as the assent of the parties has supplied this ingredient, there is *at once* a Contract. The Consensus draws with it the Obligation, performing, in transactions of the sort specified, the exact functions which are discharged, in the other contracts, by the *Res* or Thing, by the *Verba* stipulationis, and by the *Literæ* or written entry in a ledger. Consensual is therefore a term which does not involve the slightest anomaly, but is exactly analogous to Real, Verbal, and Literal.

In the intercourse of life the commonest and most important of all the contracts are unquestionably the four styled Consensual. The larger part of the collective existence of every community is consumed in transactions of buying and selling, of letting and hiring, of alliances between men for purposes of business, of delegation of business from one man to another; and this is no doubt the consideration which led the Romans, as it has led most societies, to relieve these transactions from technical incumbrance, to abstain as much as possible from clogging the most efficient springs of social movement. Such motives were not of course confined to Rome, and the commerce of the Romans with their neighbours must have given them abundant opportunities for observing that the contracts before us tended everywhere to become *Consensual*, obligatory on the mere signification of mutual assent. Hence, following their usual practice, they distinguished these contracts as contracts *Juris Gentium*. Yet I do not think that they were so named at a very early period. The first notions of a Jus Gentium may have been deposited in the minds of the Roman lawyers long before the appointment of a Prætor Peregrinus, but it would only be through extensive and regular trade that they would be familiarized with the contractual system of other Italian communities, and such a trade would scarcely attain considerable proportions before Italy had been thoroughly pacified, and the supremacy of Rome conclusively assured. Although, however, there is strong probability that the Consensual Contracts were the latest-born into the Roman system, and though it is likely that the qualification, *Juris Gentium*, stamps the recency of their origin, yet this very expression, which attributes them to the ' Law of Nations ', has in modern times produced the notion of their extreme antiquity. For, when the ' Law of Nations ' had been converted into the ' Law of Nature ', it seemed to be implied that the Consensual Contracts were the type of the agreements most congenial to the natural state; and hence arose the singular belief that the younger the civilization, the simpler must be its forms of contract.

The Consensual Contracts, it will be observed, were extremely limited in number. But it cannot be doubted that they constituted the stage in the history of Contract-law from which all modern conceptions of contract took their start. The motion of the will which constitutes agreement was now completely insulated, and became the subject of separate contemplation; forms were entirely eliminated from the notion of contract, and external acts were only regarded as symbols of the internal act of volition. The Consensual Contracts had, moreover, been classed in the Jus Gentium, and it was not long before this classification drew with it the inference that they were the species of agreement which represented the engagements approved of by Nature and included in her code. This point once reached, we are prepared for several celebrated doctrines and distinctions of the Roman lawyers. One of them is the distinction between Natural and Civil Obligations. When a person of full intellectual maturity had deliberately bound hmself by an engagement, he was said to be under a *natural obligation*, even though he had omitted some necessary formality, and even though through some technical impediment he was devoid of the formal capacity for making a valid contract. The law (and this is what the distinction implies) would not enforce the obligation, but it did not absolutely refuse to recognize it; and *natural obligations* differed in many respects from obligations which were merely null and void, more particularly in the circumstance that they could be civilly confirmed, if the capacity for contract were subsequently acquired. Another very peculiar doctrine of the jurisconsults could not have had its origin earlier than the period at which the Convention was severed from the technical ingredients of Contract. They taught that though nothing but a Contract could be the foundation of an *action*, a mere Pact or Convention could be the basis of a *plea*. It followed from this, that though nobody could sue upon an agreement which he had not taken the

precaution to mature into a Contract by comply-
ing with the proper forms, nevertheless a claim
arising out of a valid contract could be rebutted
by proving a counter-agreement which had never
got beyond the state of a simple convention. An
action for the recovery of a debt could be met by
showing a mere informal agreement to waive or
postpone the payment.

The doctrine just stated indicates the hesitation
of the Prætors in making their advances towards
the greatest of their innovations. Their theory
of Natural law must have led them to look with
especial favour on the Consensual Contracts and
on those Pacts or Conventions of which the Consensual Contracts were only particular instances;
but they did not at once venture on extending to
all Conventions the liberty of the Consensual Contracts. They took advantage of that special superintendence over procedure which had been confided to them since the first beginnings of Roman
law, and, while they still declined to permit a suit
to be launched which was not based on a formal
contract, they gave full play to their new theory
of agreement in directing the ulterior stages of
the proceeding. But, when they had proceeded
thus far, it was inevitable that they should proceed farther. The revolution of the ancient law
of Contract was consummated when the Prætor
of some one year announced in his Edict that he
would grant equitable actions upon Pacts which
had never been matured at all into Contracts,
provided only that the Pacts in question had been
founded on a consideration (*causa*). Pacts of this
sort are always enforced under the advanced
Roman jurisprudence. The principle is merely
the principle of the Consensual Contract carried

to its proper consequence; and, in fact, if the technical language of the Romans had been as plastic as their legal theories, these Pacts enforced by the Prætor would have been styled new Contracts, new Consensual Contracts. Legal phraseology is, however, the part of the law which is the last to alter, and the Pacts equitably enforced continued to be designated simply Prætorian Pacts. It will be remarked that unless there were consideration for the Pact, it would continue *nude* so far as the new jurisprudence was concerned; in order to give it effect, it would be necessary to convert it by a stipulation into a Verbal Contract.

The extreme importance of this history of Contract, as a safeguard against almost innumerable delusions, must be my justification for discussing it at so considerable a length. It gives a complete account of the march of ideas from one great landmark of jurisprudence to another. We begin with the Nexum, in which a Contract and a Conveyance are blended, and in which the formalities which accompany the agreement are even more important than the agreement itself. From the Nexum we pass to the Stipulation, which is a simplified form of the older ceremonial. The Literal Contract comes next, and here all formalities are waived, if proof of the agreement can be supplied from the rigid observances of a Roman household. In the Real Contract a moral duty is for the first time recognised, and persons who have joined or acquiesced in the partial performance of an engagement are forbidden to repudiate it on account of defects in form. Lastly, the Consensual Contracts emerge, in which the mental attitude of the contractors is solely regarded, and external circumstances have no title to notice except as evidence of the inward undertaking. It is of course uncertain how far this progress of Roman ideas from a gross to a refined conception exemplifies the necessary progress of human thought on the subject of Contract. The Contract-law of all other ancient societies but the Roman is either too scanty to furnish information, or else is entirely lost; and modern jurisprudence is so thoroughly leavened with the Roman notions that it furnishes us with no contrasts or parallels from which instruction can be gleaned. From the absence, however, of everything violent, marvellous, or unintelligible in the changes I have described, it may be reasonably believed that the history of ancient Roman Contracts is, up to a certain point, typical of the history of this class of legal conceptions in other ancient societies. But it is only up to a certain point that the progress of Roman law can be taken to represent the progress of other systems of jurisprudence. The theory of Natural law is exclusively Roman. The notion of the *vinculum juris*, so far as my knowledge extends, is exclusively Roman. The many peculiarities of the mature Roman law of Contract and Delict which are traceable to these two ideas, whether singly or in combination, are therefore among the exclusive products of one particular society. These later legal conceptions are important, not because they typify the necessary results of advancing thought under all conditions, but because they have exercised perfectly enormous influence on the intellectual diathesis of the modern world.

I know nothing more wonderful than the variety of sciences to which Roman law, Roman Contract-law more particularly, has contributed modes of thought, courses of reasoning, and a technical language. Of the subjects which have whetted the intellectual appetite of the moderns, there is scarcely one, except Physics, which has not been filtered through Roman jurisprudence. The science of pure Metaphysics had, indeed, rather a Greek than a Roman parentage, but Politics, Moral Philosophy, and even Theology, found in Roman law not only a vehicle of expression, but a nidus in which some of their profoundest inquiries were nourished into maturity. For the purpose of accounting for this phenomenon, it is not absolutely necessary to discuss the mysterious relation between words and ideas, or to explain how it is that the human mind has never grappled with any subject of thought, unless it has been provided beforehand with a proper store of language and with an apparatus of appropriate logical methods. It is enough to remark, that, when the philosophical interests of the Eastern and Western worlds were separated, the founders of Western thought belonged to a society which spoke Latin and reflected in Latin. But in the Western provinces the only language which retained sufficient precision for philosophical purposes was the language of Roman law, which by a singular fortune had preserved nearly all the purity of the Augustan age, while vernacular Latin was degenerating into a dialect of portentous barbarism. And if Roman jurisprudence supplied the only means of exactness in speech, still more emphatically did it furnish the only means of exactness, subtlety, or depth in thought. For at least three centuries, philosophy and science were without a home in the West; and though metaphysics and meta-

physical theology were engrossing the mental
energies of multitudes of Roman subjects, the
phraseology employed in these ardent inquiries
was exclusively Greek, and their theatre was the
Eastern half of the Empire. Sometimes, indeed,
the conclusions of the Eastern disputants became
so important that every man's assent to them, or
dissent from them, had to be recorded, and then
the West was introduced to the results of Eastern
controversy, which it generally acquiesced in
without interest and without resistance. Meanwhile, one department of inquiry, difficult enough
for the most laborious, deep enough for the
most subtle, delicate enough for the most
refined, had never lost its attractions for the
educated classes of the Western provinces. To
the cultivated citizen of Africa, of Spain, of Gaul,
and of Northern Italy, it was jurisprudence, and
jurisprudence only, which stood in the place of
poetry and history, of philosophy and science.
So far then from there being anything mysterious
in the palpably legal complexion of the earliest
efforts of Western thought it would rather be
astonishing if it had assumed any other hue. I
can only express my surprise at the scantiness of
the attention which has been given to the difference between Western ideas and Eastern, between
Western theology and Eastern, caused by the
presence of a new ingredient. It is precisely
because the influence of jurisprudence begins to
be powerful that the foundation of Constantinople
and the subsequent separation of the Western
Empire from the Eastern, are epochs in philosophical history. But continental thinkers are
doubtless less capable of appreciating the importance of this crisis by the very intimacy with

which notions derived from Roman Law are mingled up with their everyday ideas. Englishmen, on the other hand, are blind to it through the monstrous ignorance to which they condemn themselves of the most plentiful source of the stream of modern knowledge, of the one intellectual result of the Roman civilisation. At the same time, an Englishman, who will be at the pains to familiarise himself with the classical Roman law, is perhaps, from the very slightness of the interest which his countrymen have hitherto taken in the subject, a better judge than a Frenchman or a German of the value of the assertions I have ventured to make. Anybody who knows what Roman jurisprudence is, as actually practised by the Romans, and who will observe in what characteristics the earliest Western theology and philosophy differ from the phases of thought which preceded them, may be safely left to pronounce what was the new element which had begun to pervade and govern speculation.

The part of Roman law which has had most extensive influence on foreign subjects of inquiry has been the law of Obligation, or what comes nearly to the same thing, of Contract and Delict. The Romans themselves were not unaware of the offices which the copious and malleable terminology belonging to this part of their system might be made to discharge, and this is proved by their employment of the peculiar adjunct *quasi* in such expressions as Quasi-Contract and Quasi-Delict. ' Quasi ', so used, is exclusively a term of classification. It has been usual with English critics to identify the Quasi-contracts with *implied* contracts, but this is an error, for implied contracts are true contracts, which quasi-contracts

are not. In implied contracts, acts and circumstances are the symbols of the same ingredients
which are symbolised, in express contracts, by
words; and whether a man employs one set of
symbols or the other must be a matter of indiffer-
ence so far as concerns the theory of agreement.
But a Quasi-Contract is not a contract at all.
The commonest sample of the class is the relation
subsisting between two persons one of whom has
paid money to the other through mistake. The
law, consulting the interests of morality, imposes
an obligation on the receiver to refund, but the
very nature of the transaction indicates that it is
not a contract, inasmuch as the Convention, the
most essential ingredient of Contract, is wanting.
This word ' quasi ', prefixed to a term of Roman
law, implies that the conception to which it serves
as an index is connected with the conception with
which the comparison is instituted by a strong
superficial analogy or resemblance. It does not
denote that the two conceptions are the same or
that they belong to the same genus. On the contrary, it negatives the notion of an identity between
them; but it points out that they are sufficiently
similar for one to be classed as the sequel to the
other, and that the phraseology taken from one
department of law may be transferred to the
other, and employed without violent straining in
the statement of rules which would otherwise be
imperfectly expressed.

It has been shrewdly remarked, that the confusion between Implied Contracts, which are true
contracts, and Quasi Contracts, which are not
contracts at all, has much in common with the
famous error which attributed political rights and
duties to an Original Compact between the

governed and the governor. Long before this
theory had clothed itself in definite shape, the
phraseology of Roman contract-law had been
largely drawn upon to describe that reciprocity of
rights and duties which men had always conceived as existing between sovereigns and subjects. While the world was full of maxims setting
forth with the utmost positiveness the claims of
kings to implicit obedience—maxims which pretended to have had their origin in the New Testament, but which were really derived from in-
delible recollections of the Cæsarian despotism—
the consciousness of correlative rights possessed
by the governed would have been entirely without
the means of expression if the Roman law of
Obligation had not supplied a language capable
of shadowing forth an idea which was as yet
imperfectly developed. The antagonism between
the privileges of kings and their duties to their
subjects was never, I believe, lost sight of since
Western history began, but it had interest for few
except speculative writers so long as feudalism
continued in vigour, for feudalism effectually controlled by express customs the exorbitant theoretical pretensions of most European sovereigns. It
is notorious, however, that as soon as the decay
of the Feudal System had thrown the mediæval
constitutions out of working order, and when
the Reformation had discredited the authority
of the Pope, the doctrine of the divine right
of Kings rose immediately into an importance
which had never before attended it. The vogue
which it obtained entailed still more constant
resort to the phraseology of Roman law, and a
controversy which had originally worn a theological aspect assumed more and more the air of

a legal disputation. A phenomenon then appeared which has repeatedly shown itself in the history of opinion. Just when the argument for monarchical authority rounded itself into the definite doctrine of Filmer, the phraseology, borrowed from the Law of Contract, which had been used in defence of the rights of subjects, crystallised into the theory of an actual original compact between king and people, a theory which, first in English and afterwards, and more particularly, in French hands, expanded into a comprehensive explanation of all the phenomena of society and law. But the only real connection between political and legal science had consisted in the last giving to the first the benefit of its peculiarly plastic terminology. The Roman jurisprudence of Contract had performed for the relation of sovereign and subject precisely the same service which, in a humbler sphere, it rendered to the relation of persons bound together by an obligation of ' quasi-contract.' It had furnished a body of words and phrases which approximated with sufficient accuracy to the ideas which then were from time to time forming on the subject of political obligation. The doctrine of an Original Compact can never be put higher than it is placed by Dr. Whewell, when he suggests that, though unsound, ' it may be a *convenient* form for the expression of moral truths.'

The extensive employment of legal language on political subjects previously to the invention of the Original Compact, and the powerful influence which that assumption has exercised subsequently, amply account for the plentifulness in political science of words and conceptions, which were the exclusive creation of Roman jurisprudence. Of their plentifulness in Moral Philosophy a rather different explanation must be given, inasmuch as ethical writings have laid Roman law under contribution much more directly than political speculations, and their authors have been much more conscious of the extent of their obligation. In speaking of moral philosophy as extraordinarily indebted to Roman jurisprudence, I must be understood to intend moral philosophy as understood previously to the break in its history effected by Kant, that is, as the science of the rules governing human conduct, of their proper interpretation and of the limitations to which they are subject. Since the rise of the Critical Philosophy, moral science has almost wholly lost its older meaning, and, except where it is preserved under a debased form in the casuistry still cultivated by Roman Catholic theologians, it seems to be regarded nearly universally as a branch of ontological inquiry. I do not know that there is a single contemporary English writer, with the exception of Dr. Whewell, who understands moral philosophy as it was understood before it was absorbed by metaphysics and before the groundwork of its rules came to be a more important consideration than the rules themselves. So long, however, as ethical science had to do with the practical regimen of conduct, it was more or less saturated with Roman law. Like all the great subjects of modern thought, it was originally incorporated with theology. The science of Moral Theology, as it was at first called, and as it is still designated by the Roman Catholic divines, was undoubtedly constructed, to the full knowledge of its authors, by taking principles of conduct from the system of the Church, and by using the language and methods of jurisprudence for their expression and expansion. While this process went on, it was inevitable that jurisprudence, though merely intended to be the vehicle of thought, should communicate its colour to the thought itself. The tinge received through contact with legal conceptions is perfectly perceptible in the earliest ethical literature of the modern world, and it is evident, I think, that the Law of Contract, based as it is on the complete reciprocity and indissoluble connection of rights and duties, has acted as a wholesome corrective to the predispositions of writers who, if left to themselves, might have exclusively viewed a moral obligation as the public duty of a citizen in the Civitas Dei. But the amount of Roman Law in moral theology becomes sensibly smaller at the time of its cultivation by the great Spanish moralists. Moral theology, developed by the juridical method of doctor commenting on doctor, provided itself with a phraseology of its own, and Aristotelian peculiarities of reasoning and expression, imbibed doubtless in great part from the Disputations on Morals in the academical schools, take the place of that special turn of thought and speech which can never be mistaken by any person conversant with the Roman law. If the credit of the Spanish school of moral theologians had continued, the juridical ingredient in ethical science would have been insignificant, but the use made of their conclusions by the next generation of Roman Catholic writers on these subjects almost entirely destroyed their influence. Moral Theology, degraded into Casuistry, lost all interest for the leaders of European speculation; and the new science of Moral Philosophy, which was entirely in the hands of the Protestants, swerved greatly aside from the path which the moral theologians had followed. The effect was vastly to increase the influence of Roman law on ethical inquiry.

' Shortly after the Reformation, we find two great schools of thought dividing this class of subjects between them. The most influential of the two was at first the sect or school known to us as the Casuists, all of them in spiritual communion with the Roman Catholic Church, and nearly all of them affiliated to one or other of her religious orders. On the other side were a body of writers connected with each other by a common intellectual descent from the great author of the treatise *De Jure Belli et Pacis*, Hugo Grotius. Almost all of the latter were adherents of the Reformation, and though it cannot be said that they were formally and avowedly at conflict with the Casuists, the origin and object of their system were nevertheless essentially different from those of Casuistry. It is necessary to call attention to this difference, because it involves the question of the influence of Roman law on that department of thought with which both systems are concerned. The book of Grotius, though it touches questions of pure Ethics in every page, and though it is the parent immediate or remote of innumerable volumes of formal morality, is not, as is well known, a professed treatise on Moral Philosophy; it is an attempt to determine the Law of Nature, or Natural Law. Now, without entering upon the question, whether the conception of a Law Natural be not exclusively a creation of the Roman jurisconsults, we may lay down that, even on the admission of Grotius himself, the dicta of the Roman jurisprudence as to

what parts of known positive law must be taken
to be parts of the Law of Nature, are, if not
infallible, to be received at all events with the
profoundest respect.   Hence   the   system   of
Grotius is implicated with Roman law at its very
foundation, and this connection rendered inevitable—what the legal training of the writer
would perhaps have entailed without it—the free
employment in every paragraph of technical
phraseology, and of modes of reasoning, defining,
and illustrating, which must sometimes conceal
the sense, and almost always the force and
cogency, of the argument from the reader who is
unfamiliar with the sources whence they have
been derived.   On the other hand, Casuistry
borrows little from Roman law, and the views of
morality contended for have nothing whatever
in common with the undertaking of Grotius. All
that philosophy of right and wrong which has
become famous, or infamous, under the name of
Casuistry, had its origin in the distinction between
Mortal and Venial Sin. A natural anxiety to
escape the awful consequences of determining a
particular act to be mortally sinful, and a desire,
equally intelligible, to assist the Roman Catholic
Church in its conflict with Protestantism by dis-
burthening it of an inconvenient theory, were the
motives which impelled the authors of the Casuis-
tical philosophy to the invention of an elaborate
system of criteria, intended to remove immoral
actions, in as many cases as possible, out of the
category of mortal offences, and to stamp them
as venial sins. The fate of this experiment is
matter of ordinary history. We know that the
distinctions of Casuistry, by enabling the priest-
hood to adjust spiritual control to all the varieties

of human character, did really confer on it an influence with princes, statesmen, and generals, unheard of in the ages before the Reformation, and did really contribute largely to that great reaction which checked and narrowed the first successes of Protestantism. But beginning in the attempt, not to establish, but to evade—not to discover a principle, but to escape a postulate— not to settle the nature of right and wrong, but to determine what was not wrong of a particular nature,—Casuistry went on with its dexterous refinements till it ended in so attenuating the moral features of actions, and so belying the moral instincts of our being, that at length the conscience of mankind rose suddenly in revolt against it, and consigned to one common ruin the system and its doctors. The blow, long pending, was finally struck in the *Provincial Letters* of Pascal, and since the appearance of those memorable Papers, no moralist of the smallest influence or credit has ever avowedly conducted his speculations in the footsteps of the Casuists. The whole field of ethical science was thus left at the exclusive command of the writers who followed Grotius; and it still exhibits in an extraordinary degree the traces of that entanglement with Roman law which is sometimes imputed as a fault, and sometimes the highest of its recommendations, to the Grotian theory. Many inquirers since Grotius's day have modified his principles, and many, of course, since the rise of the Critical Philosophy, have quite deserted them; but even those who have departed most widely from his fundamental assumptions have inherited much of his method of statement, of his train of thought, and of his mode of illustration;

and these have little meaning and no point to the person ignorant of Roman jurisprudence*.'

I have already said that, with the exception of the physical sciences, there is no walk of knowledge which has been so slightly affected by Roman law as Metaphysics. The reason is that discussion on metaphysical subjects has always been conducted in Greek, first in pure Greek, and afterwards in a dialect of Latin expressly constructed to give expression to Greek conceptions. The modern languages have only been fitted to metaphysical inquiries by adopting this Latin dialect, or by imitating the process which was originally followed in its formation. The source of the phraseology which has been always employed for metaphysical discussion in modern times was the Latin translations of Aristotle, in which, whether derived or not from Arabic versions, the plan of the translator was not to seek for analogous expressions in any part of Latin literature, but to construct anew from Latin roots a set of phrases equal to the expression of Greek philosophical ideas. Over such a process the terminology of Roman law can have exercised little influence; at most, a few Latin law terms in a transmuted shape have made their way into metaphysical language. At the same time it is worthy of remark that whenever the problems of metaphysics are those which have been most strongly agitated in Western Europe, the thought, if not the language, betrays a legal parentage. Few things in the history of speculation are more impressive than the fact that no Greek-speaking

* The passage quoted is transcribed with slight alterations from a paper contributed by the author to the *Cambridge Essays* for 1856.

people has ever felt itself seriously perplexed by the great question of Free-will and Necessity. I do not pretend to offer any summary explanation of this, but it does not seem an irrelevant suggestion that neither the Greeks, nor any society speaking and thinking in their language, ever showed the smallest capacity for producing a philosophy of law. Legal science is a Roman creation, and the problem of Free-will arises when we contemplate a metaphysical conception under a legal aspect. How came it to be a question whether invariable sequence was identical with necessary connection? I can only say that the tendency of Roman law, which became stronger as it advanced, was to look upon legal consequences as united to legal causes by an inexorable necessity, a tendency most markedly exemplified in the definition of Obligation which I have repeatedly cited, ' Juris vinculum quo necessitate adstringimur alicujus solvendæ rei.'

But the problem of Free-will was theological before it became philosophical, and, if its terms have been affected by jurisprudence, it will be because Jurisprudence has made itself felt in Theology. The great point of inquiry which is here suggested has never been satisfactorily elucidated. What has to be determined, is whether jurisprudence has ever served as the medium through which theological principles have been viewed; whether, by supplying a peculiar language, a peculiar mode of reasoning, and a peculiar solution of many of the problems of life, it has ever opened new channels in which theological speculation could flow out and expand itself. For the purpose of giving an answer it is necessary to recollect what is already agreed upon

by the best writers as to the intellectual food
which theology first assimilated. It is conceded
on all sides that the earliest language of the
Christian Church was Greek, and that the problems to which it first addressed itself were those
for which Greek philosophy in its later forms had
prepared the way. Greek metaphysical literature contained the sole stock of words and ideas
out of which the human mind could provide
itself with the means of engaging in the profound
controversies as to the Divine Persons, the Divine
Substance, and the Divine Natures. The Latin
language and the meagre Latin philosophy were
quite unequal to the undertaking, and accordingly
the Western or Latin-speaking provinces of the
Empire adopted the conclusions of the East without disputing or reviewing them. ' Latin Christianity ', says Dean Milman, ' accepted the creed
which its narrow and barren vocabulary could
hardly express in adequate terms. Yet, throughout, the adhesion of Rome and the West was a
passive acquiescence in the dogmatic system
which had been wrought out by the profounder
theology of the Eastern divines, rather than a
vigorous and original examination on her part of
those mysteries. The Latin Church was the
scholar as well as the loyal partizan of Athana-
sius.' But when the separation of East and
West became wider, and the Latin-speaking
Western Empire began to live with an intellectual
life of its own, its deference to the East was all
at once exchanged for the agitation of a number
of questions entirely foreign to Eastern speculation. ' While Greek theology (Milman, *Latin
Christianity*, Preface, 5) went on defining with
still more exquisite subtlety the Godhead and the

nature of Christ '—' while the interminable controversy still lengthened out and cast forth sect
after sect from the enfeebled community '—the
Western Church threw itself with passionate
ardour into a new order of disputes, the same
which from those days to this have never lost
their interest for any family of mankind at any
time included in the Latin communion. The
nature of Sin and its transmission by inheritance—the debt owed by man and its vicarious
satisfaction—the necessity and sufficiency of the
Atonement—above all the apparent antagonism
between Free-will and the Divine Providence—
these were the points which the West began to
debate as ardently as ever the East had discussed
the articles of its more special creed. Why is it
then that on the two sides of the line which
divides the Greek-speaking from the Latin-speaking provinces there lie two classes of theological
problems so strikingly different from one another?
The historians of the Church have come close
upon the solution when they remark that the
new problems were more ' practical ', less absolutely speculative, than those which had torn
Eastern Christianity asunder, but none of them,
so far as I am aware, has quite reached it. I
affirm without hesitation that the difference between the two theological systems is accounted
for by the fact that, in passing from the East
to the West, theological speculation had passed
from a climate of Greek metaphysics to a climate
of Roman law. For some centuries before these
controversies rose into over vhelming importance,
all the intellectual activity of the Western
Romans had been expended on jurisprudence
exclusively. They had been occupied in applying

a peculiar set of principles to all the combinations in which the circumstances of life are capable of being arranged. No foreign pursuit or taste called off their attention from this engrossing occupation, and for carrying it on they possessed a vocabulary as accurate as it was copious, a strict method of reasoning,* a stock of general propositions on conduct more or less verified by experience, and a rigid moral philosophy. It was impossible that they should not select from the questions indicated by the Christian records those which had some affinity with the order of speculations to which they were accustomed, and that their manner of dealing with them should borrow something from their forensic habits. Almost everybody who has knowledge enough of Roman law to appreciate the Roman penal system, the Roman theory of the obligations established by Contract or Delict, the Roman view of Debts and of the modes of incurring, extinguishing, and transmitting them, the Roman notion of the continuance of individual existence by Universal Succession, may be trusted to say whence arose the frame of mind to which the problems of Western theology proved so congenial, whence came the phraseology in which these problems were stated, and whence the description of reasoning employed in their solution. It must only be recollected that the Roman law which had worked itself into Western thought was neither the archaic system of the ancient city, nor the pruned and curtailed jurisprudence of the Byzantine Emperors; still less, of course, was it the mass of rules, nearly buried in a parasitical overgrowth of modern speculative doctrine, which passes by the name of Modern Civil Law. I speak only of

that philosophy of jurisprudence, wrought out by
the great juridical thinkers of the Antonine age,
which may still be partially reproduced from the
Pandects of Justinian, a system to which few
faults can be attributed except it perhaps aimed
at a higher degree of elegance, certainty, and precision, than human affairs will permit to the limits
within which human laws seek to confine them.

It is a singular result of that ignorance of
Roman law which Englishmen readily confess,
and of which they are sometimes not ashamed to
boast, that many English writers of note and
credit have been led by it to put forward the most
untenable of paradoxes concerning the condition
of human intellect during the Roman Empire. It
has been constantly asserted, as unhesitatingly as
if there were no temerity in advancing the proposition, that from the close of the Augustan era
to the general awakening of interest on the points
of the Christian faith, the mental energies of the
civilised world were smitten with a paralysis. Now
there are two subjects of thought—the only two
perhaps with the exception of physical science—
which are able to give employment to all the
powers and capacities which the mind possesses.
One of them is Metaphysical inquiry, which
knows no limits so long as the mind is satisfied to
work on itself; the other is Law, which is as extensive as the concerns of mankind. It happens
that, during the very period indicated, the Greek-
speaking provinces were devoted to one, the
Latin-speaking provinces to the other, of these
studies. I say nothing of the fruits of speculation in Alexandria and the East, but I confidently
affirm that Rome and the West had an occupation in hand fully capable of compensating them

for the absence of every other mental exercise, and I add that the results achieved, so far as we know them, were not unworthy of the continuous and exclusive labour bestowed on producing them. Nobody except a professional lawyer is perhaps in a position completely to understand how much of the intellectual strength of individuals Law is capable of absorbing, but a layman has no difficulty in comprehending why it was that an unusual share of the collective intellect of Rome was engrossed by jurisprudence. ' The proficiency of a given community in jurisprudence depends in the long run on the same conditions as its progress in any other line of inquiry; and the chief of these are the proportion of the national intellect devoted to it, and the length of time during which it is so devoted. Now, a combination of all the causes, direct and indirect, which contribute to the advancing and perfecting of a science continued to operate on the jurisprudence of Rome through the entire space between the Twelve Tables and the severance of the two Empires,—and that not irregularly or at intervals, but in steadily increasing force and constantly augmenting number. We should reflect that the earliest intellectual exercise to which a young nation devotes itself is the study of its laws. As soon as the mind makes its first conscious efforts towards generalization, the concerns of every-day life are the first to press for inclusion within general rules and comprehensive formulas. The popularity of the pursuit on which all the energies of the young commonwealth are bent is at the outset unbounded; but it ceases in time. The monopoly of mind by law is broken down. The crowd at the morning audience of the great Roman jurisconsult lessens. The students are counted by hundreds instead of thousands in the English Inns of Court. Art, Literature, Science, and Politics, claim their share of the national intellect; and the practice of jurisprudence is confined within the circle of a profession, never indeed limited or insignificant, but attracted as much by the rewards as by the intrinsic recommendations of their science. This succession of changes exhibited itself even more strikingly at Rome than in England. To the close of the Republic the law was the sole field for all ability except the special talent of a capacity for generalship. But a new stage of intellectual progress began with the Augustan age, as it did with our own Elizabethan era. We all know what were its achievements in poetry and prose; but there are some indications, it should be remarked, that, besides its efflorescence in ornamental literature, it was on the eve of throwing out new aptitudes for conquest in physical science. Here, however, is the point at which the history of mind in the Roman State ceases to be parallel to the routes which mental progress had since then pursued. The brief span of Roman literature, strictly so called, was suddenly closed under a variety of influences, which though they may partially be traced it would be improper in this place to analyse. Ancient intellect was forcibly thrust back into its old courses, and law again became no less exclusively the proper sphere for talent than it had been in the days when the Romans despised philosophy and poetry as the toys of a childish race. Of what nature were the external inducements which, during the Imperial period, tended to draw a man of inherent capacity to the pursuits of the juris-consult may best be understood by considering the option which was practically before him in his choice of a profession. He might become a teacher of rhetoric, a commander of frontier-posts, or a professional writer of panegyrics. The only other walk of active life which was open to him was the practice of the law. Through that lay the approach to wealth, to fame, to office, to the council-chamber of the monarch—it may be to the very throne itself *.'

The premium on the study of jurisprudence was so enormous that there were schools of law in every part of the Empire, even in the very domain of Metaphysics. But, though the transfer of the seat of empire to Byzantium gave a perceptible impetus to its cultivation in the East, juris-prudence never dethroned the pursuits which there competed with it. Its language was Latin, an exotic dialect in the Eastern half of the Em-pire. It is only of the West that we can lay down that law was not only the mental food of the ambitious and aspiring, but the sole aliment of all intellectual activity. Greek philosophy had never been more than a transient fashionable taste with the educated class of Rome itself, and when the new Eastern capital had been created, and the Empire subsequently divided into two, the divorce of the Western provinces from Greek speculation, and their exclusive devotion to juris-prudence, became more decided than ever. As soon then as they ceased to sit at the feet of the Greeks and began to ponder out a theology of their own, the theology proved to be permeated

* *Cambridge Essays*, 1856.

with forensic ideas and couched in a forensic phraseology. It is certain that this substratum of law in Western theology lies exceedingly deep. A new set of Greek theories, the Aristotelian philosophy, made their way afterwards into the West and almost entirely buried its indigenous doctrines. But when at the Reformation it partially shook itself free from their influence, it instantly supplied their place with Law. It is difficult to say whether the religious system of Calvin or the religious system of the Arminians has the more markedly legal character.

The vast influence of the specific jurisprudence of Contract produced by the Romans upon the corresponding department of modern Law belongs rather to the history of mature jurisprudence than to a treatise like the present. It did not make itself felt till the school of Bologna founded the legal science of modern Europe. But the fact that the Romans, before their Empire fell, had so fully developed the conception of Contract becomes of importance at a much earlier period than this. Feudalism, I have repeatedly asserted, was a compound of archaic barbarian usage with Roman law; no other explanation of it is tenable, or even intelligible. The earliest social forms of the feudal period differ in little from the ordinary associations in which the men of primitive civilizations are everywhere seen united. A Fief was an organically complete brotherhood of associates whose proprietary and personal rights were inextricably blended together. It had much in common with an Indian Village Community and much in common with a Highland clan. But still it presents some phenomena which we never find in the associations which are spontaneously

formed by beginners in civilization. True archaic
communities are held together not by express
rules, but by sentiment, or, we should perhaps
say, by instinct; and new comers into the brotherhood are brought within the range of this instinct
by falsely pretending to share in the good-rela-
tionship from which it naturally springs. But the
earliest feudal communities were neither bound
together by mere sentiment nor recruited by a
fiction. The tie which united them was Contract,
and they obtained new associates by contracting
with them. The relation of the lord to the vassals
had originally been settled by express engagement, and a person wishing to engraft himself on
the brotherhood by *commendation* or *infeudation*
came to a distinct understanding as to the conditions on which he was to be admitted. It is
therefore the sphere occupied in them by Contract which principally distinguishes the feudal
institutions from the unadulterated usages of
primitive races. The lord had many of the characteristics of a patriarchal chieftain, but his prerogative was limited by a variety of settled customs traceable to the express conditions which
had been agreed upon when the infeudation took
place. Hence flow the chief differences which
forbid us to class the feudal societies with true
archaic communities. They were much more
durable and much more various; more durable,
because express rules are less destructible than
instinctive habits, and more various, because the
contracts on which they were founded were adjusted to the minutest circumstances and wishes
of the persons who surrendered or granted away
their lands. This last consideration may serve to
indicate how greatly the vulgar opinions current

among us as to the origin of modern society stand in need of revision. It is often said that the irregular and various contour of modern civilization is due to the exuberant and erratic genius of the Germanic races, and it is often contrasted with the dull routine of the Roman Empire. The truth is that the Empire bequeathed to modern society the legal conception to which all this irregularity is attributable; if the customs and institutions of barbarians have one characteristic more striking than another, it is their extreme uniformity.

CHAPTER X

THE EARLY HISTORY OF DELICT AND CRIME

THE Teutonic Codes, including those of our Anglo-Saxon ancestors, are the only bodies of archaic secular law which have come down to us in such a state that we can form an exact notion of their original dimensions. Although the extant fragments of Roman and Hellenic codes suffice to prove to us their general character, there does not remain enough of them for us to be quite sure of their precise magnitude or of the proportion of their parts to each other. But still on the whole all the known collections of ancient law are characterised by a feature which broadly distinguishes them from systems of mature jurisprudence. The proportion of criminal to civil law is exceedingly different. In the German codes, the civil part of the law has trifling dimensions as compared with the criminal. The traditions which speak of the sanguinary penalties inflicted by the code of

Draco seem to indicate that it had the same
characteristic. In the Twelve Tables alone, produced by a society of greater legal genius and at
first of gentler manners, the civil law has something like its modern precedence; but the relative
amount of space given to the modes of redressing
wrong, though not enormous, appears to have
been large. It may be laid down, I think, that
the more archaic the code, the fuller and the
minuter is its penal legislation. The phenomenon
has often been observed, and has been explained,
no doubt to a great extent correctly, by the
violence habitual to the communities which for
the first time reduced their laws to writing. The
legislator, it is said, proportioned the divisions of
his work to the frequency of a certain class of
incidents in barbarian life. I imagine, however,
that this account is not quite complete. It should
be recollected that the comparative barrenness of
civil law in archaic collections is consistent with
those other characteristics of ancient jurisprudence which have been discussed in this treatise.
Nine-tenths of the civil part of the law practised
by civilized societies are made up of the Law of
Persons, of the Law of Property and of Inheritance
and of the Law of Contract. But it is plain
that all these provinces of jurisprudence must
shrink within narrower boundaries, the nearer we
make our approaches to the infancy of social
brotherhood. The Law of Persons, which is
nothing else than the Law of Status, will be
restricted to the scantiest limits as long as all
forms of status are merged in common subjection
to Paternal Power, as long as the Wife has no
rights against her Husband, the Son none against
his Father, and the infant Ward none against the

Agnates who are his Guardians. Similarly, the rules relating to Property and Succession can never be plentiful, so long as land and goods devolve within the family, and, if distributed at all, are distributed inside its circle. But the greatest gap in ancient civil law will always be caused by the absence of Contract, which some archaic codes do not mention at all, while others significantly attest the immaturity of the moral notions on which Contract depends by supplying its place with an elaborate jurisprudence of Oaths. There are no corresponding reasons for the poverty of penal law, and accordingly, even if it be hazardous to pronounce that the childhood of nations is always a period of ungoverned violence, we shall still be able to understand why the modern relation of criminal law to civil should be inverted in ancient codes.

I have spoken of primitive jurisprudence as giving to *criminal* law a priority unknown in a later age. The expression has been used for convenience' sake, but in fact the inspection of ancient codes shows that the law which they exhibit in unusual quantities is not true criminal law. All civilized systems agree in drawing a distinction between offences against the State or Community and offences against the Individual, and the two classes of injuries, thus kept apart, I may here, without pretending that the terms have always been employed consistently in jurisprudence, call Crimes and Wrongs, *crimina* and *delicta*. Now the penal law of ancient communities is not the law of Crimes; it is the law of Wrongs, or, to use the English technical word, of Torts. The person injured proceeds against the wrong-doer by an ordinary civil action, and recovers compensation in the shape of money-damages if he succeeds. If the Commentaries of Gaius be opened at the place where the writer treats of the penal jurisprudence founded on the Twelve Tables, it will be seen that at the head of the civil wrongs recognized by the Roman law stood *Furtum* or *Theft*. Offences which we are accustomed to regard exclusively as *crimes* are exclusively treated as *torts*, and not theft only, but assault and violent robbery, are associated by the jurisconsult with trespass, libel and slander. All alike gave rise to an Obligation or *vinculum juris*, and were all requited by a payment of money. This peculiarity, however, is most strongly brought out in the consolidated Laws of the Germanic tribes. Without an exception, they describe an immense system of money compensations for homicide, and with few exceptions, as large a scheme of compensations for minor injuries. ' Under Anglo-Saxon law ' writes Mr. Kemble (*Anglo-Saxons*, i, 177) ' a sum was placed on the life of every free man, according to his rank, and a corresponding sum on every wound that could be inflicted on his person, for nearly every injury that could be done to his civil rights, honour or peace; the sum being aggravated according to adventitious circumstances.' These compositions are evidently regarded as a valuable source of income; highly complex rules regulate the title to them and the responsibility for them; and, as I have already had occasion to state, they often follow a very peculiar line of devolution, if they have not been acquitted at the decease of the person to whom they belong. If therefore the criterion of a *delict*, *wrong*, or *tort* be that the person who suffers it, and not the State, is conceived to be wronged, it may be asserted that in the infancy of jurisprudence the citizen depends for protection against violence or fraud not on the Law of Crime but on the Law of Tort.

Torts then are copiously enlarged upon in primitive jurisprudence. It must be added that Sins are known to it also. Of the Teutonic codes it is almost unnecessary to make this assertion, because those codes, in the form in which we have received them, were compiled or recast by Christian legislators. But it is also true that non-Christian bodies of archaic law entail penal consequences on certain classes of acts and on certain classes of omissions, as being violations of divine prescriptions and commands. The law administered at Athens by the Senate of Areopagus was probably a special religious code, and at Rome, apparently from a very early period, the Pontifical jurisprudence punished adultery, sacrilege and perhaps murder. There were therefore in the Athenian and in the Roman States laws punishing *sins*. There were also laws punishing *torts*. The conception of offence against God produced the first class of ordinances; the conception of offence against one's neighbour produced the second; but the idea of offence against the State or aggregate community did not at first produce a true criminal jurisprudence.

Yet it is not to be supposed that a conception so simple and elementary as that of wrong done to the State was wanting in any primitive society. It seems rather that the very distinctness with which this conception is realized is the true cause which at first prevents the growth of a criminal law. At all events, when the Roman community conceived itself to be injured, the analogy of a personal wrong received was carried out to its consequences with absolute literalness, and the State avenged itself by a single act on the individual wrong-doer. The result was that, in the infancy of the commonwealth, every offence vitally touching its security or its interests was punished by a separate enactment of the legislature. And this is the earliest conception of a *crimen* or Crime—an act involving such high issues that the State, instead of leaving its cognisance to the civil tribunal or the religious court, directed a special law or *privilegium* against the perpetrator. Every indictment therefore took the form of a bill of pains and penalties, and the trial of a *criminal* was a proceeding wholly extraordinary, wholly irregular, wholly independent of settled rules and fixed conditions. Consequently, both for the reason that the tribunal dispensing justice was the sovereign state itself and also for the reason that no classification of the acts prescribed or forbidden was possible, there was not at this epoch any *Law* of crimes, any criminal jurisprudence. The procedure was identical with the forms of passing an ordinary statute; it was set in motion by the same persons and conducted with precisely the same solemnities. And it is to be observed that, when a regular criminal law with an apparatus of Courts and officers for its administration had afterwards come into being, the old procedure, as might be supposed from its conformity with theory, still in strictness remained practicable; and, much as resort to such an expedient was discredited, the people of Rome always retained the power of punishing by a special law offences against its majesty. The classical scholar does not require to be reminded that in exactly the same manner the Athenian Bill of Pains and Penalties, or *εἰσαγγελία,* survived the establishment of regular tribunals. It is known too that when the freemen of the Teutonic races assembled for legislation, they also claimed authority to punish offences of peculiar blackness or perpetrated by criminals of exalted station. Of this nature was the criminal jurisdiction of the Anglo-Saxon Witenagemot.

It may be thought that the difference which I have asserted to exist between the ancient and modern view of penal law has only a verbal existence. The community, it may be said, besides interposing to punish crimes legislatively, has from the earliest times interfered by its tribunals to compel the wrong-doer to compound for his wrong, and, if it does this, it must always have supposed that in some way it was injured through his offence. But, however rigorous this inference may seem to us now-a-days, it is very doubtful whether it was actually drawn by the men of primitive antiquity. How little the notion of injury to the community had to do with the earliest interferences of the State *through its tribunals,* is shown by the curious circumstances that in the original administration of justice, the proceedings were a close imitation of the series of acts which were likely to be gone through in private life by persons who were disputing, but who afterwards suffered their quarrel to be appeased. The magistrate carefully simulated the demeanour of a private arbitrator casually called in.

In order to show that this statement is not a mere fanciful conceit, I will produce the evidence on which it rests. Very far the most ancient judicial proceeding known to us is the Legis Actic

Sacramenti of the Romans, out of which all the
later Roman Law of Actions may be proved to
have grown. Gaius carefully describes its ceremonial. Unmeaning and grotesque as it appears
at first sight, a little attention enables us to
decipher and interpret it.

The subject of litigation is supposed to be in
Court. If it is moveable, it is actually there. If
it be immoveable, a fragment or sample of it is
brought in its place; land, for instance, is represented by a clod, a house by a single brick. In
the example selected by Gaius, the suit is for a
slave. The proceeding begins by the plaintiff's
advancing with a rod, which, as Gaius expressly
tells, symbolized a spear. He lays hold of the
slave and asserts a right to him with the words,
' *Hunc ego hominem ex Jure Quiritium meum
esse dico secundum suam causam sicut dixi* ';
and then saying ' *Ecce tibi Vindictam imposui* ',
he touches him with the spear. The defendant
goes through the same series of acts and gestures.
On this the Prætor intervenes, and bids the litigants relax their hold, ' *Mittite ambo hominem.*'
They obey, and the plaintiff demands from the
defendant the reason of his interference, ' *Pos-
tulo anne dicas quâ ex causâ vindicaveris* ', a
question which is replied to by a fresh assertion of
right, ' *Jus peregi sicut vindictam imposui.*' On
this, the first claimant offers to stake a sum of
money, called a Sacramentum, on the justice of
his own case, ' *Quando tu injuriâ provocasti,
D æris Sacramento te provoco* ', and the defendant, in the phrase ' *Similiter ego te* ', accepts
the wager. The subsequent proceedings were
no longer of a formal kind, but it is to be
observed that the Prætor took security for the

Sacramentum, which always went into the coffers
of the State.

Such was the necessary preface of every ancient
Roman suit. It is impossible, I think, to refuse
assent to the suggestion of those who see in it a
dramatization of the Origin of Justice. Two
armed men are wrangling about some disputed
property. The Prætor, *vir pietate gravis*, happens
to be going by, and interposes to stop the contest.
The disputants state their case to him, and agree
that he shall arbitrate between them, it being
arranged that the loser, besides resigning the
subject of the quarrel, shall pay a sum of money
to the umpire as remuneration for his trouble and
loss of time. This interpretation would be less
plausible than it is, were it not that, by a surprising coincidence, the ceremony described by
Gaius as the imperative course of proceeding in a
Legis Actio is substantially the same with one of
the two subjects which the God Hephæstus is
described by Homer as moulding into the First
Compartment of the Shield of Achilles. In the
Homeric trial-scene, the dispute, as if expressly
intended to bring out the characteristics of primitive society, is not about property but about the
composition for a homicide. One person asserts
that he has paid it, the other that he has never
received it. The point of detail, however, which
stamps the picture as the counterpart of the
archaic Roman practice is the reward designed for
the judges. Two talents of gold lie in the
middle, to be given to him who shall explain the
grounds of the decision most to the satisfaction
of the audience. The magnitude of this sum as
compared with the trifling amount of the Sacramentum seems to me indicative of the difference

between fluctuating usage and usage consolidated into law. The scene introduced by the poet as a striking and characteristic, but still only occasional, feature of city-life in the heroic age has stiffened, at the opening of the history of civil process, into the regular, ordinary formalities of a lawsuit. It is natural therefore that in the Legis Actio the remuneration of the Judge should be reduced to a reasonable sum, and that, instead of being adjudged to one of a number of arbitrators by popular acclamation, it should be paid as a matter of course to the State which the Prætor represents. But that the incidents described so vividly by Homer, and by Gaius with even more than the usual crudity of technical language, have substantially the same meaning, I cannot doubt; and, in confirmation of this view, it may be added that many observers of the earliest judicial usages of modern Europe have remarked that the fines inflicted by Courts on offenders were originally *sacramenta*. The State did not take from the defendant a composition for any wrong supposed to be done to itself, but claimed a share in the compensation awarded to the plaintiff simply as the fair price of its time and trouble. Mr. Kemble expressly assigns this character to the Anglo-Saxon *bannum* or *fredum*.

Ancient law furnishes other proofs that the earliest administrators of justice simulated the probable acts of persons engaged in a private quarrel. In settling the damages to be awarded, they took as their guide the measure of vengeance likely to be exacted by an aggrieved person under the circumstances of the case. This is the true explanation of the very different penalties imposed by ancient law on offenders caught in the act or soon after it and on offenders detected after considerable delay. Some strange exemplifications of this peculiarity are supplied by the old Roman law of Theft. The Laws of the Twelve Tables seem to have divided Thefts into Manifest and Non-Manifest, and to have allotted extraordinarily different penalties to the offence according as it fell under one head or the other. The Manifest Thief was he who was caught within the house in which he had been pilfering, or who was taken while making off to a place of safety with the stolen goods; the Twelve Tables condemned him to be put to death if he were already a slave, and, if he was a freeman, they made him the bondsman of the owner of the property. The Non-Manifest Thief was he who was detected under any other circumstances than those described; and the old code simply directed that an offender of this sort should refund double the value of what he had stolen. In Gaius's day the excessive severity of the Twelve Tables to the Manifest Thief had naturally been much mitigated, but the law still maintained the old principle by mulcting him in fourfold the value of the stolen goods, while the Non-Manifest Thief still continued to pay merely the double. The ancient lawgiver doubtless considered that the injured proprietor, if left to himself, would inflict a very different punishment when his blood was hot from that with which he would be satisfied when the Thief was detected after a considerable interval; and to this calculation the legal scale of penalties was adjusted. The principle is precisely the same as that followed in the Anglo-Saxon and other Germanic codes, when they suffer a thief chased down and caught with the booty to be

hanged or decapitated on the spot, while they
exact the full penalties of homicide from anybody
who kills him after the pursuit has been inter-
mitted. These archaic distinctions bring home to
us very forcibly the distance of a refined from a
rude jurisprudence. The modern administrator of
justice has confessedly one of his hardest tasks
before him when he undertakes to discriminate
between the degrees of criminality which belong
to offences falling within the same technical description. It is always easy to say that a man
is guilty of manslaughter, larceny, or bigamy, but
it is often most difficult to pronounce what extent
of moral guilt he has incurred, and consequently
what measure of punishment he has deserved.
There is hardly any perplexity in casuistry, or in
the analysis of motive, which we may not be
called upon to confront, if we attempt to settle
such a point with precision; and accordingly the
law of our day shows an increasing tendency to
abstain as much as possible from laying down
positive rules on the subject. In France, the
jury is left to decide whether the offence which
it finds committed has been attended by extenu-
ating circumstances; in England, a nearly unbounded latitude in the selection of punishments
is now allowed to the judge; while all States have
in reserve an ultimate remedy for the miscarriages of law in the Prerogative of Pardon,
universally lodged with the Chief Magistrate. It
is curious to observe how little the men of primitive times were troubled with these scruples, how
completely they were persuaded that the impulses
of the injured person were the proper measure of
the vengeance he was entitled to exact, and how
literally they imitated the probable rise and fall

of his passions in fixing their scale of punishment.
I wish it could be said that their method of legislation is quite extinct. There are, however,
several modern systems of law which, in cases of
graver wrong, admit the fact of the wrong doer
having been taken in the act to be pleaded in
justification of inordinate punishment inflicted on
him by the sufferer—an indulgence which, though
superficially regarded it may seem intelligible, is
based, as it seems to me, on a very low morality.

Nothing, I have said, can be simpler than the
considerations which ultimately led ancient
societies to the formation of a true criminal jurisprudence. The State conceived itself to be
wronged, and the Popular Assembly struck
straight at the offender with the same movement
which accompanied its legislative action. It is
further true of the ancient world—though not
precisely of the modern, as I shall have occasion
to point out—that the earliest criminal tribunals
were merely subdivisions, or committees, of the
legislature. This, at all events, is the conclusion
pointed at by the legal history of the two great
states of antiquity, with tolerable clearness in one
case, and with absolute distinctness in the other.
The primitive penal law of Athens entrusted the
castigation of offences partly to the Archons, who
seem to have punished them as *torts*, and partly
to the Senate of Areopagus, which punished them
as *sins*. Both jurisdictions were substantially
transferred in the end to the Heliæa, the High
Court of Popular Justice, and the functions of
the Archons and of the Areopagus became either
merely ministerial or quite insignificant. But
' Heliæa ' is only an old word for Assembly; the
Heliæa of classical times was simply the Popular

Assembly convened for judicial purposes, and the famous Dikasteries of Athens were only its sub-divisions or panels. The corresponding changes which occurred at Rome are still more easily interpreted, because the Romans confined their experiments to the penal law, and did not, like the Athenians, construct popular courts with a civil as well as a criminal jurisdiction. The history of Roman criminal jurisprudence begins with the old Judicia Populi, at which the Kings are said to have presided. These were simply solemn trials of great offenders under legislative forms. It seems, however, that from an early period the Comitia had occasionally delegated its criminal jurisdiction to a Quæstio or Commission, which bore much the same relation to the Assembly as a Committee of the House of Commons bears to the House itself, except that the Roman Commissioners or Quæstores did not merely *report* to the Comitia, but exercised all powers which that body was itself in the habit of exercising, even to the passing sentence on the Accused. A Quæstio of this sort was only appointed to try a particular offender, but there was nothing to prevent two or three Quæstiones sitting at the same time; and it is probable that several of them were appointed simultaneously, when several grave cases of wrong to the community had occurred together. There are also indications that now and then these Quæstiones approached the character of our *Standing* Committees, in that they were appointed periodically, and without waiting for occasion to arise in the commission of some serious crime. The old Quæstores Parricidii, who are mentioned in connection with transactions of very ancient date, as being deputed to try (or, as some take it, to search out and try) all cases of parricide and murder, seem to have been appointed regularly every year; and the Duumviri Perduellionis, or Commission of Two for trial of violent injury to the Commonwealth, are also believed by most writers to have been named periodically. The delegations of power to these latter functionaries bring us some way forwards. Instead of being appointed *when and as* state-offences were committed, they had a general, though a temporary jurisdiction over such as *might* be perpetrated. Our proximity to a regular criminal jurisprudence is also indicated by the general terms ' Parricidium ' and ' Perduellio ' which mark the approach to something like a classification of crimes.

The true criminal law did not however come into existence till the year B.C. 149, when L. Calpurnius Piso carried the statute known as the Lex Calpurnia de Repetundis. The law applied to cases Repetundarum Pecuniarum, that is, claims by Provincials to recover monies improperly received by a Governor-General, but the great and permanent importance of this statute arose from its establishing the first Quæstio Perpetua. A Quæstio Perpetua was a *Permanent* Commission as opposed to those which were occasional and to those which were temporary. It was a regular criminal tribunal, whose existence dated from the passing of the statute creating it and continued till another statute should pass abolishing it. Its members were not specially nominated, as were the members of the older Quæstiones, but provision was made in the law constituting it for selecting from particular classes the judges who were to officiate, and for renewing them in conformity with definite rules. The offences of which it took cognisance were also expressly named and defined in this statute, and the new Quæstio had authority to try and sentence all persons in future whose acts should fall under the definitions of crime supplied by the law. It was therefore a regular criminal judicature, administering a true criminal jurisprudence.

The primitive history of criminal law divides itself therefore into four stages. Understanding that the conception of *Crime*, as distinguished from that of *Wrong* or *Tort* and from that of *Sin*, involves the idea of injury to the State or collective community, we first find that the commonwealth, in literal conformity with the conception, itself interposed directly, and by isolated acts, to avenge itself on the author of the evil which it had suffered. This is the point from which we start; each indictment is now a bill of pains and penalties, a special law naming the criminal and prescribing his punishment. A *second* step is accomplished, when the multiplicity of crimes compels the legislature to delegate its powers to particular Quæstiones or Commissions, each of which is deputed to investigate a particular accusation, and if it be proved, to punish the particular offender. Yet *another* movement is made when the legislature, instead of waiting for the alleged commission of a crime as the occasion of appointing a Quæstio, periodically nominates Commissioners like the Quæstores Parricidii and the Duumviri Perduellionis, on the chance of certain classes of crimes being committed, and in the expectation that they *will* be perpetrated. The *last* stage is reached when the Quæstiones from being periodical or occasional become permanent Benches or

Chambers—when the judges, instead of being named in the particular law nominating the Commission, are directed to be chosen through all future time in a particular way and from a particular class—and when certain acts are described in general language and declared to be crimes, to be visited, in the event of their perpetration, with specified penalties appropriated to each description.

If the Quæstiones Perpetuæ had had a longer history, they would doubtless have come to be regarded as a distinct institution, and their relation to the Comitia would have seemed no closer than the connection of our own Courts of Law with the Sovereign, who is theoretically the fountain of justice. But the Imperial despotism destroyed them before their origin had been completely forgotten, and, so long as they lasted, these Permanent Commissions were looked upon by the Romans as the mere depositaries of a delegated power. The cognisance of crimes was considered a natural attribute of the legislature, and the mind of the citizen never ceased to be carried back from the Quæstiones, to the Comitia which had deputed them to put into exercise some of its own inalienable functions. The view which regarded the Quæstiones, even when they became permanent, as mere Committees of the Popular Assembly—as bodies which only ministered to a higher authority—had some important legal consequences which left their mark on the criminal law to the very latest period. One immediate result was that the Comitia continued to exercise criminal jurisdiction by way of bill of pains and penalties, long after the Quæstiones had been established. Though the legislature had consented

to delegate its powers for the sake of convenience
to bodies external to itself, it did not follow that
it surrendered them. The Comitia and the Quæstiones went on trying and punishing offenders side
by side; and any unusual outburst of popular
indignation was sure, until the extinction of the
Republic, to call down upon its object an indictment before the Assembly of the Tribes.

One of the most remarkable peculiarities of the
institutions of the Republic is also traceable to
this dependance of the Quæstiones on the Comitia.
The disappearance of the punishment of Death
from the penal system of Republican Rome used
to be a very favourite topic with the writers of
the last century, who were perpetually using it to
point some theory of the Roman character or of
modern social economy. The reason which can be
confidently assigned for it stamps it as purely fortuitous. Of the three forms which the Roman
legislature successively assumed, one, it is well
known—the Comitia Centuriata—was exclusively
taken to represent the State as embodied for
military operations. The Assembly of the centuries, therefore, had all powers which may be
supposed to be properly lodged with a General
commanding an army, and, among them, it had
authority to subject all offenders to the same correction to which a soldier rendered himself liable
by breaches of discipline. The Comitia Centuriata
could therefore inflict capital punishment. Not
so, however, the Comitia Curiata or Comitia
Tributa. They were fettered on this point by the
sacredness with which the person of a Roman
citizen, inside the walls of the city, was invested
by religion and law; and, with respect to the last
of them, the Comitia Tributa, we know for certain

that it became a fixed principle that the Assembly
of the Tribes could at most impose a fine. So
long as criminal jurisdiction was confined to the
legislature, and so long as the assemblies of the
Centuries and of the Tribes continued to exercise
co-ordinate powers, it was easy to prefer indict-
ments for graver crimes before the legislative body
which dispensed the heavier penalties; but then
it happened that the more democratic assembly,
that of the Tribes, almost entirely superseded the
others, and became the ordinary legislature of the
later Republic. Now the decline of the Republic
was exactly the period during which the Quæstiones Perpetuæ were established, so that the
statutes creating them were all passed by a legislative assembly which itself could not, at its
ordinary sittings, punish a criminal with death. It
followed that the Permanent Judicial Commissions,
holding a delegated authority, were circumscribed
in their attributes and capacities by the limits of
the powers residing with the body which deputed
them. They could do nothing which the Assembly
of the Tribes could not have done; and, as the
Assembly could not sentence to death, the Quæstiones were equally incompetent to award capital
punishment. The anomaly thus resulting was not
viewed in ancient times with anything like the
favour which it has attracted among the moderns,
and indeed, while it is questionable whether the
Roman character was at all the better for it, it is
certain that the Roman Constitution was a great
deal the worse. Like every other institution which
has accompanied the human race down the current of its history, the punishment of death is a
necessity of society in certain stages of the civiliz-
ing process. There is a time when the attempt

to dispense with it baulks both of the two great instincts which lie at the root of all penal law. Without it, the community neither feels that it is sufficiently revenged on the criminal, nor thinks that the example of his punishment is adequate to deter others from imitating him. The incompetence of the Roman Tribunals to pass sentence of death led distinctly and directly to those frightful Revolutionary intervals, known as the Proscriptions, during which all law was formally suspended simply because party violence could find no other avenue to the vengeance for which it was thirsting. No cause contributed so powerfully to the decay of political capacity in the Roman people as this periodical abeyance of the laws; and, when it had once been resorted to, we need not hesitate to assert that the ruin of Roman liberty became merely a question of time. If the practice of the Tribunals had afforded an adequate vent for popular passion, the forms of judicial procedure would no doubt have been as flagrantly perverted as with us in the reigns of the later Stuarts, but national character would not have suffered as deeply as it did, nor would the stability of Roman institutions have been as seriously enfeebled.

I will mention two more singularities of the Roman Criminal System which were produced by the same theory of judicial authority. They are, the extreme multiplicity of the Roman criminal tribunals, and the capricious and anomalous classification of crimes which characterised Roman penal jurisprudence throughout its entire history. Every *Quæstio*, it has been said, whether Perpetual or otherwise, had its origin in a distinct statute. From the law which created it, it derived its authority; it rigorously observed the limits which its charter prescribed to it, and touched no form of criminality which that charter did not expressly define. As then the statutes which constituted the various Quæstiones were all called forth by particular emergencies, each of them being in fact passed to punish a class of acts which the circumstances of the time rendered particularly odious or particularly dangerous, these enactments made not the slightest reference to each other, and were connected by no common principle. Twenty or thirty different criminal laws were in existence together, with exactly the same number of Quæstiones to administer them; nor was any attempt made during the Republic to fuse these distinct judicial bodies into one, or to give symmetry to the provisions of the statutes which appointed them and defined their duties. The state of the Roman criminal jurisdiction at this period, exhibited some resemblances to the administration of civil remedies in England at the time when the English Courts of Common Law had not as yet introduced those fictitious averments into their writs which enabled them to trespass on each other's peculiar province. Like the Quæstiones, the Courts of Queen's Bench, Common Pleas, and Exchequer were all theoretical emanations from a higher authority, and each entertained a special class of cases supposed to be committed to it by the fountain of its jurisdiction; but then the Roman Quæstiones were many more than three in number, and it was infinitely less easy to discriminate the acts which fell under the cognisance of each Quæstio, than to distinguish between the provinces of the three Courts in Westminster

Hall. The difficulty of drawing exact lines between the spheres of the different Quæstiones made the multiplicity of Roman tribunals something more than a mere inconvenience; for we read with astonishment that when it was not immediately clear under what general description a man's alleged offences ranged themselves, he might be indicted at once or successively before several different Commissions, on the chance of some one of them declaring itself competent to convict him; and, although conviction by one Quæstio ousted the jurisdiction of the rest, acquittal by one of them could not be pleaded to an accusation before another. This was directly contrary to the rule of the Roman civil law; and we may be sure that a people so sensitive as the Romans to anomalies (or, as their significant phrase was, to *inelegancies*) in jurisprudence, would not long have tolerated it, had not the melancholy history of the Quæstiones caused them to be regarded much more as temporary weapons in the hands of factions than as permanent institutions for the correction of crime. The Emperors soon abolished this multiplicity and conflict of jurisdiction; but it is remarkable that they did not remove another singularity of the criminal law which stands in close connection with the number of the Courts. The classifications of crimes which are contained even in the Corpus Juris of Justinian are remarkably capricious. Each Quæstio had, in fact, confined itself to the crimes committed to its cognisance by its charter. These crimes, however, were only classed together in the original statute because they happened to call simultaneously for castigation at the moment of passing it. They had not therefore anything necessarily in common; but the fact of their constituting the particular subject-matter of trials before a particular Quæstio impressed itself naturally on the public attention, and so inveterate did the association become between the offences mentioned in the same statute that, even when formal attempts were made by Sylla and by the Emperor Augustus to consolidate the Roman criminal law, the legislator preserved the old grouping. The Statutes of Sylla and Augustus were the foundation of the penal jurisprudence of the Empire, and nothing can be more extraordinary than some of the classifications which they bequeathed to it. I need only give a single example in the fact that *perjury* was always classed with *cutting and wounding* and with *poisoning*, no doubt because a law of Sylla, the Lex Cornelia de Sicariis et Veneficis, had given jurisdiction over all these three forms of crime to the same Permanent Commission. It seems too that this capricious grouping of crimes affected the vernacular speech of the Romans. People naturally fell into the habit of designating all the offences enumerated in one law by the first name on the list, which doubtless gave its style to the Law Court deputed to try them all. All the offences tried by the Quæstio De Adulteriis would thus be called Adultery.

I have dwelt on the history and characteristics of the Roman Quæstiones because the formation of a criminal jurisprudence is nowhere else so instructively exemplified. The last Quæstiones were added by the Emperor Augustus, and from that time the Romans may be said to have had a tolerably complete criminal law. Concurrently with its growth, the analogous process had gone on, which I have called the conversion of Wrongs into Crimes, for, though the Roman legislature did not extinguish the civil remedy for the more heinous offences, it offered the sufferer a redress which he was sure to prefer. Still, even after Augustus had completed his legislation, several offences continued to be regarded as Wrongs, which modern societies look upon exclusively as Crimes; nor did they become criminally punishable till some late but uncertain date, at which the law began to take notice of a new description of offences called in the Digest *crimina extraordinaria*. These were doubtless a class of acts which the theory of Roman jurisprudence treated merely as wrongs; but the growing sense of the majesty of society revolted from their entailing nothing worse on their perpetrator than the payment of money damages, and accordingly the injured person seems to have been permitted, if he pleased, to pursue them as crimes *extra ordinem*, that is by a mode of redress departing in some respect or other from the ordinary procedure. From the period at which these *crimina extraordinaria* were first recognised, the list of crimes in the Roman State must have been as long as in any community of the modern world.

It is unnecessary to describe with any minuteness the mode of administering criminal justice under the Roman Empire, but it is to be noted that both its theory and practice have had powerful effect on modern society. The Emperors did not immediately abolish the Quæstiones, and at first they committed an extensive criminal jurisdiction to the Senate, in which, however servile it might show itself in fact, the Emperor was no more nominally than a Senator like the rest. But some sort of collateral criminal jurisdiction had been claimed by the Prince from the first; and this, as recollections of the free commonwealth decayed, tended steadily to gain at the expense of the old tribunals. Gradually the punishment of crimes was transferred to magistrates directly nominated by the Emperor and the privileges of the Senate passed to the Imperial Privy Council, which also became a Court of ultimate criminal appeal. Under these influences the doctrine, familiar to the moderns, insensibly shaped itself that the Sovereign is the fountain of all Justice and the depositary of all Grace. It was not so much the fruit of increasing adulation and servility as of the centralisation of the Empire which had by this time perfected itself. The theory of criminal justice had, in fact, worked round almost to the point from which it started. It had begun in the belief that it was the business of the collective community to avenge its own wrongs by its own hand; and it ended in the doctrine that the chastisement of crimes belonged in an especial manner to the Sovereign as representative and mandatary of his people. The new view differed from the old one chiefly in the air of awfulness and majesty which the guardianship of justice appeared to throw around the person of the Sovereign.

This later Roman view of the Sovereign's relation to justice certainly assisted in saving modern societies from the necessity of travelling through the series of changes which I have illustrated by the history of the Quæstiones. In the primitive law of almost all the races which have peopled Western Europe there are vestiges of the archaic notion that the punishment of crimes belongs to

the general assembly of freemen; and there are
some States—Scotland is said to be one of them—
in which the parentage of the existing judicature
can be traced up to a Committee of the legislative
body. But the development of the criminal law
was universally hastened by two causes, the
memory of the Roman Empire and the influence
of the Church. On the one hand traditions of
the majesty of the Cæsars, perpetuated by the
temporary ascendency of the House of Charlemagne, were surrounding Sovereigns with a prestige which a mere barbarous chieftain could never
otherwise have acquired and were communicating
to the pettiest feudal potentate the character of
guardian of society and representative of the
State. On the other hand, the Church, in its
anxiety to put a curb on sanguinary ferocity,
sought about for authority to punish the graver
misdeeds, and found it in those passages of Scripture which speak with approval of the powers of
punishment committed to the civil magistrate.
The New Testament was appealed to as proving
that secular rulers exist for the terror of evil-
doers; the Old Testament, as laying down that
'whoso sheddeth man's blood, by man shall his
blood be shed.' There can be no doubt, I
imagine, that modern ideas on the subject of
crime are based upon two assumptions contended
for by the Church in the Dark Ages—first, that
each feudal ruler, in his degree, might be assimilated to the Roman Magistrates spoken of by Saint
Paul; and next, that the offences which he was
to chastise were those selected for prohibition in
the Mosaic Commandments, or rather such of
them as the Church did not reserve to her own
cognisance. Heresy (supposed to be included in

the First and Second Commandments) Adultery,
and Perjury were ecclesiastical offences, and the
Church only admitted the co-operation of the
secular arm for the purpose of inflicting severer
punishment in cases of extraordinary aggravation.
At the same time, she taught that murder and
robbery with their various modifications were
under the jurisdiction of civil rulers, not as an
accident of their position but by the express
ordinance of God.

There is a passage in the writings of King
Alfred (Kemble, ii, 209) which brings out into
remarkable clearness the struggle of the various
ideas that prevailed in his day as to the origin of
criminal jurisdiction. It will be seen that Alfred
attributes it partly to the authority of the Church
and partly to that of the Witan, while he expressly claims for treason against the lord the
same immunity from ordinary rules which the
Roman Law of Majestas had assigned to treason
against the Cæsar. ' After this it happened '
he writes, ' that many nations received the faith
of Christ, and there were many synods assembled
throughout the earth, and among the English
race also after they had received the faith of
Christ, both of holy bishops and of their exalted
Witan. They then ordained that, out of that
mercy which Christ had taught, secular lords,
with their leave, might without sin take for every
misdeed the *bot* in money which they ordained;
except in cases of treason against a lord, to which
they dared not assign any mercy because Almighty
God adjudged none to them that despised Him,
nor did Christ adjudge any to them which sold
Him to death: and He commanded that a lord
should be loved like Himself.'

INDEX